GREAT FRUIT & VEGETABLE GUIDE

LONDON, NEW YORK, MUNICH, MELBOURNE, DELHI

Project Editor Becky Shackleton
Project Art Editor Rebecca Tennant
Senior Editor Helen Fewster
Senior Art Editor Joanne Doran
Managing Editor Esther Ripley
Managing Art Editor Alison Donovan
Jacket Designer Mark Cavanagh
Picture Researcher Sarah Hopper
DK Images Claire Bowers
Database Manager David Roberts
Production Editor Joanna Byrne
Production Controller Mandy Inness
Associate Publisher Liz Wheeler
Publisher Jonathan Metcalf
Art Director Peter Luff

North American Consultant Pamela Ruch
US Editors Shannon Beatty, Margaret Parrish, Rebecca Warren

Writers Ann Baggaley, Guy Barter, Helena Caldon,
R.L. Rosenfeld, Pamela Ruch, Diana Vowles, Rosemary Ward

First American Edition, 2011

Published in the United States by DK Publishing
375 Hudson Street, New York, New York 10014

10 9 8 7 6 5 4 3 2
004—179521—Feb/11

Discover more at
www.dk.com

GREAT FRUIT & VEGETABLE GUIDE

VEGETABLE

CONTENTS

HOW TO USE THIS GUIDE

This guide showcases over 1,000 of the best available fruit and vegetable cultivars, chosen for their flavor, reliability, and ease of cultivation. More than 100 different crops are covered, and each has a guide to successful growing. Every entry includes a description of the cultivar's important features and qualities, and many are also pictured.

ICON KEY

Each fruit or vegetable entry is accompanied by a set of icons that offer information on essentials such as when to plant and harvest, hardiness, and disease resistance. These help you see at a glance which plants are the right choice for your garden.

🪴 The pot icon indicates whether the cultivar can or cannot be container grown.

🔲 The trowel icon indicates the best season to sow or plant.

✳️ The bug icon is accompanied by the level of resistance to common pests and diseases.

❄️ The snowflake icon denotes hardiness information: hardy, fairly hardy, or not hardy.

🌳 Used only in the fruit section, the tree icons give pollination information. A single tree indicates the cultivar is self-fertile; two trees mean that another plant is needed for fertilization to occur. The flowering season is included where applicable.

🔲 The basket icon shows when the crop is ready to harvest.

WHY GROW YOUR OWN

There is nothing quite like pulling your own carrots from the ground or eating juicy plums straight from the tree. More and more people are discovering the satisfaction of growing their own, and it's easy to see why—it's not only rewarding, but it can be cost-effective, eco-friendly, and organic, too. Whatever your plot size, whether you have a large backyard or a windowbox, you will be able to grow crops yourself—your options are only as limited as your imagination.

HOW TO CHOOSE
Nurturing healthy and happy crops is hugely enjoyable, but it will also take time and effort so you need to make sure that you grow the tastiest, most productive crops possible. That's what this book is all about: we've researched the best crop varieties and identified their key features and advantages, from flavor through to disease resistance. You can handpick the crops you really want to grow and make the best of your time

and space. Most importantly, this book showcases superior and sometimes unusual and little known fruits and vegetables that you'll never find in the one-or-two-types-fits-all produce section of your local supermarket. Plants are also featured that are readily available, particularly hearty or disease-resistant, and easy to grow. Don't limit your choices—there is a huge range of fruits and vegetables out there, and this book will help you to discover them and learn to grow them yourself.

WHERE TO SHOP
All the plants and seeds featured in this book should be readily available. When buying plants ensuring that they are healthy is of the utmost importance. Be cautious if you are buying plants over the Internet—if possible, try to buy from reputable companies so that you can guarantee the quality. If you are buying from a garden center or specialized nursery, check for signs of pests and diseases and be vigilant with pest control and garden hygiene after planting (see growing guides for advice).

PLANNING YOUR PLOT

If you have the luxury of a large backyard or urban garden, make the most of it by ensuring that you plan your plot carefully. Bear in mind that some crops require differing soil types, locations, and microclimates, and that some will spread and become quite large (see individual growing guides for details). Keep a record of what you grow year to year and consider rotating crops to get the best from your soil and ensure high yields.

DESIGN YOUR LAYOUT

Sketch out the dimensions and boundaries of your plot and decide which crops you want to grow. Start by inserting the features that will be permanent, such as compost bins, sheds, paths, and fruit trees. Think next about the microclimates that exist in your garden, such as frost pockets where plants are less likely to thrive, or a south-facing wall that could act as a shelter for cordons of delicate fruit. When planning your plot, make sure that you create an environment that will be easy for you to work in.

Leave pathways between rows so that you can reach crops easily for watering and weeding. Make beds an accessible size to avoid damaging surrounding plants; the ideal width is about 4 ft (1.2 m).

PLANT YOUR CROPS

Some crops require specific planting formations; corn, for example, is best planted in a fairly dense grid formation to increase its chances of pollination, while crops such as potatoes are traditionally grown in rows—consider which crops you want to grow and how their specific needs might affect your planning. Think also about the way that light hits your plot during the day—you don't want to cast small crops such as lettuce into shadow if they become stranded behind a tall crop such as runner beans.

INTEGRATE YOUR GARDEN

Even if you have a smaller space, there is a design to suit, whatever your taste—from formal kitchen garden layouts to more flexible cottage garden or mixed planting systems. If you are growing crops in your backyard

A carefully planned plot makes full use of available space and can look attractive.

and are sharing the space with, perhaps, a dining area or children's play space, consider this when you construct your plan. If you don't want a fence, a row of bean poles or fruit trees might protect your other crops from an errant football, while growing salad leaves close to a patio area might serve as an easy-access outdoor salad bowl. Consider mixing crops into flowerbeds for a more naturalized look—plants such as marigolds, nasturtiums, or basil act as companion plants, and can help to divert insect predators. Keep in mind that you might need to plan ahead to prevent gaps in your flowerbed after harvesting.

RAISE YOUR BEDS

Creating raised beds for your crops not only provides them with deeper, better-draining soil that may warm up quicker in spring, but also adds architectural interest to your garden. Use old railroad ties, bricks, slates, or even wooden boards as edging, and then build up the level of the soil with good quality compost.

GROWING IN SMALL SPACES

A flowerpot on a windowsill is all the space you need to grow a shallow-rooted plant such as a lettuce, so don't despair if you don't have much room to play with. Make the most of whatever space you have; create a raised bed in a compact garden, or plant flowerpots and containers for a patio, decking, or even a balcony. Be creative; grow crops such as tomatoes in hanging baskets, or grow fruit trees in tubs.

Plant a basket of decorative tomatoes.

VERTICAL GARDENING

Don't feel limited to growing at ground level. If you have a large unused space, a backyard wall or sturdy fence, for example, consider fastening pots and baskets to it, and grow tiers of crops while using no floor space at all. Hanging baskets are an attractive and resourceful use of space, although be careful that they are mounted well enough to support their eventual weight. Not all plants will tolerate this relative lack of soil, but some, such as strawberries and salad greens, will thrive quite happily. Consider planting your crops in with other trailing plants; a mixture of tumbling tomatoes

Grow a bowl of blackberries on your patio.

Fill a raised bed with salad greens.

and upright colorful flowers can look incredibly attractive. If you decide to attach pots to a wall, ensure that you leave enough space for the crops to grow, and try to ensure that the lowest aren't cast into permanent shade. Fasten securely, bearing in mind the eventual weight.

CLIMATE

Examine your space, however small, and work out the best situations for your crops. Many prefer full sun, but others, such as raspberries and blackberries, will flourish in shade. If you are growing crops in pots or baskets you have the flexibility to move them around, which in some cases can be highly beneficial—

citrus trees, for example, enjoy a sunny position in summertime, and can then be moved inside or under cover in colder months.

STYLISH RECYCLING

We all know that recycling is important, so think creatively when acquiring flowerpots and containers for your garden. Create stylish and unique growing locations by reusing anything from tin cans, for shallow-rooted plants such as radishes, to buckets, bins, and rain boots. You'll need to create drainage holes, and keep in mind that you'll need to water your crops frequently, since the soil will dry out much quicker than in a regular bed.

TIP   VALUE FOR MONEY

We all want to feel that we're getting the most for our money, so why not try these tasty, high value options:
- raspberries—plant three canes to a pot and support with trellis;
- blueberries—ensure that plants have acidic, well-drained conditions;
- corn—grow dwarfing types in a warm, sunny position;
- salad greens—harvest as cut-and-come-again crops for a large yield.

Raspberries taste delicious, are easy to grow, and are expensive to buy in stores.

WATERING

All your crops will need to be watered frequently, especially during critical stages in their growth (see individual growing guides for details). The most effective way to water a large plot is with a soaker hose, which dribbles water where it is needed at the base of the plant above its roots. A watering can may be all you need for a small plot or patio, but keep in mind that crops in cultivation dry out more quickly than in the ground. Consider a microirrigation system, which allows you to tailor a precise network of pipes or sprays to your containers or beds and can be automated using a timer.

Water in the cool of the morning or evening to reduce evaporation. Direct the water at the soil and not at the leaves—this is not only ineffectual, but if you water plants on a hot day, you also risk burning them. Remember, too, that soaking plants twice a week is better than spraying them lightly every day, and it will encourage stronger, deeper roots.

Keep young, leafy crops well supplied with water.

IMPROVING THE SOIL

To produce healthy crops, fruit and vegetable plants remove a lot of the nutrients from the soil. It's vital to replenish these by digging in an organic material such as compost or manure and applying fertilizer during growth.

COMPOST AND MANURE

Fill a compost bin with plant matter and kitchen waste, ensuring that you provide it with air, warmth, and moisture, and over the following months microorganisms will break down the waste into crumbly, sweet-smelling compost.

Making leaf mold is a slower process, taking up to a year. Pile decaying leaves into wire cages or punctured plastic bags containing a small amount of garden soil, and leave to rot down.

Farmyard and stable manures are packed with nutrients and are highly beneficial to the soil but need to rot for at least six months so that the ammonia doesn't "scorch" young plants.

Apply your compost or manure by either spreading a 4 in (10 cm) layer on the surface of the soil as a mulch, or by digging it into the soil the fall before planting.

Turn your kitchen waste into compost.

Mulch plants with nutrient-rich leaf mold.

Apply well-rotted farmyard manure.

WEEDING

Weeds make your garden look messy and can be hard to control. But in addition to being unsightly, they also compete with your crops for water, nutrients, light, and space, often harboring pests and diseases. It's vitally important to keep them under control.

THE NEED TO WEED

Annual weeds, such as speedwell and chickweed, can be controlled by hoeing. Slice weed stems just below the soil surface. Be careful to do this before they flower or they will create a fresh generation of seed. Preferably, weed on a dry day so that the sun will dry out and kill any upturned roots.

Perennial weeds, such as bindweed and brambles, are much harder to destroy. To remove them completely you will need to dig out every trace of root or rhizome from the soil, or they will regenerate. Do this diligently, as soon as you see weeds reshooting and you will win the battle eventually, but on a very overgrown patch you may want to use a chemical weedkiller. Use protective clothing and a mask, and spray carefully to prevent it from reaching nearby crops.

MULCHING

A mulch is a layer of material spread around the base of a plant that can serve a number of useful purposes in the fruit or vegetable garden. Black plastic sheeting or old carpet can be used to warm the ground, trap moisture, or suppress weeds by depriving them of light. Mulching with compost and manure improves soil structure and boosts it with vital nutrients. Using a straw mulch helps by raising crops such as strawberries or zucchini out of the mud, allowing air to circulate beneath them, and keeping them out of the path of pests such as slugs. See individual growing guides for details on mulching specific crops.

Protect strawberries with a straw mulch.

FROST PROTECTION

If you are planning year-round crops or just want to get ahead in spring, some kind of frost protection is essential. Not everyone has access to a greenhouse, but there are plenty of other solutions.

CONTROL YOUR CLIMATE

Cold frames and cloches (see right) are ideal for use when your seedlings are young and at their most vulnerable. They help to maintain a constant temperature for your crops, and at the same time provide protection from pests such as birds, mice, and insects. If you are sowing into modules indoors before planting out, keep crops in a cold frame until they harden up before transferring them into the ground. Ensure your cold frame is well-insulated and can be partially opened to provide good ventilation. Before sowing seed into the ground, cover the soil with a cloche to warm it beforehand, then place a cloche over the plant to help to maintain a constant temperature while the seeds are germinating. You can improvise a cheap and easy cloche by cutting a plastic bottle

in half and using the top part to cover a seed or young plant. Unscrew the lid to ventilate. For larger areas of crops, create your own polytunnel by stretching plastic wrap or horticultural fleece over wire or plastic hoops, and pinning down securely.

Protect your plants with a cold frame.

Recycle to create your own cloches.

A HEALTHY GARDEN

The varieties of fruits and vegetables in this book have been chosen for taste and reliability but also in many cases for their resistance to pests and diseases. However, no plant can be completely resistant and all will benefit from good growing conditions, vigilance, and fast action at the first sign of damage.

PESTS

The pests in your garden range from slugs or snails that love to feed on young seedlings to aphids that secrete honeydew on plants on which gray mold can develop. Methods of control can be biological, organic, or chemical.

Slugs target vulnerable new plants.

PREVENTION

Try to pest-proof your plot with a few of these methods:
• Cover seeds or young plants with a protective enclosure, such as a cloche or polytunnel, to prevent attack from insects, birds, and small mammals.
• Interplant your crops with companion plants, such as marigolds, to divert insect pests.
• Encourage insect predators such as ladybugs by providing them with a wildlife habitat.
• Set up traps or other deterrents to thwart slugs and snails.
• Hang old CDs, or place upturned plastic bottles on sticks—as the wind catches them, the noise and movement will help to discourage unwanted visitors.
• Use netting to deter birds.
• Place grease bands around the trunks of susceptible fruit trees.

TREATMENT

• Use a chemical pesticide. Be aware though that these often kill more than just your pests, and might cause a knock-on effect in your garden's food chain.
• Use parasitic nematodes, which enter the bodies of slugs and snails and trigger a fatal infection.

DISEASES

Plant diseases are caused by viruses, fungi, or bacteria. They are often more difficult to prevent and contain than pests; they can be spread by spores in the air, rainwater splash, animals and insects, and also by poor garden hygiene. Diseases vary in severity—some are fairly superficial and can be treated, while others are severe enough to cause the plant to die (see growing guides for specific information and advice).

Gray mold coats and rots crops.

PREVENTION

• Rotate your crops to prevent a buildup of diseases in the soil.
• Seedlings and young plants are especially vulnerable to the microorganisms that are sometimes present in stored water. Instead, use tap water while plants are young.
• Give crops plenty of space so that air can circulate freely around and between them.
• Destroy any diseased plant matter that you remove—do not compost it, since this risks further contamination.
• Keep your plants strong and healthy with regular feeding, watering, and weeding.
• When pruning fruit trees, remove diseased or dead material immediately. Be careful not to tear the wood, since this creates an open wound through which diseases might enter.
• Make sure that you clean and sterilize your tools and equipment regularly. If you use a greenhouse or potting shed, keep it clean and ventilated—diseases will reproduce rapidly in warm, wet, stagnant conditions.

TREATMENT

• Some fungal diseases are preventable with fungicides, but these may not be effective if the disease has already taken hold. Plants with bacterial infections may survive if diseased plant parts are removed quickly, but a plant with a viral disease should be removed and destroyed.

Fruit

Tree Fruits

- Apples
- Pears
- Plums, Damsons, and Gages
- Cherries
- Peaches and Nectarines
- Apricots
- Figs
- Medlars and Quinces
- Citrus
- Nuts

APPLES *Malus domestica*

The quintessential tree fruit, apples offer an astounding array of varieties, wide-ranging fruit flavors, and a large choice of training forms, from freestanding trees and wall-trained cordons, to compact stepovers and standards. Choose a baking apple such as 'Bramley's Seedling' for a classic apple crisp, or choose a dessert variety such as 'Jonagold' or 'Cox's Orange Pippin' for a tasty snack straight from the tree.

	SPRING	SUMMER	FALL	WINTER
PLANT				
HARVEST				

PLANTING

If you are buying a container-grown tree, ensure that it is healthy and has not become root-bound. Although container-grown trees can be planted at any time of year, it is preferable to plant them either in spring or fall. Bare-root trees should be planted between the fall and early spring, as long as the soil is not frozen.

Select certified disease-free trees.

Apple tree cultivars vary in fertility—some are self-fertile, some are diploid, requiring another pollenizer, and some are triploid, requiring two other pollenizers (see individual cultivar entries for specific information), so make sure that you plan carefully, and, if in doubt, seek the advice of a specialist when buying your trees.

Although they are not as frost-sensitive as other fruit trees, apples like a warm, sheltered site, with full sun for dessert varieties. Give trees a fertile, well-drained soil with a pH of about 6.5 and ensure that trees have enough space to develop comfortably: dwarfing trees may need as little as 4 ft (1.2 m) of space between

each other, while vigorous trees will become very large and may require as much as 25 ft (8 m).

Dig in well-rotted manure or compost before planting. Trees will need staking for the first three or four years, so ensure that the stake is sturdy before you plant your tree. Attach any horizontal training wires before planting cordons or espaliers.

CROP CARE

Young apple trees need to be kept well watered while their fruits are developing, especially those that are trained into fans and cordons or growing in pots.

Feed trees in early spring with a balanced fertilizer, and consider applying extra nitrogenous fertilizer to culinary apple trees.

Beautiful apple blossom in springtime.

Mulch after feeding with a layer of well-rotted manure or compost. If soil is particularly poor you may want to apply a mulch biannually; if soil is rich, bark chippings may suffice.

Although apples generally blossom later in the season than trees such as pears or cherries, and are therefore less vulnerable

TIP GROW IN CONTAINERS

If grown on a dwarfing or non-vigorous rootstock, apples will thrive in containers and in limited space. Feed with fertilizer in early spring, and ensure that you keep your tree well-watered, since containers will dry out faster than the open ground. Pot up every few years. Growing trees in containers enables you to cover them with netting against pests, or protect against frost with fleece.

Dwarfing apples will happily produce a crop in a confined growing space.

to frosts, you may want to cover container-grown or wall-trained trees with horticultural fleece.

HARVESTING

Depending on the variety you grow, you may have apples ready to harvest as early as midsummer, but the timing of the harvest is crucial. If you harvest fruits too soon, you may keep them from developing their full flavor; too late and they may not store well. Ripe apples should pull away from the tree easily; do not rip them away or you could damage the spur. Be careful not to bruise the fruits as you remove and store them. Fruits will not all ripen at exactly the same time, and if you have varieties with different harvesting seasons, you may be able to pick for many months.

STORING

Generally, the later the season, the longer the apple will store. When apples are ripe, remove them gently from the tree and, spacing them so that they are not touching, lay them out on trays, or wrap them in tissue paper and hang in plastic bags. Store them in a cool, dark, place and check the fruits regularly for signs of decay.

PESTS AND DISEASES

Apples are prone to a range of diseases, including canker, scab, fire blight, and infectious rots. If any of these occur, increase the air flow through the tree's branches by pruning out the diseased wood. Spray with an appropriate fungicide.

Apples are prone to pests such as wasps, birds, winter moth caterpillars, aphids, and capsid bugs. Net to deter birds; set up a jam-trap to attract wasps; use grease bands on the tree and its stake to keep winter moth caterpillars from climbing the trunk and laying eggs in the tree; and if aphids or apple sawfly are detected, remove damaged fruits and spray trees with a pyrethroid insecticide. Resistance to pests and diseases can vary between cultivars, so check catalog for specific advice.

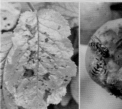
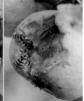

Capsid bugs (left) target young leaves, creating spots and ragged holes. Wasps (right) will target damaged fruits to feast on the sweet, ripe flesh.

'Cox's Orange Pippin'

Championed by many as the finest English eating apple, the orangey-yellow skin is tinged with red and covers a crisp, juicy, and superbly flavored flesh. The blossom is sensitive to frost, however, and the trees have poor resistance to diseases.

🪣	on a dwarfing rootstock
🔧	early spring or fall
🕷	some resistance
❄	hardy
🌼	self-fertile (mid)
🔒	mid-fall

'Golden Delicious'

This trouble-free variety is best grown in a warm, sheltered site for the most flavorsome crop. The large, yellow-green apples have a light, crisp flesh and sweet flavor; they are best eaten fresh. They store for up to eight months.

🪣	on a dwarfing rootstock
🔧	early spring or fall
🕷	excellent resistance
❄	hardy
🌼	needs 1 pollenizer (mid)
🔒	mid-fall

'Jonagold'

A widely grown tree, it produces heavy yields but has some susceptibility to scab and canker. The large, yellow-green, red-flushed fruits are crisp and juicy and their creamy flesh has a sweet, honeyed flavor. The fruit will store until the new year.

 on a dwarfing rootstock
 early spring or fall
some resistance
hardy
needs 2 pollenizers (mid)
late fall

'Enterprise'

The crisp, full flavor of 'Enterprise' gets even better after a month or two of cold storage. Its immunity to scab and resistance to cedar apple rust and fire blight make it an excellent backyard choice. The dark red apples mature late.

 on a dwarfing rootstock
 early spring (or fall in the south)
 excellent resistance
hardy
fertile (mid)
mid-fall

'Laxton's Fortune'

An old British variety, the yellowish-green apples are flushed with red stripes. Fruits have a firm, aromatic flesh that has a good blend of sweetness and acidity. The apples will keep until well into the new year.

on a dwarfing rootstock
early spring or fall
 good resistance
hardy
partially self-fertile (mid)
early fall

'Gala'

One of the most widely grown dessert apples, these shiny orange-red fruits have a sweet flavor and crisp, juicy flesh. The trees crop heavily, producing apples that keep well once picked, although this variety is susceptible to scab and canker.

- 🪣 on a dwarfing rootstock
- 🍂 early spring or fall
- 🕷 some resistance
- ❄️ hardy
- 👥 needs 1 pollenizer (mid)
- 🔒 mid-fall

'Pixie'

This easy-to-grow variety bears very high yields of yellow-green apples with red stripes and flushes. The diminutive fruits are crisp, aromatic, and juicy—perfect for children—and will store into the new year.

- 🪣 on a dwarfing rootstock
- 🍂 early spring or fall
- 🕷 excellent resistance
- ❄️ hardy
- 👥 needs 1 pollenizer (mid)
- 🔒 mid-fall

'William's Pride'

An extended bloom period makes this early-maturing variety an excellent pollenizer for other cultivars. It is immune to scab, with varying resistance to other diseases; exceptionally crisp and flavorful for a summer apple.

- 🪣 on a dwarfing rootstock
- 🍂 early spring (or fall in the South)
- 🕷 good resistance
- ❄️ hardy
- 👤 self-fertile (early to mid)
- 🔒 mid- to late summer

'Mother'

This old American variety, also known as 'American Mother', bears slightly conical yellow-green fruits with red stripes and a soft, yellow, juicy, sweet flesh. It is a slow-growing tree with good scab resistance. Early fruits will store well until the new year.

🪣	on a dwarfing rootstock
🏷	early spring or fall
🕷	good resistance
❄	hardy
👬	partially self-fertile (late)
🔒	early fall

'Herefordshire Russet'

A relatively new, heavy-cropping variety of exceptional quality, the tree produces golden brown fruits, which are small, but are rich and aromatic. Although they are best eaten fresh, they will store well until the new year.

🪣	on a dwarfing rootstock
🏷	early spring or fall
🕷	good resistance
❄	hardy
👬	partially self-fertile (mid)
🔒	early fall

'Honeycrisp'

Known for the crisp, aromatic flavor that develops when the mottled red fruits ripen on the tree, 'Honeycrisp' is winter-hardy and somewhat resistant to scab and fire blight. It can be harvested over a long period and stores well.

🪣	on a dwarfing rootstock
🏷	early spring (or fall in the South)
🕷	good resistance
❄	hardy
👬	self-fertile (mid)
🔒	early fall

'Adam's Pearmain'

This trouble-free old variety produces conical-shaped fruits with yellow-green, red-striped skin. The aromatic yellow flesh is crisp and firm with a nutty flavor. Stored correctly, the fruit will keep well into the new year.

- 🪣 on a dwarfing rootstock
- 🌱 early spring or fall
- 🐞 excellent resistance
- ❄️ hardy
- 👯 needs 1 pollenizer (early)
- 🔒 mid-fall

'Helena'

A clone of the classic 'Braeburn', this excellent crisp and juicy apple crops about 10 days earlier. The red and green apples are ready for picking from mid-fall and can be stored for up to four months.

- 🪣 on a dwarfing rootstock
- 🌱 early spring or fall
- 🐞 good resistance
- ❄️ hardy
- 👯 needs 1 pollenizer (mid)
- 🔒 mid-fall

'Ribston Pippin'

A classic English apple and one of the parents of 'Cox's Orange Pippin', its fruits have a firm, crisp flesh and a strong aromatic flavor. Trees produce heavy yields of red-flushed, yellow-green fruits with some russeting. Fruits store well until the new year.

- on a dwarfing rootstock
- early spring or fall
- good resistance
- hardy
- needs 2 pollenizers (early)
- early fall

'Worcester Pearmain'

This old favorite produces medium-sized, bright red-flushed apples whose sweet, aromatic flavor is enhanced if left on the tree until fully ripe. Although hardy and resistant to mildew, it is susceptible to scab and canker.

- on a dwarfing rootstock
- early spring or fall
- good resistance
- hardy
- partially self-fertile (mid)
- early fall

'Lord Lambourne'

This early-fruiting, compact tree is good for small gardens. The round fruits are a gold-green color with a touch of russet, and their aromatic flesh is crisp and juicy and pleasantly acidic. The apples keep well until Christmas.

- on a dwarfing rootstock
- early spring or fall
- good resistance
- hardy
- partially self-fertile (early)
- late summer

'Ashmead's Kernel'

A classic old variety, this apple is still one of the best late dessert varieties. The pretty blossoms make way for aromatic-tasting fruit, with crisp yellow flesh and russet coloring. It is relatively low-yielding, but has good scab resistance. Fruits store well.

🪣	on a dwarfing rootstock
🔪	early spring or fall
🐛	excellent resistance
❄️	hardy
👭	needs 1 pollenizer (mid)
🔒	mid-fall

'Jonafree'

The crisp taste of the glossy red 'Jonafree' closely resembles heirloom favorite 'Jonathan', but this updated variety is far less susceptible to disease. The fine-grained flesh holds its quality for up to 10 weeks in cold storage.

🪣	on a dwarfing rootstock
🔪	early spring (or fall in the South)
🐛	good resistance
❄️	hardy
🌸	fertile (mid)
🔒	early fall

'Scrumptious'

This modern variety is excellent for all gardens, but is particularly good in frosty sites. The crisp, juicy flesh of this bright red apple has a honeylike sweetness with a hint of strawberry and a touch of acidity.

🪣	on a dwarfing rootstock
🔪	early spring or fall
🐛	good resistance
❄️	hardy
🌸	self-fertile (mid)
🔒	late summer

'Greensleeves'

This pretty tree for the garden produces heavy yields of greeny-yellow fruits early in the season. The apples have a sharp flavor that mellows as they ripen, but they will only store for a few weeks. These very hardy trees are ideal for colder regions.

- on a dwarfing rootstock
- early spring or fall
- excellent resistance
- hardy
- partially self-fertile (mid)
- early fall

'Priscilla'

Bred for scab resistance, this variety shows moderate resistance to fire blight, cedar apple rust, and powdery mildew. Fruits display a blush of red over yellow. The crisp flesh keeps its aromatic flavor for up to three months in cold storage.

- on a dwarfing rootstock
- early spring (or fall in the South)
- excellent resistance
- hardy
- fertile (mid)
- late summer

'Tydeman's Late Orange'

A reliable, easy-to-grow, and late-cropping variety, this tree produces small, orange-red fruits with touches of russet. Their rich and aromatic flavor is similar to that of a 'Cox', but sharper. Apples will keep until early spring.

- on a dwarfing rootstock
- early spring or fall
- good resistance
- hardy
- needs 1 pollenizer (mid)
- mid-fall

'Kidd's Orange Red'

A rival to 'Cox's Orange Pippin', this green, red-flushed dessert apple is similar, but its yellowy-cream, juicy flesh has a sweeter, aromatic taste. It produces good, regular yields that will keep until Christmas. It is generally untroubled by scab and mildew.

- on a dwarfing rootstock
- early spring or fall
- good resistance
- hardy
- needs 1 pollenizer (mid)
- late fall

'Pristine'

One of the best early, disease-resistant varieties for the home garden, 'Pristine' bears lots of small to medium-sized yellow apples if not thinned early and heavily. Excellent for eating and baking, fruits store well for up to six weeks.

- on a dwarfing rootstock
- early spring (or fall in the South)
- excellent resistance
- hardy
- fertile (mid)
- mid- to late summer

'Liberty'

Since its release in 1978, 'Liberty' has been the standard for disease resistance. The firm, juicy red fruits are as good for eating as for cooking; its long-storage capabilities and low-maintenance add to the variety's all-star status.

- on a dwarfing rootstock
- early spring (or fall in the South)
- excellent resistance
- hardy
- fertile (mid)
- early to mid-fall

'Blenheim Orange'

This excellent dual-purpose tree produces heavy yields of red- and russet-striped golden fruits with white flesh and a nutty flavor. It is vigorous, so is best on a dwarfing rootstock. It has good mildew resistance, although scab can be a problem.

- on a dwarfing rootstock
- early spring or fall
- good resistance
- hardy
- needs 2 pollenizers (mid)
- late fall

'James Grieve'

One of the finest early fruiters, this popular dual-purpose variety produces heavy crops of yellow- and red-speckled apples. The juicy fruits are acidic on picking, but after a few weeks the flavor will sweeten and become milder.

- on a dwarfing rootstock
- early spring or fall
- some resistance
- hardy
- partially self-fertile (mid)
- early fall

'Belmac'

This productive, Canadian-bred cultivar combines cold-hardiness with resistance to scab, mildew, and cedar apple rust. The late-ripening fruits have a sweet-tart flavor excellent for fresh use; fruits keep for three months.

- on a dwarfing rootstock
- early spring (or fall in the South)
- good resistance
- hardy
- fertile (mid)
- early fall

'Bramley's Seedling'

The most popular cooker, it bears heavy crops of extra-large yellow-green fruits in mid-fall, although it tends to crop biennially. The apples have creamy, juicy, and full-flavored flesh. It is a vigorous variety and has poor scab resistance.

- 🪴 on a dwarfing rootstock
- 🍃 early spring or fall
- 🐛 some resistance
- ❄️ hardy
- 🌼 needs 2 pollenizers (mid)
- 🔒 mid-fall

'Arthur Turner'

Beautiful blossom makes way for heavy yields of yellow-green apples flushed orange-brown. This outstanding baking apple has a good sweet flavor. A particularly hardy tree, it does well in colder regions.

- 🪴 on a dwarfing rootstock
- 🍃 early spring or fall
- 🐛 some resistance
- ❄️ hardy
- 🌼 partially self-fertile (mid)
- 🔒 mid-fall

'Wolf River'

It is said that one 'Wolf River' apple makes a pie. The enormous fruits are pale red with tender, creamy flesh, and used for cooking and baking. Trees are long-lived, very cold-hardy, and resistant to scab, mildew, rust, and fire blight.

- 🪴 unsuitable for containers
- 🍃 early spring or fall
- 🐛 good resistance
- ❄️ hardy
- 🌼 needs 1 pollinator (mid)
- 🔒 early fall

'Golden Noble'

The juicy flesh of this large yellow-green apple cooks to a golden purée and has a sharp flavor and creamy texture. A reliable cropper, this tree is fairly vigorous and does well in cooler areas. The fruit keeps well, too.

  on a dwarfing rootstock

early spring or fall

excellent resistance

hardy

needs 1 pollenizer (mid)

mid-fall

'Rhode Island Greening'

This historic American apple, also known as 'Burlington', 'Ganges', and 'Green Winter Pippin', produces hard, green-skinned, tart fruits that are excellent winter keepers. The vigorous, long-lived heirloom is a triploid.

unsuitable for containers

early spring or fall

no resistance

hardy

needs 2 pollinators (mid)

early to mid fall

'Gravenstein'

This crisp, juicy apple has been grown for centuries; it is a favorite for sauces and baking. Hardy and large, the vigorous tree is usually sold on semi-dwarfing rootstock. Plant two other early-blooming varieties nearby for best yield.

unsuitable for containers

early spring or fall

some resistance

hardy

needs 2 pollinators (early)

mid- to late summer

PEARS *Pyris communis*

When harvested at their sweet and juicy best, pears are simply unbeatable. They are delicious eaten fresh, used in cooking, or bottled in alcohol and stored for later use. Although less widely grown than apples, they can be just as easy, are vulnerable to fewer pests and diseases, and are arguably much tastier—just give them a sheltered site and provide them with some frost protection in winter.

	SPRING	SUMMER	FALL	WINTER
PLANT				
HARVEST				

PLANTING

Choose your trees carefully: if you have only a small space, pears can be grown on a semi-dwarfing rootstock. These types will need around 10 ft (3 m) of space between trees, whereas more vigorous types need about 15 ft (5 m). They can be grown as free-standing trees or trained; fans, cordons, or espaliers are ideal for a south-facing wall, since pears require more heat and sunshine than apples.

Although some pear cultivars are classified as partially self-fertile, all will benefit from pollination from another tree, so choose carefully, selecting trees that will flower within the same period. Bear in mind that pear pollination can be complicated:

Allow trees plenty of space to develop.

there are some trees that produce very poor pollen and make unsatisfactory pollenizers (although they are not suggested in the pear catalog of this book). Some combinations of trees will simply not pollinate each other, such as 'Doyenné du Comice' and 'Onward', while others are triploid—meaning that they need at least two other pollenizers to produce fruit.

Seek advice from a specialist at the time of purchase.

Container-grown trees can be planted at any time of year, although spring or fall are preferable; ensure that they have not become pot-bound when you choose your tree. Plant bare-root trees between fall and early spring as long as the ground is not frozen. Pears need a warm, sheltered, sunny site with well-draining, fertile soil, and a pH of around 6.5. Dig in plenty of well-rotted manure or compost before planting—a thin, acidic, or chalky soil can encourage lime-induced chlorosis.

Thin out fruits to encourage large growth.

CROP CARE

Pear trees will require careful watering, especially while young or during their growing season— do not allow them to dry out. Pears will need to be fed with a balanced or nitrogenous fertilizer in late winter, and then weeding and mulching with well-rotted manure or compost in spring.

If your tree produces lots of fruits, thin them out to encourage the tree to channel its energy into

TIP   PRUNING

Pear trees should be pruned in winter while the tree is dormant to reduce the risk of infection. Cut back any diseased wood and aim to improve ventilation through the branches. If training the tree, prune to encourage directed growth and tie in where necessary (see right). Do not overprune, since too much pruning can encourage an excess of leafy growth and fewer fruits.

Tie in branches with twine or garden string to guide growth for training.

the remaining fruits, producing the largest possible. Thin them to leave about 4–6 in (10–15 cm) between fruits (see image, left).

Pear trees are more susceptible to frost damage than apple trees because they produce their blossom earlier in the season—so, if possible, protect trees with horticultural fleece.

HARVESTING

It is crucial to time the harvesting of your pears carefully; if you harvest early or midseason pears too early and leave them indoors for too long, or harvest them too late, they may become grainy and unpalatable, or rot prematurely. Test fruits to check that they are sweet, and then pick them while they are still slightly underripe. When late-season pears pull easily away from the tree they can be brought inside and stored.

STORING

Pears store for varying times—some varieties will keep until the following spring, so see individual cultivar entries for more specific information. Pears need to be kept in a cool, dark place. Ensure that fruits are not touching each other, and check regularly for signs of rot.

PESTS AND DISEASES

Comparisons are often made between apples and pears, and when it comes to fighting off pests and diseases pears are the clear winners. Although they are not completely invincible, they face far fewer problems.

If aphids are spotted or pear leaf midge suspected, use a plant oil wash in winter and, if necessary, spray trees with a pyrethroid insecticide after blossom has dropped. Place grease bands around the trunks to keep winter moth caterpillars from climbing up and laying eggs.

Trees may be vulnerable to diseases such as scab, brown rot, and fire blight—prune diseased plant parts and pick off damaged fruits. Destroy rather than compost infected material. Using sterilized tools when pruning will help reduce the risk and spread of disease.

Wasps (left) will target existing holes in fruits to feast on the sweet flesh. Pear leaf midge (right) cause leaves to roll and turn to red then black in color.

'Gorham'

Bearing a dual-purpose pear with a sweet, musky flavor and smooth-textured, juicy flesh, this is a moderate to good cropper with upright growth. It is a good pollenizer for other varieties, especially 'Doyenne du Comice', and is partially self-fertile.

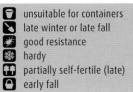

🪣	unsuitable for containers
🍂	late winter or late fall
🐛	good resistance
❄️	hardy
🌸	partially self-fertile (late)
🔒	early fall

'Packham's Triumph'

A tree of relatively weak growth, it crops so heavily that fruits may need thinning. They have pale yellow-green, smooth, juicy flesh. For the best flavor, leave on the tree as long as possible. Plant in a warm, sheltered location.

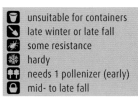

🪣	unsuitable for containers
🍂	late winter or late fall
🐛	some resistance
❄️	hardy
🌸	needs 1 pollenizer (early)
🔒	mid- to late fall

'Conference'

This reliable and heavy cropper is partially self-fertile. The long, greenish-russet fruits have creamy-white, very crisp flesh for dessert or culinary use. It is good for cordon and espalier training but is susceptible to canker, mildew, and scab.

🪣	unsuitable for containers
🔪	late winter or late fall
🐛	poor resistance
❄️	hardy
👬	partially self-fertile (mid)
🔒	late fall

'Magness'

Vigorous, fire blight-resistant 'Magness' bears excellent, greenish-brown, lightly russeted fruits with un-gritty flesh. This 'Seckel' and 'Comice' hybrid should be planted with two other varieties to ensure that all trees are pollinated.

🪣	unsuitable for containers
🔪	early spring
🐛	excellent resistance
❄️	hardy
👬	needs 1 pollenizer (early)
🔒	early fall

'Bosc'

Easily recognized by its long-necked shape and yellow-brown, russeted skin, this classic dessert pear is known for excellent flavor and juicy, smooth-textured flesh, and is considered the best pear for poaching. It is at risk of fire blight.

🪣	unsuitable for containers
🔪	early spring
🐛	poor resistance
❄️	hardy
🔒	fertile (mid)
🔒	early fall

'Concorde'

This new, partially self-fertile variety bears a very heavy crop on a compact tree, with pale green fruits turning pale yellow-green with russet patches. The flesh is juicy and sweet with a very good flavor, and fruits can be stored until midwinter.

🪣	unsuitable for containers
🔪	late fall to late winter
🕷	good resistance
❄	hardy
👥	partially self-fertile (mid)
🔒	mid-fall

'Williams' Bon Chrétien'

The fruits of this vigorous, hardy tree have bright yellow-green skin and white, very smooth, juicy flesh with a musky flavor. They are borne in profusion and are dual-purpose. Pick promptly when ripe or they may rot.

🪣	unsuitable for containers
🔪	late winter or late fall
🕷	excellent resistance
❄	hardy
👥	partially self-fertile (mid)
🔒	late summer to early fall

'Beurré Hardy'

This variety may be slow
to bear its first crops, but from
then on produces an abundance
of medium to large fruits with
green, bronze-russeted skin
and aromatic, juicy flesh.
Pick while hard and ripen
in storage.

- unsuitable for containers
- late fall to late winter
- good resistance
- hardy
- needs 1 pollenizer (mid)
- early fall

'Luscious'

Bred for fire blight resistance,
this is a good choice for colder
areas. The excellent fruits are
bright yellow with a red blush.
Its pollen is sterile, so plant it
near two other varieties to ensure
that all trees are pollinated.

- unsuitable for containers
- early spring
- good resistance
- hardy
- needs 1 pollenizer (mid)
- early fall

'D'Anjou'

Characterized by its green skin
even when ripe, mild, juicy
'D'Anjou' is a popular winter pear.
Pears are harvested when firm,
and improve in flavor after a
month or two of cold storage. It is
more blight-resistant than Bartlett.

- unsuitable for containers
- early spring
- some resistance
- hardy
- self-fertile (mid)
- early fall

'Clapp's Favorite'

A hardy variety with upright growth, this tree crops prolifically, producing an early yield of scarlet-flushed, yellow-green fruits with crisp, sweet, juicy flesh that is good for both cooking and eating. Pick as soon as the fruit is ripe.

🪣	unsuitable for containers
🍂	late fall to late winter
🐛	excellent resistance
❄️	hardy
🌸	needs 1 pollenizer (late)
🔒	late summer to early fall

'Moonglow'

This vigorous upright tree bears yellow-green, pink-flushed, very juicy pears with a sweet, musky flavor and smooth texture, good for both dessert and culinary use; pick before fruits are ripe. This hardy variety is resistant to scab.

🪣	unsuitable for containers
🍂	late winter or late fall
🐛	excellent resistance
❄️	hardy
🌸	needs 1 pollenizer (late)
🔒	late summer

'Catillac'

An old French variety with spreading growth and attractive blossom, 'Catillac' is one of the best culinary pears, bearing heavy crops of large greenish-yellow fruits, ready for use from late winter to mid-spring.

🪣	unsuitable for containers
🍂	late winter or late fall
🐛	excellent resistance
❄️	hardy
🌸	needs 2 pollenizers (late)
🔒	mid- to late fall

'Doyenne du Comice'

The large, gold-green fruits of
this variety have a fine flavor and
juicy, smooth flesh. They are best
when picked early and ripened
indoors. It has some resistance to
mildew, but is susceptible to scab.
Grow in a warm location for the
best crop.

- unsuitable for containers
- late winter or late fall
- some resistance
- hardy
- needs 1 pollenizer (late)
- mid-fall

'Orient'

Named for the similarity of its
large, round fruits to Asian pears,
'Orient' is noted for its beauty as
a landscape tree as well as for its
productiveness and resistance to
fire blight. Pears have yellow skin
with a red blush and a mild flavor.

- unsuitable for containers
- early spring
- good resistance
- hardy
- self-fertile (mid)
- late summer

'Nijisseiki'

An Asian apple pear from Japan,
'Nijisseiki' has fruits that resemble
an apple in shape and crispness
but have the juiciness and sweet
flavor of a pear. They will store in
the refrigerator for several months
with no loss of quality.

- unsuitable for containers
- late winter or late fall
- good resistance
- hardy
- needs 1 pollenizer (mid)
- late summer to early fall

PLUMS, DAMSONS, AND GAGES

Prunus spp.

With their beautiful blossom and their sweet, juicy fruits that are excellent for use in jams, desserts, pies, and crisps, there is every reason to want to grow your own plum tree. Their close relative the gages are even richer in flavor and are wonderful eaten fresh from the tree. Damsons are too sharp to eat raw but are delicious cooked.

	SPRING	SUMMER	FALL	WINTER
PLANT				
HARVEST				

PLANTING

Plums, damsons, and gages all need a well-drained soil with a pH of about 6.5, and a warm, sunny position. A south-facing wall is ideal; frost pockets should be avoided. You need to select the right variety and rootstock for your garden, since not all plum trees are self-fertile. If you opt for trees that aren't, ensure that they flower at the same time in the season and that the combination you choose are compatible, since some trees will simply not pollinate each other. If in doubt, seek the advice of a specialist when you buy your trees.

Choose a rootstock that works for your space. Plum trees can grow quite large, so if you don't have a large plot choose a

Protect blossom from early frosts

semi-dwarfing rootstock. If you choose a semi-vigorous type, ensure that trees have enough room to spread as they get older. Leave about 22 ft (7 m) between freestanding trees, but less if you are training the tree into a fan or cordon shape, since it will require less space.

Container-grown trees can be planted at any time of year, provided that the weather is

not too hot, but ensure that trees have not become pot-bound. Bare-root trees should be planted between late fall and early spring, unless the soil is frozen.

Dig in plenty of well-rotted manure or compost before planting, since plums, damsons, and gages all prefer a fertile soil. Water in well, and apply an organic mulch around the base. Young trees need staking for their first few years of growth.

Thin out fruits to encourage strong growth.

CROP CARE

Keep trees well-watered to help prevent fruits from splitting (see box, right). Feed trees with a balanced fertilizer in late winter and a nitrogenous fertilizer in early spring. Mulch around the base of trunks with well-rotted manure, compost, or bark chippings after feeding.

Plums, damsons, and gages flower relatively early in the season, and may need protection with fleece if frosts occur—this may not be feasible for larger trees, but will be much easier for container-grown or wall-trained types. Plums, damsons, and

TIP PRUNING

Whether you are training your tree or simply pruning it, only do so between late spring and early fall to reduce the risk of infection from silver leaf or bacterial canker. Use sterilized tools, and prune out diseased wood first to promote an open, well-ventilated branch structure. Plums fruit on two- or three-year-old wood, so the aim of pruning is to clean up the tree rather then remove too much of the old wood.

Like other stone fruit, prune plums in summer while leaves are still out.

gages need far less pruning than apples or pears (see tip box, left). Freestanding trees may not require pruning at all.

Fruits may need thinning out if growth is heavy (see image, left), to encourage larger fruits to form. Some crops will fall in early summer in the "June drop." Thin out any remaining fruits to leave around 2–5 in (5–10 cm) between them.

HARVESTING

Plums and gages should be ready to harvest in midsummer; damsons in midfall. Leave plums that you plan to eat to ripen on the tree, and squeeze them gently to test—when they are soft to the touch they are ready to pick. Plums to be used for cooking can be harvested earlier and will keep a little longer in the refrigerator. Pick plums with a short amount of stalk attached to prevent the fruit skins from tearing. Fruits ripen in succession, so keep checking the tree for those that are ripe.

STORING

Plums, damsons, and gages will keep for a short time in the refrigerator, but try to use them as soon as possible after harvesting to keep them from spoiling.

PESTS AND DISEASES

Wasps, flies, and birds are drawn to sweet, ripening fruits, so do all you can to discourage them. Try to ensure that trees receive a constant level of moisture, since irregular watering can cause the plums' skins to split, leaving them open to attack from both pests and diseases, notably brown rot, which will shrivel plums, covering the skins in spores. Net container-grown or wall-trained trees to deter birds.

Winter moths can be a real problem, and will munch their way through leaves—attach sticky grease bands around the trunks of trees and pick off any caterpillars you find. If aphids are a problem, spray with insecticidal soap. Be wary of diseases such as bacterial canker, plum sawfly, plum fruit moth, and pocket plum as well.

Wasps will feast on sweet, ripe fruits (left), so set up a jam-trap to distract them. Bacterial canker (right) creates holes in, and then withers, leaves.

'Victoria'

Probably the best-known and most widely grown dual-purpose English plum, this tree reliably bears heavy yields. The pale purple-red, medium-sized fruits have a yellow-green, juicy flesh that is sweet, but has a much better flavor when cooked.

- 🪣 unsuitable for containers
- 🍂 early spring or fall
- 🐝 some resistance
- ❄️ fairly hardy
- 🌳 self-fertile (mid)
- 🔒 late summer

'Seneca'

This hardy, upright, and vigorous tree reliably bears good crops of very large, purpled-red fruits late in the season. The plums have bright yellow-orange flesh and are delicious eaten fresh from the tree.

- 🪣 unsuitable for containers
- 🍂 early spring or fall
- 🐝 good resistance
- ❄️ hardy
- 🌳 partially self-fertile (mid)
- 🔒 late summer

'Early Laxton'

One of the earliest cropping plum varieties, this compact tree produces regular crops of round, medium-sized, yellow fruits whose skins are flushed with pink. Plums have juicy golden flesh and are good eaten straight from the tree or cooked.

🪣	unsuitable for containers
🌱	early spring or fall
🕷	good resistance
❄	fairly hardy
🌺	partially self-fertile (mid)
🔒	early summer

'President'

One of the last European plums to ripen, 'President' produces blue-black, yellow-fleshed fruits famous for their big size. Resistant to black knot, the tree is a heavy producer—so heavy that its branches sometimes snap under their loads.

🪣	unsuitable for containers
🌱	early spring or fall
🕷	some resistance
❄	hardy
🌺	needs 1 pollenizer (mid)
🔒	early fall

'Santa Rosa'

This long-time favorite Japanese plum is revered for the juicy sweetness of its red-tinged flesh. The tree is fast-growing and vigorous, and a good pollenizer for other Japanese varieties, but it lacks disease resistance.

🪣	unsuitable for containers
🌱	early spring
🕷	poor resistance
❄	hardy
🌺	self-fertile (early)
🔒	mid- to late summer

'Stanley'

This variety is widely grown because of its excellent, reliable cropping nature and its tendency to produce heavy yields. The large, purple-blue plums have a sweet and juicy greenish-yellow flesh that is delicious eaten fresh or dried.

- unsuitable for containers
- early spring or fall
- good resistance
- hardy
- self-fertile (late)
- late summer

'Methley'

One of the best Japanese plums available, this variety is a very heavy cropper, and fruits often need thinning out early in the season. The tree bears medium-sized, reddish-purple fruits with juicy, mild-flavored, red flesh.

- unsuitable for containers
- early spring or fall
- good resistance
- hardy
- self-fertile (mid)
- midsummer

'Morris'

This large, red-fleshed, aromatic plum was developed at Texas A and M for commercial growers, but its high productivity and leaf scald tolerance make it a good garden choice. The ruby-red fruits grow in easily harvested clusters.

- unsuitable for containers
- early spring or fall
- good resistance
- hardy
- partially self-fertile (early)
- midsummer

'Opal'

A very hardy, vigorous, upright variety, 'Opal' bears heavy crops of dessert plums that mature early in the season. Inside the small, bite-sized, purplish-green fruits, the pale yellow flesh has a distinctly greengagelike flavor.

- unsuitable for containers
- early spring or fall
- good resistance
- fairly hardy
- self-fertile (mid)
- early to midsummer

'Superior'

This Japanese-American hybrid was selected for fruit size, vigor, and cold-hardiness. It grows larger and faster than most, and bears red fruit with yellow flesh that is excellent fresh or in jams. Pollenize with Japanese plums or hybrids.

- unsuitable for containers
- early spring
- some resistance
- hardy
- self-fertile (early)
- late summer

'Wickson'

This Chinese-Japanese plum, hybridized a century ago, bears large, yellow-and-red fruits with tasty yellow flesh. Self-fruitful, it produces bigger crops when planted by a Japanese variety. Prone to mildew and brown rot.

- unsuitable for containers
- early spring or fall
- no resistance
- hardy
- partially self-fertile (early)
- mid- to late summer

'Giant Prune'

A reliable and prolific cropper also known as 'Burbank', this tree bears large, oval, purple-red fruits that keep well. The purple flesh is excellent both for cooking and for fresh eating. This variety also has good frost tolerance and disease resistance.

- 🪴 unsuitable for containers
- 🌱 early spring or fall
- ❄️ excellent resistance
- ❄️ fairly hardy
- 🔑 self-fertile (late)
- 🔒 late summer

'Satsuma'

Medium to large oval-shaped fruits with distinctive dark skin and juicy red flesh have a sweet rather than tart flavor, and are excellent for fresh eating and for preserves. However, this variety is susceptible to brown rot.

- 🪴 unsuitable for containers
- 🌱 early spring
- ❄️ poor resistance
- ❄️ hardy
- 🔑 needs 1 pollenizer (early)
- 🔒 late summer

'Shiro'

This Japanese variety is a vigorous, reliable, easy-to-grow tree bearing very sweet, medium-sized, yellow fruits early in the season. The crisp, yellow flesh of these plums is excellent eaten fresh, cooked, or preserved.

- 🪴 unsuitable for containers
- 🌱 early spring or fall
- ❄️ good resistance
- ❄️ fairly hardy
- 🔑 needs 1 pollenizer (mid)
- 🔒 early to midsummer

'Marjorie's Seedling'

This US-only variety is popular for the quality of its fruit and its good disease and frost resistance. The large, oval, purple plums are produced late in the season. The sweet, sharp, yellow flesh is best cooked, but can be eaten fresh.

- unsuitable for containers
- early spring or fall
- excellent resistance
- fairly hardy
- self-fertile (late)
- early fall

'Castleton'

Also known as a prune plum, 'Castleton' sets heavy crops of blue-purple freestone fruits that are excellent for eating and drying. Self-fertile; better fruit set will occur when it is planted near a European plum, such as 'Stanley'.

- unsuitable for containers
- early spring
- some resistance
- hardy
- self-fertile (mid)
- midsummer

'AU Producer'

A cultivar bred for disease resistance and adaptability to Southern climates, 'AU Producer' bears small, round, firm fruits that are red inside and out. Fruit flavor is excellent; trees are resistant to black knot disease and leaf scale.

- unsuitable for containers
- early spring
- good resistance
- hardy
- self-fertile (early)
- midsummer

'Old Green Gage'

Often considered the finest of all the dessert plums, the medium-sized, yellow-green fruits produced by this variety have a superb, sweet, luscious flavor. Although not always a reliable cropper, the yields are usually of a decent size.

- unsuitable for containers
- early spring or fall
- good resistance
- fairly hardy
- partially self-fertile (late)
- midsummer

'Oullins Gage'

This gagelike plum is a reliable, heavy-cropping variety. The large, round, light-green fruits have a sweet flavor. The plums can be picked early for cooking or left to ripen for fresh eating, but are also excellent for bottling.

- unsuitable for containers
- early spring or fall
- good resistance
- fairly hardy
- self-fertile (late)
- midsummer

'Imperial Gage'

Also known as 'Denniston's Superb', this is the most reliable gage, regularly producing heavy crops. It is very hardy, so is ideal for colder locations. The medium-sized, round, green-yellow fruits have a firm, yellow, juicy flesh.

- unsuitable for containers
- early spring or fall
- good resistance
- hardy
- self-fertile (mid)
- late summer

'Cambridge Gage'

One of the most popular and reliable dual-purpose greengages, the compact trees produce decent yields in all but the coldest areas. The small, yellow-green, juicy fruits have an excellent flavor and can be eaten raw or cooked.

- unsuitable for containers
- early spring or fall
- good resistance
- fairly hardy
- partially self-fertile (late)
- late summer

'Merryweather Damson'

This very popular, heavy-cropping tree bears the largest of the damsons. The blue-black fruits look like small plums but their sharp, acidic, yellow flesh has the distinctive damson flavor. Use in jams and pickles.

- unsuitable for containers
- early spring or fall
- good resistance
- fairly hardy
- self-fertile (mid)
- midsummer

'Prune Damson'

Also known as 'Shropshire Damson', this compact variety is easy to grow even in colder areas. Heavy yields of small, deep purple fruits have a sharp flavor that mellows with cooking. They are excellent for jams and for drying.

- unsuitable for containers
- early spring or fall
- good resistance
- fairly hardy
- self-fertile (late)
- early fall

SWEET AND SOUR CHERRIES

Prunus avium and P. cerasus

Not only are sweet cherries a delicious treat picked and eaten fresh, but their trees are also renowned for their breathtaking displays of spring beauty. Although they are too sour to eat fresh, sour varieties are also worth growing—they are hardier than their sweet relatives, and the fruits are wonderful cooked and used in jams, desserts, and pies.

	SPRING	SUMMER	FALL	WINTER
PLANT				
HARVEST				

PLANTING

Select your cherry tree carefully—most are self-fertile, so if you only have space for one, ensure you invest in this type. If you are growing more than one tree, make sure that their seasons of flowering are the same—but bear in mind that there are a few varieties of sweet cherry that will not cross-pollinate each other, even if they both flower at the same time. Seek advice from a specialist at the time of purchase.

Cherry trees grow fast and can become large, so if you only have a small space choose a tree grown on a dwarfing rootstock. Trees may be bare-root or container-grown; if you are buying the latter, ensure that it has not become pot-bound.

Protect blossom from frost and rain.

Sweet cherries need a warm, sheltered site, and a well-drained, moist soil with a pH of around 6.5. Their blossoms will need protection against frost, so growing them against a south-facing wall is ideal, since they can then be easily covered over with fleece or netting, or plastic sheeting to protect the trees from rain. Sour cherries are less fussy, and although they need the same

soil conditions as sweet varieties, they will happily grow in cooler locations—even trained against a north-facing wall or fence.

Dig in some well-rotted manure or compost shortly before planting. Your trees will need support, so insert stakes for freestanding trees before planting, and stake and fix horizontal wires in place for trees to be trained. Some compact varieties of cherry can be grown in containers; ensure that your pot is at least 18 in (45 cm) deep and that the soil is well-drained.

Protect your precious crops with netting.

CROP CARE

Cherry trees should be kept well-watered while they are young and need an application of a balanced fertilizer in early spring. Mulch around the base of trees with well-rotted manure or compost after feeding. Sour cherries will also benefit from a late winter feeding with a nitrogen-rich fertilizer.

Bear in mind that due to their restricted conditions, container-grown trees will need more water than those planted outside—they

TIP   PRUNING

- When the tree is young, prune to encourage strong growth. Once the tree is established, prune in early spring to encourage growth and again in summer after fruiting.
- Use sterilized tools. Prune out any diseased or damaged wood first.
- Prune strategically so that branches are not crossing or rubbing—the tree is vulnerable to infection if the bark has been rubbed away.

Prune in spring when blossoms and new leaves are present on the tree.

will also need to be fed with a high-potash fertilizer in spring.

To discourage the spread of diseases such as silver leaf, always prune in early spring and summer. Cherries, like other stone fruit trees, produce their crop on year-old wood, so prune to remove old, fruited wood and to train the tree into shape. Cherries are commonly grown as fans or pyramids (see pruning tip box, left).

Cover both sweet and sour cherries with fleece while the delicate flowers are blossoming. Trees will also need netting to deter birds, as these will happily strip the tree of all of its fruits.

HARVESTING

When they are ripe, cut the cherries from the tree with their stalks attached using scissors or pruning shears. Hold the fruits by the stalks while you cut them to prevent the fruit from dropping and becoming damaged. You may need to go over the tree several times to collect the entire harvest.

STORING

Cherries do not store well after harvesting, so eat them fresh as soon as possible, use them for cooking or making preserves, or freeze them for later use.

PESTS AND DISEASES

Sudden changes in moisture levels can cause the cherries' skins to split, leaving them vulnerable to wasps and flies. To discourage this, ensure that you water the tree regularly and do not let it dry out. Net the trees to deter birds, and be wary of other pests such as aphids and fruit flies. If you spot signs of these, spray the affected trees with an appropriate insecticide.

Cherry trees are prone to diseases such as bacterial canker, silver leaf, and brown rot (see below). To discourage the emergence or spread of disease, practice good garden hygiene: ensure that the trees have sufficient ventilation and space, always prune with sterilized equipment, and remove and destroy any affected fruits, foliage, or branches promptly.

Cherries affected by brown rot shrivel and develop creamy-white spots.

'Emperor Francis'

A reliable and hardy tree that produces heavy crops of medium-sized, yellowish fruits with a light red blush that darkens as they ripen. The juicy cherries have an excellent sweet flavor, and are delicious eaten straight from the tree.

🪣	unsuitable for containers
🌱	early spring or fall
🕷	good resistance
❄	hardy
👥	needs 1 pollenizer (late)
🔒	midsummer

'Stella'

One of the oldest, more compact, and easy-to-grow varieties, this has long been the preferred choice for gardens. It reliably produces an abundant crop of large, dark red, almost black, juicy fruits with a sweet flavor.

🪣	unsuitable for containers
🌱	early spring or fall
🕷	good resistance
❄	hardy
🔒	self-fertile (mid)
🔒	midsummer

'Summit'

This relatively new American variety produces good crops of cherries in the middle of the cherry season. The large, slightly heart-shaped fruits are a light red color and their strong, sweet taste is delicious straight from the tree.

- 🪣 unsuitable for containers
- 🍂 early spring or fall
- 🐛 good resistance
- ❄️ hardy
- 👫 needs 1 pollenizer (late)
- 🔒 midsummer

'Hedelfinger'

This productive European variety is a favored for its vigorous growth habit and reliable, high-quality, dark fruits that resist cracking. The beautiful white spring blossoms that appear before the foliage require cross-pollination.

- 🪣 unsuitable for containers
- 🍂 early spring
- 🐛 poor resistance
- ❄️ hardy
- 👫 needs 1 pollenizer (mid to late)
- 🔒 midsummer

'WhiteGold'

Winter-hardy and frost-tolerant, 'WhiteGold' produces crack-resistant, yellow-red fruits. Trees are tolerant to cherry leaf spot and resistant to bacterial canker. Self-fertile, it is an excellent pollenizer for other sweet cherries.

- 🪣 unsuitable for containers
- 🍂 early spring
- 🐛 good resistance
- ❄️ hardy
- 🔒 self-fertile (mid to late)
- 🔒 midsummer

'Ulster'

'Ulster' produces large, dark, high-quality fruits that resist cracking. The vigorous trees have shown resistance to cherry leaf spot, and its blossoms are less likely to be damaged by spring frosts than those of other varieties. It requires a pollenizer.

- unsuitable for containers
- early spring
- some resistance
- hardy
- needs 1 pollenizer (mid)
- midsummer

'Sweetheart'

A relatively new variety, this tree produces fruits that do not ripen all at once, making the harvesting period longer than for many other types. The heavy crops of cherries ripen to a dark red color with an excellent sweet flavor.

- unsuitable for containers
- early spring or fall
- good resistance
- hardy
- self-fertile (late)
- late summer

'Kristin'

This tree bears heavy crops of extra-large dark fruits when paired with a suitable pollenizer. However it is self-infertile, and incompatible with 'Ulster' and 'Emperor Francis'. It is the recommended sweet cherry for cold-winter locations.

- unsuitable for containers
- early spring
- poor resistance
- hardy
- needs 1 pollenizer (mid)
- midsummer

'Hudson'

These medium-to-large dark-red cherries ripen later than most. Plant with another variety for cross-pollination, and canker-tolerant 'Hudson' will extend the harvest period. Prune for productive, lateral branches.

- unsuitable for containers
- early spring
- some resistance
- hardy
- needs 1 pollenizer (late)
- mid- to late summer

'Sweetheart'

'Lapins'

This upright tree bears heavy crops of large, good-quality fruits. The cherries are a dark red, almost black color when they are fully ripe and have an exquisite, sweet flavor, both straight from the tree and when cooked.

- unsuitable for containers
- early spring or fall
- good resistance
- hardy
- self-fertile (mid)
- midsummer

'BlackGold'

For areas prone to early summer rains, 'BlackGold' is a good choice; its heavy crop of drupes resists cracking. It is self-fertile and an excellent pollenizer for other sweet cherry varieties. Trees show tolerance to canker.

- unsuitable for containers
- early spring
- some resistance
- hardy
- self fertile (late)
- early summer

'Northstar'

A compact size of 10 ft (3 m) allows for easy harvesting and facilitates netting against birds. Cold-hardiness, resistance to brown rot and leaf spot, and an attractive drooping habit make 'Northstar' a great backyard choice.

- unsuitable for containers
- early spring
- good resistance
- hardy
- self-fertile (mid)
- midsummer

'Morello'

Probably the most popular sour cherry, this relatively small tree produces huge crops of large red fruits, even in slightly shaded or north-facing gardens. The cherries are sour when eaten straight from the tree and so are best when cooked.

- unsuitable for containers
- early spring or fall
- good resistance
- hardy
- self-fertile (late)
- late summer

'Montmorency'

This French heirloom variety is the standard for pie cherries. The ornamental trees are compact, with a spreading habit, and do not require a pollenizer. Dependable yields of bright red fruits have yellow flesh and clear juice.

- unsuitable for containers
- early spring
- some resistance
- hardy
- self-fertile (mid)
- midsummer

'Meteor'

This natural-dwarf variety bears large, oblong, bright red, freestone fruits. The acidic, juicy yellow flesh is excellent for pies. Bred for winter-hardiness, it is leaf spot resistant, and an easy choice for a small garden.

- unsuitable for containers
- early spring
- good resistance
- hardy
- self-fertile (late)
- midsummer

PEACHES AND NECTARINES

Prunus persica and *Prunus persica* var. *nectarina*

Sweet, juicy, and delicious, fuzzy peaches and smooth nectarines are delicious eaten fresh or used for making jams or desserts. Requiring cold weather over winter, protection from frost in spring, and sun in summer, peaches and nectarines are fussy trees, but try growing them in movable containers so that you can guarantee them the conditions they'll need.

	SPRING	SUMMER	FALL	WINTER
PLANT				
HARVEST				

PLANTING

Peaches and nectarines need a warm, sheltered site: a south-facing wall is ideal if you are growing them outside; they can then be easily protected against frost, predators, and rain with fleece, netting, or plastic sheeting. They will grow happily under cover in a greenhouse, and some types are suitable for containers so can be moved indoors or out as the weather dictates. Peaches and nectarines prefer a deep, slightly acidic soil—a pH of between 6.5 and 7 is ideal—that does not become waterlogged; plant both types in fall or early spring.

Prepare your plot by digging in well-rotted manure or compost a few months before planting. Trees can be purchased either

Plant in a sheltered site to protect blossoms.

bare-root or container-grown. If you buy container-grown trees, ensure that they have not become pot-bound. Plant both types between fall and early spring, to the same depth as the soil mark on their stems.

If you are training your tree against a wall, fix the horizontal wires before planting. Trees will need staking for a few years; insert a stake before planting.

CROP CARE

Peaches and nectarines are self-fertile, so technically you do not need more than one tree in your garden to produce a crop. That said, the trees may benefit from a little help—if the weather is especially cold you may not be able to rely on insect pollinators. Gently transfer pollen from one flower to another using a small paintbrush.

Thin out fruitlets when they are young.

Both fruits will need protection against frost, which may kill off their early blossoms. If your tree is compact or is growing against a wall, it will be relatively easy to protect with horticultural fleece. Alternatively, cover your trees with plastic sheeting over winter to keep them dry; this will help protect them from peach leaf curl, which may be transferred between trees by rain. Birds may also be a problem as fruit develops, so cover trees with netting to deter them. This may be problematic for freestanding trees, but attempt where possible.

Both peach and nectarine trees will benefit from being fed with a balanced fertilizer in late

TIP   PRUNING AND TRAINING

If you don't want a freestanding tree, peaches and nectarines can be trained into fans on walls, or grown as bushes or pyramid forms—start from scratch with a feathered maiden or buy a two- or three-year-old pretrained tree.

Prune peaches and nectarines (along with other stone fruits) in springtime. The trees fruit on year-old wood, so prune to remove old wood that bore fruit the previous year.

Train your tree along wires to allow good ventilation and easy picking access.

winter and then given a balanced liquid fertilizer while fruits are developing. Keep the trees well-weeded and well-watered.

THINNING

It is essential to thin out peaches and nectarines while the fruits are young. This will force the tree to focus its energy on forming larger, higher-quality peaches or nectarines. When the fruits are very small, thin to leave one fruit per cluster, removing all the others. When fruits have grown larger, thin them out again so that there is about 8–10 in (20–25 cm) between peaches and 6 in (15 cm) between nectarines—the space they need to grow to their full size.

HARVESTING

Peaches and nectarines are ready to harvest once they become soft—take care not to drop them, since they bruise and spoil easily. They are ready to pick when they pull easily away from the tree.

STORING

Once picked and fully ripened, peaches and nectarines will only last for a few days, before they go bad and begin to rot. Freeze or use to make jam if you cannot eat the fruits fast enough.

PESTS AND DISEASES

Peaches and nectarines can be afflicted by a range of problems. Creating a barrier will guard against some of them: covering with plastic sheeting reduces the risk of peach leaf curl, netting can help deter birds, and if it is very fine, wasps, too. Other problems are harder to combat:

- Aphids stunt growth and cause leaves to curl. Spray affected leaves with pyrethrin or insecticidal soap.
- Red spider mite cause leaves to appear "bronzed." Treat as for aphids.
- Silver leaf disease causes leaves to appear silvery. Remove the damaged plant material and destroy, being careful to keep cutting tools sterilized.
- Bacterial canker causes round holes to form in leaves and gum to ooze from the bark. Treat as for silver leaf.

Aphids (left) cause leaves to curl; they may become sticky with honeydew. Peach leaf curl (right) causes leaves to distort and become bright red in color.

'Redstar'

Resistance to bacterial spot and canker makes 'Redstar' a solid backyard choice. Spreading trees produce medium-to-large, yellow, semi-freestone peaches in midseason. Fruits have a rich, orange-red color, firm flesh, and an excellent flavor.

- unsuitable for containers
- early spring
- good resistance
- not hardy
- self-fertile
- mid- to late summer

'Red Haven'

Dark pink flowers in spring are followed in late summer by heavy crops of peaches with firm yellow flesh, reddening toward the center. The skins are yellow with a red flush. It is a hardy tree, and resistant to peach leaf curl.

- unsuitable for containers
- late fall or early winter
- good resistance
- hardy
- self-fertile
- late summer

'Arctic Supreme'

This large, white, semi-freestone peach is favored for its sweet and tangy, yet delicate, flavor. Fruits are very firm-textured for a white peach, and have a nice acid-sugar balance. It is a "low-chill" variety for warm winter climates.

- unsuitable for containers
- early spring
- some resistance
- not hardy
- self-fertile
- late summer

'Harrow Diamond'

Resistant to bacterial spot and brown rot, Canadian-bred 'Harrow Diamond' is known for its large, frost-resistant, pink blossoms and early harvest. Medium-large fruits are nearly freestone, with fairly firm flesh and a good flavor.

- unsuitable for containers
- early spring
- good resistance
- hardy
- self-fertile
- midsummer

'Red Haven'

'Saturn'

This new variety has unusual flattened peaches resembling a doughnut in shape. The white flesh is firm, very sweet, and has an excellent flavor, while the skin is white, flushed with dusky pink and red. It is susceptible to peach leaf curl.

- 🪣 unsuitable for containers
- 🍂 late fall or early winter
- 🕷 poor resistance
- ❄️ hardy
- 🌸 self-fertile
- 🔒 mid- to late summer

'Klondike White'

The white peaches have a sweeter, milder taste than yellow varieties. The vigorous trees produce good yields of large, high-quality fruits, which exhibit a purplish-red blush over creamy red skin. They are susceptible to bacterial spot.

- 🪣 unsuitable for containers
- 🍂 early spring
- 🕷 some resistance
- ❄️ not hardy
- 🌸 self-fertile
- 🔒 late summer

'Ernie's Choice'

These medium-to-large, mostly red freestone peaches are known for their luscious flavor and juicy texture, which bruises easily. Blossoms are showy, and the productive trees are moderately resistant to bacterial spot.

- 🪣 unsuitable for containers
- 🍂 early spring
- 🕷 some resistance
- ❄️ not hardy
- 🌸 self-fertile
- 🔒 late summer

'Fantasia'

This easy-to-grow, vigorous, frost-resistant variety bears large, yellow-fleshed nectarines with orange-red skin. Harvested early, they have a slightly acidic, tangy flavor. Later, a rich, sweet juiciness develops. It is resistant to bacterial canker and some pests.

🪣	unsuitable for containers
🍂	late fall or early winter
🕷	good resistance
❄	hardy
🌼	self-fertile
🔒	late summer

'Redgold'

One of the best-tasting nectarine varieties, popular 'Redgold' bears large, yellow-fleshed, freestone fruits with red and gold skin. The 15–30-ft- (4.6–9-m-) tall trees are adaptable and productive, but susceptible to bacterial spot.

🪣	unsuitable for containers
🍂	early spring
🕷	poor resistance
❄	hardy
🌼	self-fertile
🔒	late summer

'Jade'

This French variety bears small-to-medium clingstone fruits with smooth, purplish-crimson skin and firm, juicy flesh. The trees produce some of the season's first nectarines. They are moderately resistant to bacterial spot.

🪣	unsuitable for containers
🍂	early spring
🕷	some resistance
❄	not hardy
🌼	self-fertile
🔒	midsummer

APRICOTS *Prunus armeniaca*

Homegrown apricots are a delicious treat—perfect for eating fresh or for cooking or making jam. Because of their Asian origins, apricots will need adequate frost protection during colder months, and may need help with pollination. Since they are self-fertile you will only need one tree to produce a crop, and if you choose a dwarfing variety you can harvest fresh, flavorful fruit even from a tiny space.

	SPRING	SUMMER	FALL	WINTER
PLANT				
HARVEST				

PLANTING

Apricot trees prefer a warm, sheltered site—a south-facing wall is ideal, although they will grow happily in a greenhouse or in a large container that can be moved under cover in colder months. As with all fruit trees, if you are buying them container-grown, ensure that they have not become pot-bound.

Plant trees in fall–early winter. Dig in plenty of well-rotted manure or compost a few months before planting. Apricots will grow well in most fertile, well-drained soils, but prefer a pH of between 6.7–7.5. Attach some supports if you are growing your apricot against a wall. Stake young trees, and ensure that they are kept well-watered.

Colorful buds break in early spring.

CROP CARE

Apricot trees are fully hardy, but since they produce blossoms very early in the year—even as early as late winter—they may still need protection against frost. Move container-grown plants indoors, and cover wall-trained trees with fleece (see right). If you are growing your apricots indoors, or where they will receive few insect pollinators,

you may need to pollinate trees by hand—use a small paintbrush and gently transfer the pollen between flowers. Only prune trees in spring or summer, since this helps to reduce the risk of infection and dieback.

HARVESTING AND STORING
Harvest fruits when they are soft and ripe. Picked apricots will not store well for long, so eat them when they are as fresh as possible.

PESTS AND DISEASES
Ensuring that trees have enough space and are well-pruned will help to avoid common problems.

TIP PROTECTION

Training your apricot tree against a south-facing wall will make it easier for you to protect it: cover it with a layer of horticultural fleece in colder months, or waterproof sheeting against strong winds or weather.

Protect vulnerable wall-trained trees.

'Alfred'

A hardy, early-flowering variety, 'Alfred' has medium to small fruits with pink-flushed orange skin and juicy, orange flesh with an excellent flavor. It is less susceptible to die-back than other apricot varieties and is reliably productive.

- suitable for containers
- midwinter or late fall
- good resistance
- hardy
- self-fertile (early)
- mid- to late summer

'Moorpark'

Bearing large, crimson-flushed fruits with sweet, juicy, orange flesh, this 18th-century variety is reliable and crops generously. It does best against a wall, but will crop freestanding in a frost-free position. It is prone to die-back.

- suitable for containers
- midwinter or late fall
- some resistance
- hardy
- self-fertile (early)
- late summer

'Tomcot'

This is an early and heavy-cropping variety that produces very large, red-blushed, golden orange fruits, particularly noteworthy for their flavor. It bears abundant blossom. It is reliable, but for best results, grow it against a south-facing wall.

- suitable for containers
- midwinter or late fall
- some resistance
- hardy
- self-fertile (early)
- midsummer

'Early Golden'

This heirloom variety produces large, sweet, freestone fruits that can be eaten fresh or preserved by canning or drying. Well suited for the South, the tree is fast-growing and self-fertile, but produces more with another variety nearby.

- suitable for containers
- early spring
- some resistance
- hardy
- self-fertile (early)
- midsummer

'Harglow'

A disease-resistant variety from Canada, 'Harglow' produces large crops of bright orange, flavorful, freestone fruits. Self-fertile and late-blooming, the tree is excellent for locations with late frosts, and for coastal northwestern climates.

- suitable for containers
- early spring
- good resistance
- hardy
- self-fertile (late)
- mid- to late summer

FIGS *Ficus carica*

Although they look and taste exotic, figs are relatively easy to grow and will provide you with a good yearly crop as long as you contain their roots, give them plenty of sun and warmth, and keep them watered. Figs are available year-round and can be planted any time from early fall, so why not build yourself a fig pit and train your fig tree into an attractive fan shape against a south-facing wall?

	SPRING	SUMMER	FALL	WINTER
PLANT				
HARVEST				

PLANTING

Figs need a warm, sheltered site and should be located carefully, away from strong winds and frost pockets. Preferably, grow them against a south-facing wall, or grow under cover in a greenhouse. Figs will grow happily in a fig pit (see right) or in containers, and, as long as the pot is not too heavy, you may be able to alter your tree's location as the seasons change.

Figs prefer alkaline conditions, although they will grow happily in most well-drained soils; if the soil is too rich, figs may grow too rapidly, producing plenty of foliage but few fruits. If growing against a wall, you will need to provide supports for your fig tree—fix horizontal wires every 12 in (30 cm).

New leaves will burst forth in spring.

CROP CARE

Fig trees need to be watered regularly, especially if they are growing in a pot; letting them dry out encourages them to drop their fruits. Pot-grown and pit-grown trees will need to be fed with a balanced fertilizer every year, and all figs benefit from a compost mulch in early spring. Pot-grown fig trees may need to be repotted every few years. In colder regions,

protect trees against frost in winter by wrapping them, or cage them and fill cages with leaves.

HARVESTING

Harvest fruits when they are soft and fully ripe—not before— they will hang downward, and the skin will split slightly near the stem. Break them from the tree and eat as soon as possible.

PESTS AND DISEASES

Figs are a relatively trouble-free crop; the biggest problems are likely to be birds and wasps, which will be attracted to the ripened fruits. Protect with netting.

TIP   BUILD A FIG PIT

Fig trees thrive if their roots are kept in check, so dig a 24 x 24 in (60 x 60 cm) pit, line with paving slabs, and lay old brick and rubble as a base. This will encourage the tree to use its energy to produce fruits rather than foliage.

Restrain fig roots and the tree will reward you with larger crops.

'White Marseilles'

This slow-growing, hardy tree, produces medium-to-large, rounded fruits with yellowish-green, slightly ribbed skin and whitish, almost translucent flesh with a very sweet flavor. If grown in a greenhouse, it will bear two crops each year.

- suitable for containers
- late winter or late fall
- poor resistance
- hardy
- self-fertile
- early fall

'Brown Turkey'

With glossy, palmate leaves and a spreading habit, this variety is ornamental as well as productive. The most reliable US variety, it bears an abundance of sweet, juicy, pear-shaped fruits, with purplish-brown skin and red flesh.

- suitable for containers
- late winter or late fall
- some resistance
- hardy
- self-fertile
- late summer to early fall

'Brunswick'

This old English variety produces heavy crops of large, pear-shaped fruits with greenish-yellow skins and yellow flesh, red in the center. It has very large, deeply divided leaves and is more tolerant of cold, wet conditions than most figs.

- 🪣 suitable for containers
- 🌙 late winter or late fall
- 🐛 poor resistance
- ❄️ hardy
- 🔆 self-fertile
- 🔒 late summer to early fall

'Black Mission'

Named for the Spanish missionaries who planted it along the California coast, 'Mission' trees can grow to 30 ft (10 m). Black, teardrop-shaped figs with red pulp develop sweetness when daytime temperatures reach 100°F (38°C).

- 🪣 suitable for containers
- 🌙 very early spring
- 🐛 some resistance
- ❄️ hardy
- 🔆 self-fertile
- 🔒 midsummer to fall

'Celeste'

The small-to-medium, purplish-brown, red-fleshed fruits borne by this cold-hardy, US variety have tightly closed eyes that inhibit insect entry. 'Celeste' will grow well in a container or in the ground.

- 🪣 suitable for containers
- 🌙 very early spring
- 🐛 some resistance
- ❄️ hardy
- 🔆 self-fertile
- 🔒 midsummer to fall

MEDLARS AND QUINCES

Mespilus germanica and *Cydonia oblonga*

These unusual tree fruits look highly ornamental, and are an acquired taste, but are well worth growing if you have the space. Rose-hiplike medlars (see below) should be left until sweet-tasting and almost rotten before eating. Quinces (see right) are rarely soft enough to eat if grown in a cool climate, but are delicious cooked or used in jams or jellies.

	SPRING	SUMMER	FALL	WINTER
PLANT				
HARVEST				

PLANTING

As with all trees, ensure that container-grown medlars and quinces have not become pot-bound. Plant bare-root trees between late winter and early spring. You can plant container-grown trees at any time, but fall is preferred. Medlars and quinces are best planted in a warm, sheltered site and in well-drained soil; both are self-fertile, so will not need another tree to produce fruit. Dig well-rotted manure or compost into the soil a few months before planting.

CROP CARE

Young trees will need to be staked for the first few years. Quinces appreciate regular

Leave medlars to "blet" before eating.

feeding and watering, especially during spring and summer if the weather is dry. Medlars need feeding and watering while young, but after a few years will cope without any extra watering. Mulch well around young trees with compost, manure, or bark chips. Quinces and medlars will be largely untroubled by frost, provided they have been sited correctly.

HARVESTING AND STORING

Ripe medlars will lift easily from the tree in mid-fall. Dip the stems in a concentrated salt solution to preserve them, and then leave for several weeks in a cool, dark place, with "eyes" facing downward to decompose, or "blet." They will then be ready to eat—"bletting" gives the flesh an almost sickly sweet flavor.

Quinces can be harvested when fruits are golden-yellow in color, and, provided conditions are frost-free, they improve the longer they are left on the tree. Store in a cool, dark place, leaving space between the fruits.

PESTS AND DISEASES

Quinces are sometimes affected by diseases such as leaf blight and brown rot. Water regularly to prevent fruits from splitting. To discourage disease, prune in winter, and allow good airflow. Medlars are usually trouble-free.

Blight (right) discolors quince leaves.

'Royal'

More compact than other medlars, with an upright habit, this variety is ideal for smaller spaces. The medium-sized, golden brown fruits have a better flavor than most and can be eaten fresh, without the need for bletting.

- unsuitable for containers
- early spring or fall
- some resistance
- hardy
- self-fertile
- mid-fall

'Marron'

The hardy 'Marron' medlar is compact and productive, and an interesting ornamental landscape plant. Late spring flowers are white and fragrant. The chestnut-colored pulp of the fruits is custard-like, with a taste of applesauce.

- unsuitable for containers
- early spring
- some resistance
- hardy
- self-fertile
- late fall

'Macrocarpa'

The aromatic medlar ripens after frost. Right after picking, the 2.5-in (6-cm) fruits are too hard and astringent to eat. After a few weeks in a cool, lighted space, they become soft and spicy, and can be eaten or made into jam.

- unsuitable for containers
- early spring
- some resistance
- hardy
- self-fertile
- late fall

'Vranja'

A popular quince, these attractive, medium-sized trees bear an abundance of large, pale-green, pear-shaped fruits that become golden as they ripen. Leave the fruits on the tree as long as possible to develop their exceptional perfume and flavor.

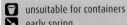	
🪣	unsuitable for containers
🍃	early spring or fall
❋	good resistance
❄	hardy
🌱	self-fertile
🔒	late fall

'Pineapple'

With a flavor that resembles its namesake, this variety produces heavy yields of large, pear-shaped, golden-yellow quinces that are best cooked or used in jellies. The attractive trees bear rose-pink blooms in spring.

🪣	unsuitable for containers
🍃	early spring
❋	some resistance
❄	hardy
🌱	self-fertile
🔒	early fall

'Smyrna'

This variety bears large, highly fragrant quinces with lemony-yellow skin. The fruits are rich in flavorful tannin and pectin, which makes them excellent for jellies and preserves. The fruits store exceptionally well.

🪣	unsuitable for containers
🍃	early spring
❋	some resistance
❄	hardy
🌱	self-fertile
🔒	early fall

CITRUS *various*

Although most citrus fruits will only grow well outdoors in very warm, sunny climates, it is possible to grow them in cooler regions if you can provide them with the heat and protection they need. For most people, this will probably mean growing them under glass. There is a wide range of citrus fruits to choose from: lemons, limes, and oranges (see image, right) are the most obvious choices.

	SPRING	SUMMER	FALL	WINTER
PLANT				
HARVEST				

PLANTING

Citrus trees should be bought as young specimens and nurtured on. Trees can be grown from seed, but it's a difficult and lengthy process. Since most citrus take a relatively long time to develop fruits, buying a young tree will ensure that you get a crop as soon as possible. Most citrus trees are self-fertile, so even if you only have space for one, you will still be rewarded with fruits.

Plant out or repot in spring. Citrus trees prefer a fertile, well-drained soil and slightly acidic conditions. If you are growing your tree outside, ensure that it has a warm, sunny site, since the amount of heat the plant receives will affect the eventual flavor of the fruits. If growing under glass,

Grow lemons in a container in a hot spot.

ensure that your tree has a sunny position, which is well-ventilated. Your tree will grow happily in a container, allowing you to move it in and out of doors as the weather dictates.

CROP CARE

Wherever you have sited your tree, do not allow it to dry out. Trees grown in containers may need more frequent watering

than those grown in open ground. Apply a nitrogen fertilizer every month while fruits are developing. If your tree is outside, it will need a minimum temperature of 59°F (15°C). Overall, try to keep the temperature as stable as possible.

HARVESTING AND STORING

When fruits have reached a good size and their rich color has fully developed, taste them to check whether they are ripe enough to harvest. Use them as soon as possible after picking; they will not keep for more than a few weeks in the refrigerator, but will keep for longer on the tree.

PESTS AND DISEASES

If you are growing under glass, citrus fruits are most likely to be affected by pests such as red spider mite and mealy bugs. Pick off bugs and spray trees with insecticide. Practice good garden hygiene and keep trees well ventilated to stop diseases from spreading.

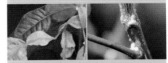

Red spider mite (left) and mealy bugs (right) attack leaves and stems.

Mexican Lime

Also known as 'Tahiti' or key lime, this medium-sized, bushy plant produces fragrant fruits popular with bartenders. The limes are produced year round, but more abundantly in summer, and have a thin, smooth skin that is yellow-green when ripe.

🪣	suitable for containers
🍃	spring or fall
🕷	some resistance
❄	not hardy
🌼	self-fertile
🔒	year round

Persian lime

This compact tree is ideal for growing in containers, producing limes with thicker skins than Mexican types, and a greater degree of hardiness. The fruits are ideal for culinary use, but are not as flavorful as some.

🪣	suitable for containers
🍃	spring or fall
🕷	some resistance
❄	not hardy
🌼	self-fertile
🔒	year round

Makrut

Although the unusual-looking, bumpy-skinned, mid-green fruits produced by this tree are largely inedible, it is worth growing for its wonderfully fragrant leaves, which are widely used in Thai cuisine.

🪣	suitable for containers
🍃	spring or fall
🕷	some resistance
❄	not hardy
🌼	self-fertile
🔒	year round

Citron

These unusual-looking, fragrant, ornamental fruits are believed in some cultures to grant good luck. What is certain is that their rind is excellent in cooking. 'Buddha's Hand' (pictured) requires higher temperatures than other citrus fruits.

- suitable for containers
- spring or fall
- some resistance
- not hardy
- self-fertile
- year round

Lemon

The quintessential citrus fruit, lemons are fast-growing, bearing acidic fruits useful for flavoring a variety of dishes. Try 'Meyer', whose compact plants produce orange-hued fruits that are sweeter than other varieties.

- suitable for containers
- spring or fall
- some resistance
- not hardy
- self-fertile
- mid- to late summer

Limequat

Hardier than a Mexican lime, but less so than a kumquat, this intergeneric cross thrives in US southeastern coastal areas. It can be container-grown and pruned to keep indoors. Its yellow fruits are juicy, with an excellent lime taste.

- suitable for containers
- spring or fall
- some resistance
- not hardy
- self-fertile
- early winter to summer

Kumquat

Winter semi-dormancy makes this subtropical tree relatively hardy. In temperate climates, the dwarf 'Nagami' kumquat can be pot-grown, and its decorative form and fragrant flowers enjoyed indoors in winter. Tart, orange fruits are eaten skin and all.

- suitable for containers
- spring or fall
- some resistance
- not hardy
- self-fertile
- winter to spring

Grapefruit

With their sharp, acidic taste, grapefruits are refreshing, but not to everyone's taste. Available in red, white, and pink types, they tolerate cold temperatures but not frost, so need to be brought inside in winter.

- suitable for containers
- spring or fall
- some resistance
- not hardy
- self-fertile
- midsummer to early winter

New Zealand grapefruit

Also known as "poor man's orange", it produces medium to large, yellow-skinned, yellow-fleshed fruits, that are less acidic than other grapefruit types. The fruits are excellent for juicing or for making marmalade.

- suitable for containers
- spring or fall
- some resistance
- not hardy
- self-fertile
- year round

Orange

Packed with vitamin C, oranges look wonderful and have a wide range of culinary uses. Try 'Valencia' (pictured), which produces sweet, medium-sized oranges that are ideal for juicing. Or try sour 'Seville' oranges, excellent for marmalade.

- suitable for containers
- spring or fall
- some resistance
- not hardy
- self-fertile
- late winter to early spring

Calamondin

This easy-to-grow citrus needs warmer outdoor temperatures to thrive or can be kept indoors year round. The shrubby, compact, evergreen tree bears fragrant white flowers followed by good crops of sour oranges.

- suitable for containers
- spring or fall
- some resistance
- not hardy
- self-fertile
- mid- to late summer

Mandarin

The mandarin family is a sprawling group that includes clementines, tangerines, and satsumas. They have thinner skins and are therefore easier to peel than oranges, and are good in fruit salads or as a snack.

- suitable for containers
- spring or fall
- some resistance
- not hardy
- self-fertile
- year round

NUTS *various*

With some trees providing architectural garden value and others beautiful spring blossoms, nuts are not as commonly grown as they ought to be. In termperate climates, a range of nuts can be homegrown: walnuts, hazelnuts (see image, left), almonds, sweet chestnuts, and cobnuts. Don't worry if you don't have a large amount of space, since some, such as almonds or cobnuts, will grow as bushes in containers.

	SPRING	SUMMER	FALL	WINTER
PLANT				
HARVEST				

PLANTING

If you buy a container-grown tree, ensure that it is healthy and has not become pot-bound. Some nut trees, such as walnuts, will eventually establish very long roots. Nut trees are generally very tolerant and will grow in a range of conditions. They prefer well-drained soil, and a pH of around 6.5.

It is important, however, to ensure that you give trees enough space to grow—walnuts, for example, will be planted at least 40–60 ft (12–18 m) away from other crops, since their roots inhibit the growth of other plants. Sweet chestnut trees will also grow large if permitted and will need a space of at least 25 ft (8 m). Cobnuts and almonds can be

Almond nuts (left) and blossom (right).

trained as fans, but will still need space; give cobnuts 15 ft (4.5 m), and almonds 15–20 ft (4.5–6 m). Stake young trees for the first few years of growth. Almonds and cobnuts are suitable for growing in containers as bushes.

CROP CARE

Keep trees well-watered, especially if the weather is dry, and feed with a balanced fertilizer

in early spring. Mulch around the base of trees for the first few years with well-rotted manure, compost, or bark, to suppress weeds and keep the soil moist.

HARVESTING AND STORING

Most nuts will be ready for harvesting in fall. If you leave them on the tree too long you risk that they will be stolen by squirrels or, in the case of walnuts, birds. Clean and dry the harvested nuts thoroughly. Store them in a cool, dark place, ensuring that no rats or mice can get to them. A net bag is ideal, as it will ensure airy conditions.

PESTS AND DISEASES

Walnuts are generally problem-free, but may come under attack from walnut leaf blight and walnut blotch, which cause black and brown spots on leaves and fruits. Remove and destroy any diseased plant material.

Cobnuts may become infected with powdery mildew—remove and destroy leaves and spray the tree with fungicide. Treat almonds as for peaches and nectarines. The biggest threat to other nut trees will probably be squirrels, so net wherever possible, and if space allows, create a wire mesh fruit cage around trees.

'Chandler'

Bred at the University of California, 'Chandler' grows to about 40 ft (12 m), and is less susceptible to walnut blight than most other varieties. It bears better crops of smooth, well-sealed nuts when another variety, such as 'Franquette', is present.

- unsuitable for containers
- early spring or fall
- good resistance
- hardy
- partially self-fertile
- mid-fall

'Franquette'

This large, slow-growing tree produces the finest-flavored walnuts. The kernels have a high oil content, which makes them sweet and moist. The trees will crop within three to four years of planting, producing good crops late in the season.

- unsuitable for containers
- late winter or late fall
- good resistance
- hardy
- self-fertile
- mid-fall

'Kwik Krop'

Over 400 cultivars of black walnut have been developed, but 'Kwik Krop' is one of the few sold. The large tree bears on alternate years; and nuts are smaller than Persian walnuts. Taste is milder if husks are removed before they soften.

- unsuitable for containers
- early spring or fall
- some resistance
- hardy
- self-fertile
- mid-fall

'Lake English'

Often called the 'English Walnut', this species originated in an area extending from the Balkans to southwest China. It is hardy, productive, and can self-pollinate; more nuts are produced if another 'Juglans Regia' variety is nearby.

- unsuitable for containers
- early spring to fall
- some resistance
- hardy
- partially self-fertile
- early to mid-fall

'Franquette'

'Hall's Hardy'

This beautiful, 15-ft (4.6-m) flowering almond tree can be grown wherever peaches thrive; it produces good yields of nuts thicker-shelled than commercial varieties. Cold-hardy and late to bloom, it is productive in regions unsuitable for most almonds.

- unsuitable for containers
- early spring or fall
- some resistance
- hardy
- partially self-fertile
- mid-fall

'All-In-One'

'All in One', a self-fertile, 15-ft (4.6-m) semi-dwarf tree, bears generous crops of sweet, high-quality almonds in a small space. Although almond trees are hardy in cold weather, their early blooms and immature nuts are susceptible to spring frosts.

- unsuitable for containers
- fall
- some resistance
- hardy
- self-fertile
- early to mid-fall

'Theta'

'Theta' is part of the Greek alphabet series of blight-immune cultivars, developed for pollination. It bears small-to-medium-sized hazelnuts of fair quality. Its main function is to shed pollen and increase yields of 'Jefferson' and other producers.

- unsuitable for containers
- early spring
- excellent resistance
- hardy
- needs 1 pollenizer
- mid-fall

'Jefferson'

This blight-immune cultivar, released by Oregon State University to replace susceptible 'Barcelona', produces heavy yields of large, tasty hazelnuts on upright shrubs. A second variety must be planted nearby for pollination.

- unsuitable for containers
- early spring; fall
- excellent resistance
- hardy
- needs 1 pollenizer
- mid-fall

'Nonpareil'

This very popular almond tree has an upright to spreading habit and produces abundant crops when planted near a second variety, such as 'All-In-One', for pollination. The nuts are poorly sealed, making them susceptible to bird and insect damage.

- unsuitable for containers
- fall
- poor resistance
- fairly hardy
- needs 1 pollenizer
- late summer to early fall

'Sumner'

Ideal for the South, 'Sumner' has high resistance to pecan scab and leaf diseases, but is susceptible to aphids. It is a "type II" upright tree, with female flowers receptive before male pollen is shed; it requires a "type I" to produce its late crop of thin-shelled nuts.

- unsuitable for containers
- fall to winter
- excellent resistance
- fairly hardy
- needs 1 pollenizer
- late fall

'Pawnee'

'Pawnee' is a "type I" pecan: its male flowers give off pollen before female flowers are receptive, so it needs a "type II" for pollination. It is cold-hardy, resistant to yellow aphids, and small. Its quality nuts mature earlier than most pecans.

- unsuitable for containers
- fall to winter
- good resistance
- fairly hardy
- needs 1 pollenizer
- mid-fall

'Hican'

This hickory-pecan hybrid has the spreading habit of the pecan, but the cold tolerance of the hickory. Cultivars produce rough-shelled nuts with a flavor that combines the two. Plant two or more varieties of hican or pecan for a good yield.

- unsuitable for containers
- early spring; fall
- good resistance
- hardy
- needs 1 pollenizer
- fall

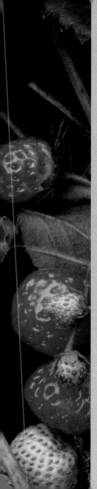

Soft Fruits

- Grape vines
- Strawberries
- Raspberries
- Blackberries and hybrid berries
- Gooseberries
- Black currants, White currants, and Red currants
- Blueberries
- Cranberries
- Melons

GRAPE VINES *Vitis vinifera*

Scrambling grape vines are highly ornamental as well as productive, and look wonderful trained over an arch or used to create a screen. Grapes can be grown for wine-making or for eating fresh—some grape varieties are suitable for both—although sweet dessert grapes will need to be grown under cover in cool climates. If you don't have much space, grow a vine in a container and train it into a standard.

	SPRING	SUMMER	FALL	WINTER
PLANT				
HARVEST				

PLANTING INDOORS

Vines can be planted under cover in a greenhouse, or planted just outside and trained through a hole in the wall or vent. Planting outside and training in will mean that you do not need to water the vine, since its roots will run deep outside. However, the soil will warm up more slowly.

If you plant vines inside, you will need to ensure that you give the plant the water, nutrients, and soil conditions that it needs. Grow indoor grape vines as cordons, and allow them about 3–4 ft (1–1.2 m) space. Some varieties suit containers.

PLANTING OUTDOORS

Grape vines are quite tolerant of most soil types: ideally, they like

Buy only certified disease-free plants.

a neutral pH. Plant vines out in early spring, at a depth of about 12 in (30 cm). Grapes are vigorous plants both above and below ground—and however you choose to train your vine you will need to give it plenty of space: cordons 3–4 ft (1–1.2 m); guyots 3 ft (1 m); and double guyots 5–6 ft (1.5–2 m) (see tip box on p.110 for details).

CARE OF INDOOR VINES

Ensure your vines receive enough water, especially while the fruits are developing, but do not allow them to become waterlogged. Feed the vines with a high-nitrogen fertilizer, and mulch around them with well-rotted manure or garden compost in late winter. Do not allow the mulch to touch the vine stems.

Ensure that vines are kept well-ventilated by opening greenhouse vents over winter to allow air to circulate. It is important not to allow the air to become stagnant, since diseases will thrive in these conditions. Do not allow the temperature to drop below 41°F (5°C).

In winter, scrape away any old bark, where pests such as red

Thin bunches to encourage larger fruits.

spider mite and mealy bug may be hiding. Remove bugs by hand and use insecticide, if necessary. Plants will become heavy over time and will need careful pruning and training (see tip box below). Dessert grapes will need to be thinned to encourage larger fruits—using scissors, reduce each bunch by about a third.

TIP PRUNING AND TRAINING

All grape vines will require annual pruning in winter while the plant is dormant. Vines can be trained into cordons, which are the most common greenhouse form, with the fruiting stems branching from a vertical main stem. For guyot shapes, the fruiting stems branch upward from the main horizontal branches. Ensure that you provide your plant with adequate supports, and tie in stems securely.

Remove the weakest side-shoots, leaving the strongest two to be trained on wires.

Although most grape vines are self-fertile, those grown under cover need help because they are not exposed to the wind—their usual method of pollination. Shake the vine gently to help it transfer its pollen. Move container-grown plants outside for a month in winter—the cold induces flowering.

CARE OF OUTDOOR VINES

Feed and mulch outdoor vines as for indoor-grown types, and water newly planted vines in dry spells; once established, they will not require further watering.

Thin foliage in late summer to allow sunlight to reach the fruits; trim back with sterile pruners, taking care not to touch the delicate fruits. Prune and train as for indoor vines (see tip box).

HARVESTING AND STORING

As fruits ripen, their skins become slightly translucent and develop a bloom. Sample the fruits to check whether they are fully ripe, and use scissors or pruners to cut a whole bunch free at a time. This helps to prevent damage to the fruits. Once picked, grapes will not keep fresh for more than a few days, so eat them or use them as soon as possible after harvesting.

PESTS AND DISEASES

Due to the higher temperatures, grapes grown in greenhouses are more at risk from pests and diseases than those grown outside, although outside vines may need to be netted to keep birds from stealing the fruits.

It is especially important to maintain good garden hygiene in the warm climate of the greenhouse: ensure that plants have sufficient space and ventilation, and ensure that plants are neither over- or underwatered. Also be aware that vines are easily damaged by chemical weedkillers, and that many are prone to magnesium deficiency.

Common diseases include: gray mold, and downy and powdery mildews. Common pests include mealy bugs and red spider mites. Be vigilant, and inspect for early signs of damage.

Vine leaf blister mites (left) create yellow-brown blisters on leaves. Powdery mildew (right) coats the fruits, causing them to split.

'New York Muscat'

This black grape grows well outdoors on a sunny wall, producing good yields of high-quality fruits that can be eaten fresh or used to make sweet white wine. The oval, reddish-blue grapes have a black currant flavor and few seeds.

- unsuitable for containers
- early spring
- excellent resistance
- hardy
- self-fertile
- early fall

'Reliance'

One of the best red, seedless table grapes, 'Reliance' sets large crops of thin-skinned fruits that pass through an array of colors before ripening to pink-purple. Cold-hardiness and resistance to disease make it a good garden variety.

- unsuitable for containers
- early spring
- good resistance
- hardy
- self-fertile
- late summer

'Bluebell'

A Lambrusca-type grape, 'Bluebell' produces medium-to-large, blue-black seeded grapes with tender skins, good for eating, juice, and jam. Resistant to disease and cold-hardy, this versatile variety is good in cold climates.

- unsuitable for containers
- early spring
- good resistance
- hardy
- self-fertile
- early fall

'Regent'

This is a fairly vigorous hybrid vine that bears good yields of very large, blue-black grapes with a sweet, refreshing flavor. In hot summers, the fruit ripens to true black. The fall foliage takes on a fiery orange and red color.

- unsuitable for containers
- early spring
- excellent resistance
- hardy
- self-fertile
- early to mid-fall

'Himrod'

This hybrid American variety bears loose clusters of small-to-medium sized, yellow fruits of outstanding flavor. It is one of the best white, seedless table grapes for colder areas. Fruits can also be used for juice or raisins.

- unsuitable for containers
- early spring
- some resistance
- hardy
- self-fertile
- late summer to early fall

'Vidal Blanc'

A variety of choice for makers of ice wine, 'Vidal blanc' is disease-resistant and productive, and grows well where growing seasons are long and winters moderate. It bears narrow clusters of golden grapes suited for many wines.

- unsuitable for containers
- early spring
- good resistance
- not hardy
- self-fertile
- early to mid-fall

'Niagara'

The huge, handsome, thick-skinned white grapes of this North American variety are produced in large, compact clusters. The tangy but delicate flavor is excellent for fresh eating, as well as for making wines, juice, and jam. 'Niagara' is susceptible to fungal diseases.

- unsuitable for containers
- early spring
- poor resistance
- hardy
- self-fertile
- early fall

'Concord'

This reliable table and juice grape is a favorite of home gardeners. The intensely flavored blue-black skin with a lighter "bloom" slips easily from the sweet, gelatinous interior of the fruits. Seeded and seedless varieties are available.

- unsuitable for containers
- early spring
- poor resistance
- hardy
- self-fertile
- early fall

'Siegerrebe'

This hybrid variety's parentage includes the spicy 'Gewürztraminer' grape. The medium-sized, golden brown grapes mature early with a sweet, aromatic taste. The fruits can be left to ripen on the vine for a more intense flavor.

- unsuitable for containers
- early spring
- good resistance
- hardy
- self-fertile
- early fall

'Mars'

This vigorous table grape has shown good resistance to black rot and mildews. Medium-to-large fruits are blue, round, and seedless and, as with 'Concord', the tough outer skins slip easily from the pulpy flesh for eating.

- unsuitable for containers
- early spring
- good resistance
- hardy
- self-fertile
- late summer to early fall

'Siegerrebe'

STRAWBERRIES *Fragaria x ananassa*

Picked and eaten fresh from the garden, served up with cream
and meringue, or used for jams and desserts, strawberries are the
quintessential summer treat. They are classified according to their fruiting
habits: June-bearing; everbearing, which produce a crop through into fall;
and day-neutral, which will grow at any time of year, provided that you
give them the right amounts of warmth and protection.

	SPRING	SUMMER	FALL	WINTER
PLANT				
HARVEST				

PLANTING

Although it is possible to grow
strawberries from seed, it is much
easier to buy healthy, disease-free
plants or runners. Runners will
either be fresh and dug up just
before purchase, or will have
been cold-stored—kept at just
below freezing point until they
are thawed out and ready to sell.

Firm plants in gently after planting.

Plant out summer-fruiting and
perpetual types mid- to late
summer; plant cold-stored
runners in late spring, fresh
June-bearing or everbearing
plants in fall, and day-neutral
types at any time of year.
Strawberries prefer a sunny,
frost-free site with free-draining
soil, and they will tolerate
slightly acidic conditions. They
can also be grown in a variety of

containers (see tip box on p.119).
Dig in well-rotted manure
or compost before planting to
improve the soil structure and
increase fertility. Ensure that
crops have enough space—they
need about 18 in (45 cm) between
plants, and about 30 in (75 cm)
between rows. When planting,
ensure that the crowns of the
plants are kept above soil level,
and water in well. Strawberries

are sometimes grown through plastic sheeting, since this warms the soil, prevents the fruits from being splashed with mud, and also suppresses weeds. Create a 3 ft (1 m) wide mound of soil the length of your desired row. Lay a sheet of plastic over it and then bury the sheet's edges so that it is weighed down tight. Cut slits and plant the runners through it.

If there is a risk of frost, cover young plants with a cloche or cold frame (see image, right). When you buy your plants, be sure that they are certified disease-free.

CROP CARE

Ensure that plants are kept well-watered—especially those in containers, since their soil will dry out much faster than those

Protect young plants with a cloche.

planted in the ground. However, be careful not to overwater the plants. Take care not to splash the berries when watering, since this may encourage them to rot. Feed plants with a balanced fertilizer in early to mid-spring.

To prevent unprotected fruits from sitting directly in the soil, it is common to mulch around

TIP MULCHING

Mulching around your plants with straw serves many useful purposes: it keeps fruits ventilated and dry, while keeping them from getting covered with soil, and protects crowns from cold in winter.

- Carefully lift the plant's leaves and fruits and tuck a thick layer of clean, dry straw underneath them.
- Place strawberry mats around plant stems. Mats can be dried, brushed off, and reused the following year.

Keeping fruits dry and cushioned minimizes the risk of them rotting.

them with straw, or use fiber strawberry mats around the base of plants (see tip box, left).

Rotate your strawberry crops every few years to prevent a buildup of diseases in the soil. Plants should last for about two to three years, their yields gradually decreasing, so plant replacements in a fresh bed, and do not reuse the original plot for strawberries or for raspberries for several years.

HARVESTING AND STORING

Strawberries are relatively quick to ripen and are ready to pick when the fruits have become fully red. They do not store well, however, so be prepared to eat them or use them for cooking as soon as possible after harvesting.

PESTS AND DISEASES

Strawberries are most commonly afflicted by viruses, gray mold, slugs and snails, and birds. Buy plants that are healthy and disease-free, and rotate every few years to reduce the risk of diseases spreading. Do not water the fruits or foliage and keep plants well-ventilated to prevent gray mold. Mulching with straw helps to improve ventilation. Use slug bait to deter slugs and snails, and netting to deter birds.

TIP CONTAINERS

Strawberry plants will grow happily in containers as long as you ensure that their soil is well-drained and that they have enough root space. Give plants full sun, and make sure that containers do not dry out. You can experiment and grow strawberries in unusual recycled containers (see p.15).

- It is fairly common to see strawberries planted in hanging baskets—which has the added advantage of keeping the plants out of the path of slugs and snails.
- Growing bags are useful, since they come preprepared with their own form of "plastic sheeting."
- Terra-cotta strawberry pots are also commonly used—place a plant in each of the "cups"—these are space-efficient and ornamental.

Move your strawberry pots to give them the best possible conditions: they need protection against late frosts and full sun when fruits are ripening.

'Albion'

'Albion'

This new variety is popular with organic growers because of its excellent disease resistance and high yields. This everbearing strawberry produces mouth-wateringly sweet, large, bright red berries from early summer right into the fall.

- suitable for containers
- early spring
- good resistance
- hardy
- self-fertile
- early summer to late fall

'Ozark Beauty'

This vigorous and cold-hardy everbearing variety produces wedge-shaped, large berries that are semi-firm and full of flavor. Suited for northern climates, the plants are resistant to leaf scorch and leaf spot, and produce better when runners are removed.

- suitable for containers
- early spring
- some resistance
- hardy
- self-fertile
- early summer and early fall

'Alpine'

Known also as "fraises des bois," alpine strawberries are seed-grown plants that bear small fruits with an intense wild strawberry flavor. A compact habit, all-season production, and few runners make it excellent for containers.

- suitable for containers
- early spring
- some resistance
- hardy
- self-fertile
- early summer to fall

'Ogalalla'

One of the hardiest strawberries, 'Ogalalla' bears heavy yields of medium-to-large fruits with the rich, tangy flavor of wild strawberries. Runners on this everbearing variety should be four per plant; fewer if planted in a pot.

- suitable for containers
- early spring
- some resistance
- hardy
- self-fertile
- early summer and early fall

'Aromel'

This traditional favorite is a perpetual-fruiting variety that is still popular today. Moderate yields of medium to large, bright red, juicy fruits are borne over a long season in small flushes, and the berries produced have an outstanding flavor.

- 🪣 suitable for containers
- 🌱 early spring
- 🕷 some resistance
- ❄ hardy
- ♂ self-fertile
- 🔒 midsummer

'Jewel'

This June bearer, bred for cold weather, produces large, wedge-shaped, bright-red fruits. The high-quality berries resist rot, but plants are susceptible to soil-borne fungi. Beds previously planted with strawberries should be avoided.

- 🪣 unsuitable for containers
- 🌱 early spring
- 🕷 some resistance
- ❄ hardy
- ♂ self-fertile
- 🔒 early summer

'Tristar'

This day-neutral variety delivers a steady, all-season yield of deep-red, flavorful, medium-sized berries. Planted in containers, the disease-resistant, adaptable plants can be brought inside in fall to extend the berry season.

- 🪣 suitable for containers
- 🌱 early spring
- 🕷 good resistance
- ❄ hardy
- ♂ self-fertile
- 🔒 spring to fall

'Seascape'

Developed by the University of California for warmer climates, this day-neutral variety is productive and resistant to fungal diseases. It sends out few runners, putting its energy instead into producing large, flavorful berries that ripen over a long period.

- suitable for containers
- early spring
- good resistance
- hardy
- self-fertile
- spring through fall

'Sweet Charlie'

This Florida-bred, June-bearing variety is resistant to anthracnose, a fungal disease common in humid, warm-weather regions. Vigorous and productive, 'Sweet Charlie' produces large, sweet fruits that ripen two weeks earlier than other varieties.

- unsuitable for containers
- early spring or fall in the south
- some resistance
- hardy
- self-fertile
- late spring

'Earliglow'

One of the earliest varieties to ripen, this US variety is known for its excellent flavor. Berries start out medium-sized, and get smaller as the season progresses. Plants are vigorous, adaptable, and disease-resistant.

- unsuitable for containers
- early spring
- good resistance
- hardy
- self fertile
- late spring to early summer

'Northeaster'

Vigorous 'Northeaster' is suited to conditions in the northeastern US, with plants tolerant of the heavy soils and soil-borne fungal pathogens common to the region. The aromatic, flavorful berries ripen early and freeze well.

- unsuitable for containers
- early spring
- good resistance
- hardy
- self-fertile
- early summer

'Sequoia'

Technically a June-bearer, this variety produces fruit over a long period of three to four weeks. Berries are very sweet, but soft, which makes 'Sequoia' a better choice for home gardeners than large growers. Plants are disease-resistant; good in warm climates.

- unsuitable for containers
- early spring
- good resistance
- hardy
- self-fertile
- early summer

'Allstar'

The large, firm, flavorful fruits of this widely adaptable variety have a near-perfect strawberry shape. Winter-hardy and resistant to red stele, verticillium wilt, and leaf scorch, 'Allstar' is one of the most trouble-free, June-bearing type of strawberry.

- unsuitable for containers
- early spring
- good resistance
- hardy
- self-fertile
- early summer

'Surecrop'

Known as an easy-to-grow June bearer, 'Surecrop' is sure to please in any region of the country. Produces reliably large yields of deep red berries with intense flavor and is ideal for making jams and pies.

- unsuitable for containers
- early spring
- good resistance
- hardy
- self-fertile
- early summer

'Guardian'

'Guardian' produces large, conical-shaped strawberries. Although fruits are not as brightly colored as newer varieties, the high-yielding plants are cold-hardy, resistant to red stele and verticillium wilt, and perform well on poor soil.

- unsuitable for containers
- early spring
- good resistance
- hardy
- self-fertile
- early summer

'Honeoye'

This early season strawberry is the most popular variety among commercial growers. It bears heavy crops of bright red, medium-sized, very firm fruits with a superb flavor. It tolerates colder conditions, but is susceptible to verticillium wilt.

 suitable for containers

late summer to early spring

some resistance

hardy

self-fertile

midsummer

'Lateglow'

This June-bearing variety's large, firm, symmetrical berries have great flavor and aroma and ripen late in the season. The vigorous plants are resistant to soil-borne root diseases and leaf problems, and thrive in warm climates.

unsuitable for containers

early spring

good resistance

hardy

self-fertile

early to midsummer

'Sparkle'

Developed over 60 years ago, June-bearing 'Sparkle' is popular with home gardeners because of its cold-hardiness and excellent taste. Medium-sized berries are soft, and their smooth texture makes them perfect for jam.

unsuitable for containers

early spring

some resistance

hardy

self-fertile

early summer

RASPBERRIES *Rubus idaeus*

Fresh, juicy raspberries are both tangy and delicious, perfect for eating fresh or using in jams or desserts. Since they are happy to grow in large containers, they can be accommodated in almost any garden. There are two main types of raspberry: summer-fruiting and fall-fruiting, and for pruning purposes it is important to keep the two types separate—summer types fruit on the previous year's canes, and fall types on new growth.

	SPRING	SUMMER	FALL	WINTER
PLANT				
HARVEST				

PLANTING

Raspberry plants are supplied as canes and, although they look very small and neat at this early stage, it won't be long before they become large and trailing, so ensure that you allocate them enough space in your plot or container. Raspberries need a good support system, so prepare this before planting in the ground (see tip box, p.129)—use sturdy posts and horizontal wires, since plants can become quite heavy.

Raspberries need a sheltered location to protect the upright plants from the wind, and full sun. They prefer a pH of between 6 and 6.5, and well-drained, fertile soil, so dig in some well-rotted manure or compost before planting. Plant raspberry

Canes will produce leafy growth in spring.

canes at a depth of about 2–3 in (5–8 cm), and then cut the cane down to a height of approximately 12 in (30 cm). Leave 16 in (40 cm) between each cane and 6 ft (2 m) between rows.

It may be easier to provide the required acidic conditions if you grow the canes in containers, although they will not produce

as large a crop. Container-grown canes will also need support—consider growing them against a trellis or intersperse them with bamboo canes and secure plants with string or garden twine. Plant two or three canes per 12 in (30 cm) container.

CROP CARE

Keep canes well-watered, especially during fruiting, bearing in mind that container-grown plants will dry out more quickly than those planted directly in the ground.

Feed with a general, balanced fertilizer in early spring and then mulch with well-rotted manure or compost. Mulch again with straw in early summer. When plants reach

Tie developing stems in to bamboo canes

about 30 in (75 cm) in height, thin them out. Remove any weak or diseased looking canes first. You may need to construct netting to protect the fruits from birds, which can strip a bush in no time.

Prune summer-fruiting types in late summer, as for blackberries (see p.132), after harvesting. Tie in the new growth, and lightly

PESTS AND DISEASES

Although cane spot and fungal leaf spots are a potential problem for raspberries, resistant cultivars are available. Other problems include:

- Birds—use netting to deter them.
- Raspberry beetle and raspberry leaf and bud mite—hoe around the soil to bring them to the soil surface, and cut down stems after fruiting.
- Raspberry viruses—remove and destroy infected canes. Rotate crops.

The virus raspberry cane spot creates purple, white-centered spots on leaves.

prune. Leave the fruited canes of fall-fruiting varieties in the ground over winter. They should be cut right back in late winter–early spring. New canes will appear in spring. Do not prune container-grown raspberries.

HARVESTING
Raspberries will either be a summer- or fall-fruiting variety, and will be ready to harvest accordingly. When berries are plump and juicy, pull them off the plant, leaving the core attached to the bush. Eat them as soon as possible. Once stems have fruited, cut them off to ground level and cover with compost to help them decompose—this helps to prevent infection from entering the plant. If growth has been particularly good, you may need to thin out the remaining stems to leave one approximately every 4 in (10 cm). New plants can be propagated from healthy, disease-free suckers or new canes, which should be carefully removed from the rootball with their roots intact and then replanted.

STORING
Raspberries will not keep long after they ripen. Freeze them to prevent them from spoiling.

TIP TRAINING

There are two good reasons for training raspberries: first, it is important that they receive adequate space and ventilation and are not allowed to trail on the ground, where they become easy prey for pests and diseases. Second, it is much easier—and much less painful—to harvest berries from a well-trained plant.

There are many different ways to train your canes—insert one or two lines of posts and fix horizontal wires between them. Canes can be planted along the bottom of each line of posts and trained upward (known as the hedgerow system), or planted down the middle of a set of two, then drawn upward and diagonally out from the center (the Scandinavian system).

When raspberries reach full height, arch them over and tie in. Plants are kept neat, are less prone to damage, and fruits are easier to harvest.

'Tulameen'

Long canes bear large, red, glossy, conical-shaped fruit with an excellent flavor over a very long season. The highest yields are produced in midsummer. This variety has good winter hardiness and its fruits are resistant to wet weather.

- suitable for containers
- fall to early spring
- good resistance
- hardy
- self-fertile
- mid- to late summer

'Prelude'

This earliest of the summer-bearing red raspberries bears a moderate crop in fall, too. The medium, round fruits are sweet and mild; the vigorous canes have sparse spines. 'Prelude' is resistant to Phytophthora root rot.

- unsuitable for containers
- early spring
- good resistance
- hardy
- self-fertile
- early to midsummer; fall

'Heritage'

This "everbearing" raspberry produces sweet, medium-sized, red berries on second and first year canes. 'Heritage' is extremely popular due to its vigor, long fruiting season, and resistance to most diseases.

- unsuitable for containers
- early spring
- good resistance
- hardy
- self-fertile
- early summer; late summer to fall

'Joan J'

This is a new, spine-free, fall-fruiting variety. The berries are produced in plentiful supply over a very long picking season—from midsummer until the first frosts. The large red fruits have an excellent flavor that is preserved well when frozen.

- suitable for containers
- fall to early spring
- good resistance
- hardy
- self-fertile
- late summer to early fall

'All Gold'

Developed from 'Autumn Bliss', this variety, also known as 'Fall Gold', bears large, golden yellow berries. Like its parent plant, the fruits are ready in fall and have a superior flavor to any red variety.

- suitable for containers
- fall to early spring
- excellent resistance
- hardy
- self-fertile
- late summer to mid-fall

BLACKBERRIES AND HYBRID BERRIES *Rubus fruticosus*

Blackberries and their many hybrids are all descended from wild brambles and will need careful training to prevent them from trailing on the ground or taking over your plot. However, the taste of these sweet, juicy berries is well worth the effort as they are very easy to grow.

	SPRING	SUMMER	FALL	WINTER
PLANT				
HARVEST				

PLANTING

Prepare your site in advance—dig in some well-rotted manure or compost, and weed well. Blackberries and other hybrid berries will need plenty of space and a good support system—both for the health of the plant, and for easy picking. There are several options: train them over an arch, or station posts along the length of your row and fix horizontal wires between them (see raspberries). The trailing stems can then be looped over the wires and tied in.

Site carefully: both blackberries and hybrid berries prefer soil that is well drained and need shelter from the wind, but while blackberries will tolerate partial shade, hybrid berries need full

Train your blackberries over wires.

sun. Plant canes to the depth of their existing soil marks, leaving 10–16 ft (3–5 m) between plants, depending on the variety chosen.

CROP CARE

Mulch plants with straw in early spring and pull up any suckers that appear. Cut down canes once they have fruited. New canes will grow in the second year. The plants are generally

undamaged by frosts, since they flower relatively late in the year.

HARVESTING
Harvest berries every few days when they are plump, taking the core with them. Do not leave them too long or they will rot.

STORING
The berries will not keep long, so freeze them, if necessary. To prevent them from forming a solid mass, space them out on a baking sheet and place in the freezer. When frozen, transfer to a container. They will keep their shape and can be used singly.

PESTS AND DISEASES

Blackberries and hybrid berries suffer the same problems as other cane fruits: raspberry spur blight, raspberry beetle, and gray mold especially. Practice good garden hygiene when pruning, and destroy affected canes.

Gray mold shrivels and rots fruits.

'Silvan'

This thorny hybrid produces the first blackberries of the season. The large, long, dark purple-black fruits ripen in mid to late summer and have a superb, sweet flavor. It is fairly tolerant of drought and has excellent disease resistance.

- unsuitable for containers
- fall to early spring
- excellent resistance
- hardy
- self-fertile
- midsummer to early fall

'Black Butte'

This new, compact variety is notable for the exceptional size of its fruits, which is twice the size of other varieties. Heavy yields of rich, full-flavored berries are borne on thorny canes, and the open habit makes picking easy.

- unsuitable for containers
- fall to early spring
- good resistance
- hardy
- self-fertile
- mid- to late summer

'Black Satin'

This thorn-free variety bears good crops of berries earlier in the season than other thornless varieties. The attractive, bright, black fruits are very juicy and have a slightly sharp flavor.

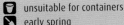 unsuitable for containers
🍂 fall to early spring
🕷 good resistance
❄ hardy
🌼 self-fertile
🔒 late summer to early fall

'Triple Crown'

This thornless variety consistently yields large, sweet berries over five weeks in summer. The plants benefit from trellising and are intolerant of wet soils. They show good resistance to bacterial and fungal diseases.

🪣 unsuitable for containers
🍂 early spring
🕷 good resistance
❄ hardy
🌼 self-fertile
🔒 midsummer

'Darrow'

This thorny blackberry is the hardiest variety for cold climates. It produces firm, flavorful berries over a long season. The vigorous plants tolerate some shade, are generally rust resistant, but susceptible to virus problems.

🪣 unsuitable for containers
🍂 early spring
🕷 some resistance
❄ hardy
🌼 self-fertile
🔒 midsummer

GOOSEBERRIES *Ribes uva-crispa*

If, like most people, you've only tasted store-bought fruits, homegrown gooseberries are often much sweeter than you might imagine. Dessert varieties are delicious eaten fresh from the bush; culinary types make excellent jams and desserts; or grow dual-purpose berries and enjoy the best of both worlds. Easy to grow, and happily trained into cordons or fans, gooseberries are an asset to any garden.

	SPRING	SUMMER	FALL	WINTER
PLANT				
HARVEST				

PLANTING

Plant bare-root gooseberries in fall or early spring, and container-grown plants at any time of year. Ensure that container-grown plants have not become pot-bound, and select bushes that have a clear 6 in (15 cm) of stem between the roots and young branches. Gooseberries need a well-drained soil, so dig in some well-rotted manure or compost to improve the structure, if necessary; they prefer a slightly acid pH. Bushes will need frost protection, since they produce blossoms early in the year, so site them carefully, avoiding frost pockets, or grow them in pots so they can be moved under cover in colder months. Gooseberries are

Prune new side-shoots in summer.

self-fertile, so you will only need one plant to produce a crop; if you grow more than one, bushes will need 5 ft (1.5 m) of space between them; space single-stemmed cordons 14 in (35 cm) apart.

CROP CARE

Stake young plants, and protect against frost. Ensure that bushes have plenty of water, apply a balanced fertilizer, and mulch

in early spring. Net against birds. Prune bushes hard in summer and winter—aim to create an open, well-ventilated structure.

HARVESTING AND STORING

Staggering your harvest by picking alternate berries will allow those left on the bush to grow larger and juicier; begin in late spring and continue throughout the summer. Early dual-purpose berries should be used for cooking; later ones for eating fresh. Dessert varieties are sweetest just after harvesting. Gooseberries will store for two weeks in the refrigerator or they can be frozen for later use.

PESTS AND DISEASES

Gooseberries are vulnerable to a number of pests and diseases, particularly gooseberry sawfly and gooseberry mildew; remove affected fruits or foliage and spray with insecticide. Use netting to deter birds.

Gooseberry sawfly larvae eat leaves.

'Hinnonmaki Red'

This vigorous, very hardy variety produces heavy crops of large, dark red fruits with an excellent flavor, suitable for both dessert and culinary purposes. Berries are similar to 'Whinham's Industry', but have a greater resistance to mildew.

- suitable for containers
- late fall to early spring
- good resistance
- hardy
- self-fertile
- midsummer

'Leveller'

This culinary and dessert variety bears exceptionally flavorful, very large, downy, yellow-green fruits, which are borne in abundance. It has a spreading, slightly drooping habit and requires fertile, well-drained soil.

- suitable for containers
- late fall to early spring
- some resistance
- hardy
- self-fertile
- early to midsummer

'Poorman'

This European-American hybrid is mildew resistant, vigorous, and not overly thorny. Annual renewal pruning helps it to keep producing good yields of medium red berries, which are excellent for eating when ripe, or in pies and jams.

- unsuitable for containers
- early spring
- good resistance
- hardy
- self-fertile
- midsummer

'Hinnonmaki Yellow'

Heavy crops of yellow fruits from medium to very large are produced from early to midsummer on vigorous, spreading bushes. A dual-purpose variety with a lovely flavor, it is suitable for organic growers, since it has some resistance to mildew.

 suitable for containers
late fall to early spring
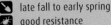 good resistance
hardy
self-fertile
early to midsummer

'Pixwell'

Productive, mildew-resistant, and nearly thornless, hybrid 'Pixwell' grows to 4–6 ft (1.2–1.8 m) and bears clusters of pale green fruits that ripen to pink. The fruits are high in sugar, and excellent for pies, jams, and preserves.

 suitable for containers
early spring
good resistance
hardy
self-fertile
late summer

'Rokula'

This early-fruiting dessert variety has attractive, dark-red berries with a sweet flavor. Bushes are moderately vigorous with a drooping habit. It is mildew-resistant, but fruit is prone to cracking if rainfall is erratic.

 suitable for containers
late fall to early spring
good resistance
hardy
self-fertile
early summer

'Captivator'

This hybrid gooseberry was developed in Canada for cold-hardiness and mildew resistance. The small, semi-thornless bush can be planted in partial shade and yields sweet, teardrop-shaped fruits that ripen from pink to red in the height of summer.

- suitable for containers
- early spring
- good resistance
- hardy
- self-fertile
- midsummer

'Invicta'

A fast-growing, mildew-resistant variety for both dessert and culinary use, it bears abundant large, yellowish-green fruits with a good flavor. Its very thorny stems are amenable to training against a wall and it is tolerant of shade and most soil types.

- suitable for containers
- late fall to early spring
- good resistance
- hardy
- self-fertile
- midsummer

'Tixia'

This recent introduction is favored for its high yields of large, bright red fruits with a sweet-tart flavor. The 4-ft (1.2-m) tall shrubs are vigorous and mildew-resistant; nearly thornless one-year shoots allow for painless picking.

- suitable for containers
- early spring
- good resistance
- hardy
- self-fertile
- midsummer

'Jahns Prairie'

This hardy North American species produces tasty, sweet-tart berries. Maturing at 5 ft (1.5 m), the shrub has few thorns and an upright growth, with sprawling branches. It is resistant to rust, mildew, and gray mold.

- unsuitable for containers
- early spring
- excellent resistance
- hardy
- self-fertile
- midsummer

'Invicta'

BLACK, WHITE, AND RED CURRANTS *Ribes nigrum* and *R. rubrum*

Delicious used in desserts, pies, or jams, these beautiful berries are an eye-catching addition to any garden. Currants are fully hardy, very tough, and tolerant of most soil types, although black currants prefer a more fertile soil, and more direct sunlight than red and white varieties.

	SPRING	SUMMER	FALL	WINTER
PLANT				
HARVEST				

PLANTING

Ensure that you buy certified one- or two-year-old disease-free plants, and ensure that container-grown plants have not become pot-bound. These can be planted at any time of year, as long as you give them enough water, but bare-root types should be planted in late fall or early spring.

Bushes can become quite large, so make sure that you give them enough space—about 5 ft (1.5 m) between plants. White and red currants can also be trained into cordons or fans, requiring less ground space. All currants are self-fertile, so will fruit with only one plant.

Dig in well-rotted manure or compost just before planting, and site in a sheltered, frost-free spot.

Mulch the currant bushes in early spring.

Remove any weeds and, if necessary, double-dig the site to improve the drainage. Black currant plants need to be planted 2 in (5 cm) lower than they were in their original pot, to encourage the plant to produce strong new stems. All currants have relatively shallow roots so can be planted in containers, if need be, and then moved under cover in colder months.

CROP CARE

Currants need plenty of water and should not be allowed to dry out. Feed with a balanced fertilizer and mulch in early spring. Bushes will need careful pruning; red and white currants in spring and summer; black currants in winter.

HARVESTING

Red and white currants will be ready to harvest from early summer. They are delicate fruits, so cut the whole string loose when they are ripe. Black currants can be harvested this way, too, from midsummer, or later individually when they are sturdier.

PESTS AND DISEASES

Birds can strip a bush of its currants, so use netting to deter them. Other common problems include aphids, gray mold, American gooseberry mildew, and reversion disease. Practice good garden hygiene.

Currant blister aphids distort leaves.

'Ben Sarek'

A dwarf bush, reaching only 4 ft (1.2 m), it bears heavy crops midseason, making it ideal for containers and small gardens. The large, black berries have an excellent flavor and are so abundant that the branches will need support.

- 🪣 suitable for containers
- 🌿 fall to early spring
- ✳ good resistance
- ❄ hardy
- 🌼 self-fertile
- 🔒 midsummer

'Titania'

This new variety from Sweden is possibly the most frost-resistant of the black currants. It has excellent disease resistance. Large, black berries with a high juice content and lots of flavor keep well on the bush over a long season.

- 🪣 suitable for containers
- 🌿 fall to early spring
- ✳ excellent resistance
- ❄ hardy
- 🌼 self-fertile
- 🔒 midsummer to mid-fall

'Baldwin'

An old and still popular favorite, this compact bush bears heavy crops in mid- to late season. The medium-large, black, tart berries are very high in vitamin C and keep well on the plant without splitting.

- 🪣 suitable for containers
- 🌿 fall to early spring
- ✳ good resistance
- ❄ hardy
- 🌼 self-fertile
- 🔒 mid- to late summer

'Ben Lomond'

A popular variety, this upright, fairly compact bush flowers late and so has the benefit of some frost resistance. As a result, very heavy yields of large, short-stalked, sweet but sour black currants are borne later in the season.

- suitable for containers
- fall to early spring
- good resistance
- hardy
- self-fertile
- late summer

'Ben Connan'

A compact but high-yielding black currant, this variety is ideal for small gardens. The bush bears unusually large fruits that are easy to pick and have an excellent, rich flavor. It has good mildew resistance and is tolerant of frost.

- suitable for containers
- fall to early spring
- good resistance
- hardy
- self-fertile
- midsummer

'Crandall'

Also known as 'Clove Currant', 'Crandall' produces clusters of sweet-tart fruits high in vitamin C and good for eating and preserves. Fragrant yellow flowers bloom in early spring; the 5-ft (1.5-m) bush is mildew- and rust-resistant.

- unsuitable for containers
- early spring
- good resistance
- hardy
- self-fertile
- midsummer

'Blanka'

This new, reliable variety produces the heaviest yields of all white currants over a long season. The large, almost transparent, ivory-white berries have the sweetest flavor and are borne on long strings that make picking easy.

- suitable for containers
- fall to early spring
- good resistance
- hardy
- self-fertile
- mid- to late summer

'White Imperial'

This old variety is popular for dessert use. Plants have a spreading habit, are resistant to mildew and white pine blister rust, and produce clusters of white, translucent fruits with a pink blush. Yields are moderate.

- unsuitable for containers
- early spring
- good resistance
- hardy
- self-fertile
- early summer

'Pink Champagne'

This cross between red and white currant produces beautiful, translucent, pink fruits known for their excellent taste. 'Pink Champagne' is recommended for home growing due to its resistance to leaf diseases.

- unsuitable for containers
- early spring
- good resistance
- hardy
- self-fertile
- early summer

'Red Lake'

A well-established, popular variety that starts off the red currant picking season, the large bushes produce heavy yields of big, juicy, red berries with an excellent flavor. The fruits are borne on long strings, which makes picking easier.

- suitable for containers
- fall to early spring
- good resistance
- hardy
- self-fertile
- midsummer

'Jonkheer van Tets'

An established, reliable variety, it is also one of the earliest red currants to ripen. The heavy crops of large, bright-red, juicy berries have an excellent, tart flavor. The fruits are borne on long strings, so are easier to pick.

- suitable for containers
- fall to early spring
- good resistance
- hardy
- self-fertile
- midsummer

BLUEBERRIES *Vaccinium corymbosum*

Deliciously sweet and packed with vitamins and antioxidants, blueberries are often described as a "superfood." Eaten fresh, cooked in pies, or used to make jams and jellies, they will not disappoint. Grow at least two or three plants to ensure effective pollination and high yields, and buy two- or three-year-old plants if possible, since blueberries do not reach their full cropping potential until they are about five years old.

	SPRING	SUMMER	FALL	WINTER
PLANT				
HARVEST				

PLANTING

Container-grown plants will establish more readily than bare-root types, but ensure that they have not become pot-bound. Plant both types between late fall and early spring, as long as the ground is not frozen. Blueberries need an acidic soil in order to thrive—a pH of between 4 and 5.5—so, if necessary, prepare your soil in advance, or plant in a container, where you can easily control the growing conditions.

Most blueberries are self-fertile, but like most crops their yield is increased and improved if they are pollinated by another variety. Plant in a sheltered location, protected from strong winds, with plenty of sunshine in the summer months.

Protect the pretty flowers against frost.

CROP CARE

If plants flower early in spring they may need protection against frost; use horticultural fleece, or bring container-grown plants under cover. Blueberries need a lot of water during growth, but use rainwater in order to maintain acidic soil conditions. Mulch around plants with bark or pine needles, and apply a balanced fertilizer after pruning.

HARVESTING AND STORING

Pick ripe berries once their blue skins have developed a whitish tinge. They can be harvested from midsummer through to early fall, depending on the variety—some fruit early and some fruit late. Once picked, blueberries can be stored in the refrigerator for over a week, or frozen.

PESTS AND DISEASES

Ripening fruits are most at risk from birds, so use netting to protect bushes, if necessary. Generally, provided that they have the right conditions, they are relatively problem-free.

TIP CONTAINERS

Provide them with a soil mix formulated for acid-loving plants, and blueberries will happily grow in pots. Water regularly and do not allow the soil to dry out. After a few years, you may need to transfer your blueberry plant to a larger pot.

Place containers in a sunny location.

'Berkeley '

This popular garden variety bears attractive, powder-blue fruits with a mild flavor. It is easy to grow and has good disease resistance. In mild climates, one bush will bear decent-sized yields, but it will be less productive in frost pockets.

🪣	suitable for containers
🖐	spring
✳	good resistance
❄	hardy
♂	self-fertile (mid)
🔒	midsummer

'Coville'

'Coville' is a vigorous and spreading variety that reliably bears large, deep-blue berries with a sweet flavor very late in the season. The fruits can be left on the bush for a long time before they fall.

🪣	suitable for containers
🖐	spring
✳	good resistance
❄	hardy
♂	self-fertile (late)
🔒	mid- to late summer

'Herbert'

This late-season variety is considered by many to produce the most flavorful blueberries. A vigorous, upright bush, it bears heavy, compact clusters of very large, firm, dark blue berries that have an exceptional, sweet flavor.

- 🪴 suitable for containers
- 🌱 spring
- 🐛 good resistance
- ❄️ hardy
- 🌸 self-fertile (late)
- 🔒 mid- to late summer

'Duke'

One of the most consistent and heaviest producers, this variety bears medium-sized, light-blue, firm berries with a mild, sweet flavor. Although late-flowering, it crops early, so it is ideal for areas where the season is short.

- 🪴 suitable for containers
- 🌱 spring
- 🐛 good resistance
- ❄️ hardy
- 🌸 self-fertile (early)
- 🔒 midsummer

'O'Neal'

This Southern hybrid withstands summer heat and winter chill, and produces an early crop of large, flavorful fruits. The plants grow to 6 ft (1.8 m) and are unaffected by disease. Self-fertile, it produces a better crop with another variety.

- 🪴 unsuitable for containers
- 🌱 early spring
- 🐛 good resistance
- ❄️ hardy
- 🌸 self-fertile (early to mid)
- 🔒 late spring to summer

'Spartan'

'Spartan' is an early to mid-season variety that bears very large, light blue fruits with a tangy, sweet flavor. For the best crops, plant another variety nearby. The upright habit makes harvesting easy; do so before the leaves turn bright red in fall.

- 🪣 suitable for containers
- 🌱 spring
- 🐛 good resistance
- ❄️ hardy
- 🌸 self-fertile (early)
- 🔒 midsummer

'Jersey'

One of the oldest and most reliable blueberry varieties, each bush produces large crops of dark blue, small-to-medium sized berries with a mild, sweet flavor. In fall, the leaves turn a fiery yellow-orange color.

- 🪣 suitable for containers
- 🌱 spring
- 🐛 good resistance
- ❄️ hardy
- 🌸 needs 1 pollenizer (early)
- 🔒 midsummer

'Bluetta'

This is a vigorous and very productive variety that bears good crops of medium-sized, light blue berries with a sweet flavor. It has a compact growth, so it is good for containers, and flowers late, making it ideal for colder areas.

	suitable for containers
	spring
	good resistance
	hardy
	self-fertile (late)
	early summer

'Bluecrop'

This is a popular, midseason variety that bears high yields of large, firm, light-blue fruits with a good flavor. It is a vigorous plant, drought- and frost-resistant, and has attractive fiery orange and copper leaves in fall.

	suitable for containers
	spring
	good resistance
	hardy
	self-fertile (mid)
	mid- to late summer

'Ochlockonee'

Rabbiteye blueberries, native to the southeastern US, are generally disease-free and more tolerant of heat than northern blueberries. 'Ochlockonee' grows to 10 ft (3 m); it produces good yields of crack-resistant, late-ripening berries.

	unsuitable for containers
	early spring
	good resistance
	hardy
	self-fertile (mid)
	mid- to late summer

CRANBERRIES *Vaccinium macrocarpon*

Cranberries are native to North American bogs, where they thrive in alternating layers of acidic organic matter and sand—as long as you can provide them with the same conditions in your garden, these attractive, spreading bushes will thrive. Although most varieties are generally too sharp to eat fresh from the bush, they are excellent used in cooking, especially in juices, jams, and, of course, cranberry sauce.

	SPRING	SUMMER	FALL	WINTER
PLANT				
HARVEST				

PLANTING

Cranberries need a constantly moist, although not waterlogged, soil with an acidic pH of between 4–5.5. It is probably unlikely that you will find these conditions naturally occurring in your garden, so consider growing cranberries in a container, where you can easily control their soil pH and moisture levels, or dig a dedicated cranberry bed, 6–8 in (15–20 cm) deep, and line the insides with plastic mesh or perforated plastic sheeting.

Cranberries are self-fertile, so you will only need one plant to produce a crop. Plants are supplied container-grown, so can be planted at any time of year. Saturate the soil with rainwater, which has a more acidic pH than

Control conditions in a cranberry container.

tap water, and then plant out the bushes 12 in (30 cm) apart. Leave 12 in (30 cm) between rows. Mulch around the plants with about 1 in (2.5 cm) of sand.

CROP CARE

Water bushes regularly with rainwater, ensuring that the soil is always kept moist. Cranberries are low, spreading plants and may need pruning, either after

harvesting or in spring, if their growth gets out of hand. Trim back any excess stems after harvesting. Careful pruning will encourage bushier growth.

HARVESTING
Cranberries should be ready to harvest from early fall. They do not need to be picked immediately and can be left on the bush for several months.

STORING
Fruits will keep longer than most other berries—up to three months in the refrigerator—and they can also be frozen or made into sauce.

PESTS AND DISEASES

Cranberries are under threat from relatively few pests and diseases; if need be, construct netting to deter birds. You may find that they suffer from lime-induced chlorosis, caused by high levels of calcium in very alkaline soils, which prevents plants from absorbing iron—leaves will turn yellow and then brown, before withering. Acidify the soil or add iron to it to combat the problem. Practice good garden hygiene when pruning bushes, and try to encourage strong, open growth and a well-ventilated structure.

'Stevens'

This hybrid, bred for productivity and disease resistance, is characterized by its vigorous habit and large red berries. Its leaves are larger than other varieties' and yields can be double those of wild cranberries. The tangy fruits ripen after 'Ben Lear' but before 'Howes'.

- unsuitable for containers
- spring or early fall
- good resistance
- hardy
- self-fertile
- early to mid-fall

'Early Black'

This is one of the easiest varieties to grow, since it is disease- and frost-resistant. The large, bell-shaped fruits are such a dark red that they are almost black, and they have a relatively sweet flavor. In fall, the blunt-tipped foliage turns a deep red.

- suitable for containers
- year round
- good resistance
- hardy
- self-fertile
- late summer to early fall

'Ben Lear'

Taken from the wild in Wisconsin in the 1900s, this variety produces early burgundy berries that are prized for sauces. Shrubs form a spreading mat of 8-10 in (20-25 cm), and are good ground cover under taller, acid-loving shrubs.

- unsuitable for containers
- spring or early fall
- some resistance
- hardy
- self-fertile
- early to mid-fall

'Howes'

This bright red berry originated in Massachusetts and is known for its long storage. The firm, tart fruits are oval and ripen later than other varieties. The ground-hugging shrubs benefit from winter snow cover or leaf mulch.

- unsuitable for containers
- spring or early fall
- some resistance
- hardy
- self-fertile
- mid-fall

'Early Black'

MELONS *Citriullus* spp.

Although melons are close relatives of the cucumber, in cool, temperate regions of the country it is almost inevitable that you will have to grow them under glass, since they need high temperatures and high humidity to thrive. Melons fall into two main categories: sweet melons—such as canteloupes, honeydews, and musk melons—which have dense, juicy flesh, and watermelons, which have crisp, pink, "watery" flesh.

	SPRING	SUMMER	FALL	WINTER
PLANT				
HARVEST				

PLANTING

Sow seed under cover in mid-spring and then plant out in early summer—keep the pots or trays warm, since the seed needs a temperature of at least 60°F (16°C) to germinate. Do not sow too early or the plant may become pot-bound. In warm climates, melons can be grown outdoors, provided that you cover young plants with a cloche or cold frame and site them in a warm and sunny position. Place cloches in position a few weeks prior to planting to warm up the soil. Be vigilant when there is any risk of frost.

Melons prefer a rich, well-draining soil with a neutral pH. Dig in well-rotted manure or compost prior to planting.

Sow three seeds to a pot in mid-spring.

CROP CARE

Keep plants well-watered, but take care to wet the soil and not the stems. If plants are in a cold frame, be sure to open it when they flower to allow for pollination. Fertilize weekly in the blooming period.

HARVESTING AND STORING

Melons should be ready for harvesting in late summer and early fall. Cut the stems with a

sharp knife. As ripening occurs, the stems will begin to crack, the fruits will soften, and their sweet smell will grow stronger. They will keep fresh for a few weeks in the refrigerator once harvested.

PESTS AND DISEASES

Greenhouse melons are at risk from general greenhouse pests and diseases, such as spider mite and whitefly. Powdery mildew and cucumber mosaic virus can also be a problem. Combat these by practicing good garden hygiene, and ensure that plants are well-spaced and well-ventilated. Try to prevent rot by keeping stems dry.

TIP **SUPPORT FRUITS**

Ripening melons can become very heavy, and if you have trained your plants to climb there is a risk of fruit falling and becoming damaged. Tie netting or a string bag to the wire supports to take their weight.

Support heavy fruits with netting.

'Edonis'

An early ripening hybrid that produces fruits of up to 1 lb (450 g) in weight, it is ideal outdoors in areas that experience colder conditions. The oval fruits have dark green grooves, and the pale orange flesh has a refreshing, delicate flavor.

- unsuitable for containers
- late spring
- good resistance
- not hardy
- self-fertile
- midsummer to early fall

'Minnesota Midget'

An ideal cantaloupe for small spaces or containers, this very early variety produces good yields of 4 in (10 cm) long fruits on compact vines. The melons have a dark green, grooved skin and sweet, orange, fragrant flesh.

- suitable for containers
- late spring
- good resistance
- not hardy
- self-fertile
- late summer

'Galia'

A popular commercial variety that can be grown outdoors, this vigorous plant bears good, successive yields of fruits, which mature early in the season. The greeny-yellow skin has a "netted" appearance, and the pale green flesh is succulent and sweet.

 unsuitable for containers

late spring

good resistance

not hardy

self-fertile

midsummer

'Halona'

Hybrid 'Halona' was bred for flavor and resistance to powdery mildews and fusarium wilts. When picked ripe, at 79 days, the ribbed, netted fruits weigh 4–5 lb (1.8–2.3 kg), boast small seed cavities and have sweet, orange flesh.

unsuitable for containers

mid-spring

good resistance

not hardy

self-fertile

late summer

'Eden's Gem'

These softball-sized, netted heirloom muskmelons have a firm texture and luscious, complex flavor. Also known as 'Rocky Ford Green Flesh', the 1–2-lb (0.5–1-kg) fruits ripen early, in 70–80 days. Vines are rust-resistant.

unsuitable for containers

mid-spring

some resistance

not hardy

self-fertile

mid- to late summer

'Athena'

These flavorful, 5–6-lb (2.7-kg) cantaloupes are best left to ripen until they detach easily from the vine. Resistant to powdery mildew and fusarium wilt, hybrid 'Athena' begins producing at 75 days and continues for a long season. Fruits store exceptionally well.

- unsuitable for containers
- mid-spring
- excellent resistance
- not hardy
- self-fertile
- mid- to late summer

'Ogen'

This very popular variety bears fruits of up to 4.4 lb (2 kg) in weight and has a superb, unrivaled flavor. As the melons mature, the skin turns from green to golden yellow, beneath which is a pale green, rich, aromatic, and sweet flesh.

- unsuitable for containers
- late spring
- good resistance
- not hardy
- self-fertile
- late summer

'Hale's Best'

This favorite variety bears large, 5–6-lb (2.3–2.7-kg) ribbed cantaloupes on vining plants up to 5 ft (1.5 m) wide. The sweet, juicy fruits have salmon-colored flesh, thin rinds, and small seed cavities. They mature in about 86 days.

- unsuitable for containers
- mid-spring
- some resistance
- not hardy
- self-fertile
- late summer

'Ambrosia'

Named for the sweet flavor and delectable aroma of their salmon-colored flesh, 'Ambrosia' hybrid cantaloupes measure about 6 in (15 cm) in diameter. Vines are resistant to mildews; fruits ripen 86 days after planting.

- unsuitable for containers
- mid-spring
- some resistance
- not hardy
- self-fertile
- late summer

'Ogen'

'Charentais'

This old variety is commonly grown commercially, but can also be grown under cover by less experienced gardeners. The medium-sized, round fruits have a smooth, pale green-gray skin and a very juicy, sweet flesh that is deep orange in color.

- 🪴 unsuitable for containers
- 🌱 late spring
- ✳️ good resistance
- ❄️ not hardy
- 🌼 self-fertile
- 🔒 early fall

'Arava'

This mildew-resistant galia-type hybrid produces 2–3 lb (1–1.5 kg) yellow-netted melons with sweet, aromatic green flesh that tastes similar to honeydew. Ready to harvest after just 75 days, 'Arava' is ideal for short-season gardeners.

- 🪴 unsuitable for containers
- 🌱 mid-spring
- ✳️ some resistance
- ❄️ not hardy
- 🌼 self-fertile
- 🔒 mid- to late summer

'Lambkin Christmas Melon'

With mottled green skin and juicy white flesh, this melon makes an unusual garden plant. It is a modest yielder, but has good vigor. The oval fruits are succulent and aromatic, and ripen in 65–75 days.

- 🪴 unsuitable for containers
- 🌱 mid spring
- ✳️ some resistance
- ❄️ not hardy
- 🌼 self-fertile
- 🔒 mid- to late summer

'Blenheim Orange'

This old favorite remains popular, thanks to its sweet, musk flavor. The fruits can grow up to 2 lb (1 kg) in weight and have a green, netted skin with flesh that is quite red. Grow under cover for the best yields.

- unsuitable for containers
- late spring
- good resistance
- not hardy
- self-fertile
- late summer to early fall

'Sangria'

Top-notch eating quality makes disease-resistant 'Sangria' a popular choice. This hybrid's deep red flesh is exceptionally high in sugars, with the voluptuous fruits often weighing 20 lb (9 kg). Melons ripen 86 days after planting.

- unsuitable for containers
- mid-spring
- good resistance
- not hardy
- self-fertile
- late summer

'Sugar Baby'

This modern, early variety bears small watermelons with a smooth, dark-green skin that turns almost black when ripe. The fine-textured red flesh is delicious and very sweet. It has short vines, so is ideal for small gardens.

- unsuitable for containers
- late spring
- good resistance
- not hardy
- self-fertile
- late summer to early fall

Vegetables

Roots

- Potatoes
- Carrots
- Parsnips
- Beets
- Sweet potatoes
- Rutabagas
- Radishes
- Turnips
- Salsify and Scorzonera
- Jerusalem artichokes

POTATOES *Solanum tuberosum*

Potatoes are a useful, adaptable kitchen vegetable, and easy to grow, even in small spaces. They are sometimes classified by how long they take to mature: new potatoes, the smallest, sweetest types, should be lifted first; midseason potatoes can be harvested shortly after; and late season potatoes, which take the longest to mature, produce tubers that are best for winter storage.

	SPRING	SUMMER	FALL	WINTER
PLANT				
HARVEST				

CHITTING

Although it is not absolutely necessary, chitting your potatoes before you plant them out will give you a headstart, and should result in a quicker harvest. Place your seed potatoes, with their "eyes" facing upward, in trays or egg cartons in a warm, light location. They will sprout short, green shoots or "chits." Move them to a cooler position about six weeks before planting, when the chits are .25–.5 in (5–10 mm) long.

PLANTING

Potatoes prefer an open, sunny, frost-free site in well-drained soil with a pH of 5–6. Practice crop rotation, and do not plant your crop where you have grown

Plant chitted potatoes "eyes" up.

potatoes, onions, or other root vegetables the previous year.

Dig some organic matter, such as compost or well-rotted manure, into the soil in the fall before planting. Just before you plant, apply a balanced fertilizer on the soil surface and work it in well. Alternatively, spread fertilizer along the rows when planting.

In spring, once there's no risk of severe frost, plant your

early crop. Midseason and late potatoes can be planted any time between spring and early summer. If you are planting tubers out individually, plant 4–6 in (10–15 cm) deep and cover each with 1 in (2.5 cm) of soil. If planting in rows, dig a shallow trench about 6 in (15 cm) deep, and press tubers into the soil with chits facing upward. Space new potatoes 12 in (30 cm) apart and larger potatoes 15 in (38 cm) apart. Cover with at least 1 in (2.5 cm) of soil. Leave about 24 in (60 cm) space between rows of new potatoes or 30 in (75 cm) between later maturing types.

Earth up your potatoes as they grow.

CROP CARE

Water your potatoes and keep them free from weeds. New types will need watering while they are young; later varieties need less attention until the tubers have started to develop. Applying an organic liquid feed or a top-dressing of fertilizer may help to increase the yield.

Potato plants need "earthing up" as they grow, to ensure that no light reaches the tubers,

TIP GROWING POTATOES IN CONTAINERS

If space is limited or you want to protect new potatoes under cover, plant them in containers or bags.
- Check there are drainage holes; put in 8 in (20 cm) of soil-based compost.
- Place one or two chitted potatoes on top. Cover with about 4 in (10 cm) of compost, and water in well.
- Earth up with compost at intervals and water regularly. Harvest when leaves start to die back.

Potatoes grow in a variety of containers, such as strong plastic bags, tubs, or pots.

otherwise, they will turn green and spoil. When the stems reach about 9 in (23 cm) tall, pile soil up around them, leaving about 4 in (10 cm) of foliage above the surface. You may need to repeat this process a couple of times, depending on how tall the plants grow. Cut back the stems of larger varieties in late summer or early fall to 2 in (5 cm) above the soil.

HARVESTING

New potatoes should be ready to harvest in 60–90 days, midseason in 90–110 days, and late varieties in 120 days, or more. Check that tubers are ready to harvest by scraping back some of the soil and examining them. It is best to lift potatoes on a dry day, and then leave them out in the sun for a few hours before storing. Ensure that no tubers are left in the soil or they are likely to regrow the following year.

STORING

Potatoes will store well in double-layered paper or burlap bags in a cool, dry, well-ventilated place. Ensure that they are properly dried out—the drier they are when you store them, the better they'll keep. Also check that potatoes are completely covered, with no light reaching them.

PESTS AND DISEASES

Pests that may damage your potatoes include cutworms, wireworms, slugs, and Colorado potato beetles. The best ways to prevent these are to control weeds, defend crops against slugs and snails, and try not to leave tubers in the ground longer than necessary.

The most serious disease is potato blight, an airborne fungus that infects plants in continuously wet weather, and usually affects later maturing varieties at the end of the summer. The stems and leaves wither and tubers rot. Other diseases include potato common scab, potato blackleg, and powdery scab.

Include potatoes in a three-year crop rotation to avoid common pests and diseases persisting in the soil. Plant potatoes where you have grown beans or peas in the previous year.

Colorado beetles (left) are a serious pest and can be controlled organically with Bt applications. Potato blight (right) causes plants to shrivel and die.

'Swift'

Possibly the earliest variety available, a good crop of white-skinned, waxy potatoes is ready for harvest just seven weeks after planting. The cream-colored flesh has a delicate, new potato flavor. This is a good variety for growing in containers.

- suitable for containers
- mid-spring after chitting
- good resistance
- fairly hardy
- early to midsummer

'Russet Norkotah'

This early-maturing variety produces high-quality, uniform tubers that store well, but vines are susceptible to diseases and environmental stresses, so need extra care. Tubers are medium-long, with dark russet skin, shallow eyes, and white flesh.

- suitable for containers
- early to mid-spring
- some resistance
- fairly hardy
- mid- to late summer

'Caribe'

This Canadian-bred potato is a good choice for gardeners in northern regions, maturing in just 70 to 90 days. The oblong, purple-skinned tubers have snow-white flesh, and score well in taste tests. Plants have high yields and are resistant to scab.

- suitable for containers
- early to mid-spring
- some resistance
- fairly hardy
- mid- to late summer

'Red Duke of York'

These distinctive red-skinned potatoes have a light yellow flesh that has a firm texture when cooked. 'Red Duke of York' can be left to mature as a midseason potato to produce bigger tubers.

- suitable for containers
- mid-spring after chitting
- excellent resistance
- fairly hardy
- early to midsummer

'Adirondack Red'

Early maturing 'Adirondack Red' potatoes have purplish-red skin and pinkish-red flesh, and are naturally high in antioxidants. The tubers are flavorful and moist, and make an attractive presentation whether roasted, mashed, or used in salads.

- suitable for containers
- early to mid-spring
- some resistance
- fairly hardy
- mid- to late summer

'Cranberry Red'

Also known as 'All Red', this early season variety produces large round tubers with cranberry-red skin. The potato has moist rose-colored flesh ideal for boiling or roasting. Plants are resistant to scab and adapted to drought conditions.

- suitable for containers
- early to mid-spring
- some resistance
- fairly hardy
- mid- to late summer

'Maxine'

A heavy cropper, 'Maxine' produces an abundance of round potatoes with smooth, bright-red skins that store well. The white, waxy flesh has an excellent flavor and stays firm when cooked, making these ideal for boiling, roasting, or baking.

- suitable for containers
- mid-spring after chitting
- good resistance
- fairly hardy
- midsummer

'Red Gold'

Renowned for early "new" potatoes, tender 'Red Gold' tubers can be dug at 70 days. The small to medium, nearly round potatoes are red on the outside with gold flesh, and have a moist texture and a sweet, nutty flavor. They do not store well.

- suitable for containers
- early to mid-spring
- some resistance
- fairly hardy
- mid- to late summer

'Yellow Finn'

An exceptional flavor that's described as sweet and buttery has gained these pear-shaped yellow tubers a reputation as a gourmet potato. The plants produce large numbers of yellow-fleshed tubers, which are spread out over a wider area than most other varieties.

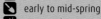
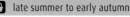

- unsuitable for containers
- early to mid-spring
- some resistance
- fairly hardy
- late summer to early autumn

'Orla'

These creamy-skinned potatoes can be grown as a midseason or early larger variety, depending on the size of tuber preferred. The pale yellow flesh has a good flavor. This variety is ideal for organic growers, since it is has very good resistance to blight.

 suitable for containers
 mid-spring after chitting
good resistance
fairly hardy
midsummer

'Red Norland'

This is the standard early-season, red-skinned potato. Plants are disease-resistant, adaptable, and have consistently high yields; the tubers, which tend to be large, have firm white flesh that can be used for a variety of purposes.

suitable for containers
early to mid-spring
some resistance
fairly hardy
mid- to late summer

'Yukon Gold'

A modern introduction, these potatoes are oval and slightly flattened with a thin, light gold skin and shallow eyes. The pale yellow flesh has a rich, buttery flavor that is good baked, roasted, or fried. Once harvested, they store well.

 suitable for containers
mid-spring after chitting
good resistance
fairly hardy
mid- to late summer

'Belle de Fontenay'

This old French salad variety is popular for its exceptional flavor, which improves on storage. It produces small, smooth, kidney-shaped, light yellow tubers with a creamy yellow, waxy flesh. Preserve their flavor by steaming.

	suitable for containers
	mid-spring after chitting
	good resistance
	fairly hardy
	midsummer

'Kestrel'

A gardeners' favorite, this is a versatile and attractive potato. The tubers produced are well-shaped with a smooth, white skin and purple rings around the eyes. The cream-colored flesh has a slightly waxy, floury texture and a good flavor.

	suitable for containers
	mid-spring after chitting
	good resistance
	fairly hardy
	midsummer

'Pentland Javelin'

Cropping later than other
new varieties, 'Pentland Javelin'
will produce a higher yield if
left to mature. The heavy
crops of oval, white-skinned
potatoes have a white, waxy
flesh with a creamy texture
that is ideal for boiling.

 suitable for containers
 early spring after chitting
 good resistance
 fairly hardy
 midsummer

'Rio Grande Russet'

This recent introduction from
Colorado State University
was bred to yield consistently
smooth, attractive, oblong tubers
with light-colored russet skin.
A deep, spreading root system
helps the disease-resistant plants
during periods of drought.

unsuitable for containers
early to mid-spring
good resistance
fairly hardy
late summer to early fall

'Purple Viking'

The purple-skinned tubers
produced by this midseason
variety can get very large, so
close planting is recommended.
The white, moist flesh is
excellent for mashing, and the
potatoes store well. Plants are
compact and resistant to scab.

 suitable for containers
 early to mid-spring
 some resistance
 fairly hardy
late summer to early fall

'Blue Danube'

Also known as 'Adam Blue', this modern 'Sarpo' introduction produces spectacular blue-skinned, oval tubers with bright white flesh. The large potatoes have a good flavor and are ideal for baking. These tubers have good disease resistance.

- suitable for containers
- mid-spring after chitting
- good resistance
- fairly hardy
- midsummer

'Princess TM Ratte'

The long, white-skinned tubers of this variety are reminiscent of 'Pink Fir Apple', but less knobbly. The creamy, yellow flesh has a similar firm and waxy texture though, and a good, nutty taste beloved of French chefs. It is good for boiling and salads.

- suitable for containers
- mid-spring after chitting
- excellent
- fairly hardy
- mid-summer

'Maris Piper'

This potato is widely grown commercially for its high yields of well-flavored tubers. The potatoes have a light yellow skin and a firm texture when cooked. It is an excellent multipurpose tuber, and is the connoisseur's choice for French fries.

- suitable for containers
- mid-spring after chitting
- excellent resistance
- fairly hardy
- early fall

'Kerr's Pink'

The "pink" in 'Kerr's Pink' refers to the color of the tubers, which are short and oval. The creamy-white flesh has a dry and floury texture when cooked, and is good for mashing and roasting. The potatoes have good blight resistance and keep well.

 suitable for containers
 mid-spring after chitting
- good resistance
- fairly hardy
 midsummer

'Red Pontiac'

Round, red-skinned tubers can get very large, but can also be harvested early for new potatoes. Also known as 'Dakota Chief', this variety is known for producing high yields of flavorful, attractive, white-fleshed potatoes that store very well.

 unsuitable for containers
- early to mid-spring
- good resistance
- fairly hardy
 midsummer to early fall

'Kennebec'

Released in 1948, 'Kennebec' remains one of the most dependable and popular potato varieties in the US. The white-fleshed tubers often get very large, and are excellent keepers. Plants tolerate drought and resist late blight and viruses, but not scab.

 unsuitable for containers
 early to mid-spring
- good resistance
- fairly hardy
 late summer to early fall

'Desiree'

This popular, scab-resistant variety produces heavy crops even in dry conditions. The red-skinned potatoes have a pale yellow flesh with a waxy texture and excellent flavor; they are good for baking and mashing, and store well once harvested.

	suitable for containers
	early to mid-spring after chitting
	good resistance
	fairly hardy
	late summer to mid-fall

'French Fingerling'

This gourmet variety produces oval-shaped 2–4-in (5–10-cm) rose-red tubers that are plumper than most fingerlings. The moist yellow flesh is lightly splashed with pink and has an exceptional flavor. Tall, spreading plants are resistant to scab.

	unsuitable for containers
	early to mid-spring
	some resistance
	fairly hardy
	late summer to early fall

'All Blue'

This unique all-purpose potato is blue inside and out. The late-maturing tubers have deep blue skin and purple-blue flesh and keep their color best when steamed or baked. 'All Blue' is moderately resistant to late blight, but susceptible to scab.

	suitable for containers
	early to mid-spring
	some resistance
	fairly hardy
	late summer to early fall

'Pink Fir Apple'

This old variety produces unusual-looking, long, knobbly, pink-skinned potatoes. Their yellow, waxy flesh has the best flavor of any salad potato. The yields are not heavy, but the tubers will store until early winter if left in the ground.

 suitable for containers
 mid-spring after chitting
good resistance
fairly hardy
late summer to early winter

'Russian Banana'

This Russian heirloom fingerling is well known to chefs, who value the plate-appeal and excellent texture and flavor of its rich yellow flesh. The golden-skinned, banana-shaped tubers grow to 4–5 in (10–13 cm), and store well.

 suitable for containers
early to mid-spring
some resistance
fairly hardy
late summer to early fall

'German Butterball'

The all-purpose golden tubers with deep yellow flesh produced by this heirloom variety are often described as "buttery" flavored. Vines are vigorous and high-yielding, and resist most diseases. 'German Butterball' potatoes store exceptionally well.

 unsuitable for containers
early to mid-spring
good resistance
fairly hardy
late summer to early fall

CARROTS *Daucus carota*

A garden favorite, carrots are a mainstay in the kitchen and are one of the most popular and easy vegetables to grow. They come in a variety of shapes, sizes, and colors, with maturity times that range from 50 days for small roots, to 90 days or more, depending on the variety. If carrot fly is a problem, growing the roots in raised containers may offer an effective solution.

	SPRING		SUMMER		FALL		WINTER	
PLANT								
HARVEST								

SOWING

Carrots favor open, dry sites and a light soil with a pH of 6.5–7.5. Ensure that the soil is free from stones so that roots have space to develop and do not become constricted or malformed. Dig in plenty of well-rotted manure or compost before planting.

Seed should be sown directly into the ground from mid-fall through to midsummer, since carrots are difficult to pot on and transplant. Sow the seeds .5–.75 in (1–2 cm) deep and space around 4 in (10 cm) apart, leaving 6 in (15 cm) between each row. By sowing successively every few weeks, it is possible to have a continuous harvest throughout the summer and fall.

Pinch out carrot leaves when thinning.

CROP CARE

Weed the area regularly by hand while the carrots are small, until their leafy canopy has grown sufficiently dense to suppress any competition. Water them during dry spells, especially if the soil starts to harden, but remember that carrots don't need as much water as some other crops; be careful not to overdo it or they will become too leafy.

HARVESTING

Thin out the carrots as they grow, eating some as baby vegetables, while allowing the others to continue growing. Early crops should be ready to harvest seven weeks after sowing, and maincrops in 10–11 weeks. Gently pull out by hand, or if the soil is too hard, ease out with a fork.

STORING

Carrots can generally be left in the ground until they are needed, or store in big wooden boxes filled with damp sand through the winter in order to protect them from frosts.

PESTS AND DISEASES

Carrot flies lay eggs in the soil and the larvae tunnel into roots, causing them to rot. Intercrop with onions to disguise the scent, erect a fine mesh fence, or grow in containers at least 18 in (45 cm) tall: higher than they can fly.

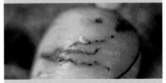

Damage caused by the carrot fly.

'Early Nantes'

The blunt-ended, deep orange roots of this variety are 5.5–6 in (14–15 cm) long, with only a minimal core and sweet, crunchy flesh. Fast-maturing, they can be picked at finger-size. 'Early Nantes' can be sown in late winter under glass or cloches.

- suitable for containers
- mid-spring to late summer
- poor resistance
- hardy
- midsummer to mid-fall

'Yaya'

This hybrid Nantes-type carrot has become the variety of choice for many market gardeners because of its crunchy sweetness and reliable performance. Tops are vigorous, and the 6-in (15-cm) blunt-tipped orange roots hold well in the ground for fall harvesting.

- suitable for containers
- mid-spring to early summer
- good resistance
- hardy biennial
- midsummer to fall

'Nelson Hybrid'

This early Nantes hybrid has 6-in (15-cm) long, smooth, blunt-ended cylindrical roots that are deep orange in color and excellent in flavor. They can be harvested young as baby carrots. Very productive, it is resistant to greentop and cracking.

- suitable for containers
- late winter to mid-spring
- poor resistance
- hardy
- early to midsummer

'Parano'

A very early Nantes hybrid, 'Parano' produces smooth-skinned, cylindrical, blunt-ended roots with good color and flavor, up to 6–7 in (15–18 cm) long. They are excellent raw, juiced, or cooked. This variety is suitable for growing under glass and for successional sowings.

- 🪣 suitable for containers
- 🌱 late winter to mid-spring
- 🐛 poor resistance
- ❄️ hardy
- 🔒 early to midsummer

'Tendersnax Hybrid'

The slightly tapered roots of 'Tendersnax' are 5–6 in (13–15 cm) long, blunt-ended, rich orange, and smooth-skinned. The flesh is exceptionally tender and juicy, delicious cooked or raw, and is high in beta-carotene. It is a disease-resistant variety.

- 🪣 suitable for containers
- 🌱 mid-spring to midsummer
- 🐛 good resistance
- ❄️ hardy
- 🔒 midsummer to late fall

'Mokum'

This high-yielding early variety produces almost coreless, very juicy, sweet, and crunchy roots that are good pulled young as baby carrots or allowed to mature to 6–7 in (15–18 cm) long. It can be sown under glass from midwinter onward.

- 🪣 suitable for containers
- 🌱 late winter to mid-spring
- 🐛 poor resistance
- ❄️ hardy
- 🔒 early to midsummer

'Parmex'

The tender, sweet roots of this variety are round, measuring only 1.5–2 in (4–5 cm) in diameter. It is ideal for containers, shallow soils, and grow bags and can be sown under glass or cloches in mid- to late winter for earlier crops.

suitable for containers
early to late spring
some resistance
hardy
late spring to early fall

'Napoli'

A very early-maturing Nantes carrot, 'Napoli' has intensely orange, tapering roots up to 8 in (20 cm) long, maturing 55 to 60 days after sowing. It can be sown under glass in late winter and early spring and is ideal for successional sowing.

unsuitable for containers
mid-spring to midsummer
poor resistance
hardy
late spring to mid-fall

'Royal Chantenay'

Chantenay carrots' thick, fat roots generally grow to 6 in (15 cm) or less, and are a good choice for heavy soils, or even for containers. This reliable, dark orange heirloom variety matures in about 70 days, is easy to harvest, and stores well.

suitable for containers
mid-spring to early summer
no resistance
hardy biennial
midsummer to fall

'Trevor'

This F1-hybrid, Nantes-type variety produces heavy yields of cylindrical roots with a good orange color. The roots can be grown for early or later crop harvests and have a good, sweet flavor and good texture. The plants have good bolt resistance.

 suitable for containers
 mid-spring to late summer
 some resistance
 hardy
midsummer to fall

'Atomic Red'

This long, slim, Imperator-type carrot is a unique red-purple color that deepens when roots are cooked in stews or roasted, and offers higher lycopene levels than most other varieties. Best planted in loose soil, its roots grow to 11 in (28 cm) long.

 unsuitable for containers
mid-spring to early summer
no resistance
 hardy biennial
 midsummer to fall

'Scarlet Nantes'

Known also as 'Nantes Scarlet', this classic orange-red carrot grows to about 8 in (20 cm) in length, and has a sweet, crisp taste and almost no inner core. The slightly tapered roots grow reliably well in a wide range of conditions.

 unsuitable for containers
 mid-spring to early summer
no resistance
 hardy biennial
 midsummer to fall

'Touchon'

This heirloom Nantes carrot produces smooth, cylindrical, stump-ended roots measuring 7–8 in (18–20 cm) long, with no core. They are crisp, sweet, and notably juicy, retaining these qualities well during winter storage. Excellent raw or juiced, the roots also freeze well.

 suitable for containers
mid- to late spring
poor resistance
hardy
midsummer to mid-fall

'Rainbow Hybrid'

The aptly named roots of this variety are diverse in color, both in the skin and the flesh, ranging from white, through yellow, to orange. They are tapered, growing to about 7–9 in (18–23 cm) long, with a sweet flavor and juicy, tender texture.

 unsuitable for containers
mid-spring to early summer
poor resistance
hardy
midsummer to early fall

'Bolero'

A heavy-yielding variety with 7-in (18-cm) long, conical, deep-orange roots with outstanding flavor, 'Bolero' is very resistant to alternaria blight and powdery mildew. The roots are sweet and crunchy, retaining these qualities well, even in long-term storage.

 suitable for containers
mid-spring to midsummer
good resistance
hardy
early to late fall

'Red Samurai'

The bright red skin and pinkish flesh of the striking 'Red Samuai' from Japan retains its beautiful, vibrant color after cooking. The tapering roots are about 10–11 in (25–28 cm) long, sweet and strong in flavor, and possess a crisp texture.

 unsuitable for containers
 early spring to midsummer
 poor resistance
 hardy
 early summer to early fall

'Crème de Lite'

The creamy-colored, tapering roots of 'Crème de Lite' have sweet, juicy flesh and are equally good raw and cooked; they do not need to be peeled. It prefers moist, rich, well-drained soils and is resistant to greentop, alternaria, and powdery mildew.

🪣 unsuitable for containers
🌱 mid-spring to early summer
🐛 good resistance
❄ hardy
🔒 midsummer to mid-fall

'Danvers Half Long'

This 19th-century American variety has roots up to 9 in (23 cm) long and 2 in (5 cm) in diameter, with sweet, tender, and crunchy flesh that retains these qualities during storage. It performs well in any soil, including clay and other heavy types.

 unsuitable for containers
 mid-spring to early summer
 poor resistance
❄ hardy
 early summer to mid-fall

'Carson'

This Chantenay-type carrot has 5-in (13-cm) long, smooth, conical roots with a rich orange core and particularly good flavor; they store well for winter use. Because of the shorter roots, this variety is a good choice for heavy soils.

	suitable for containers
	early spring to midsummer
	poor resistance
	hardy
	late spring to mid-fall

'Tonda di Parigi'

A 19th-century variety with round roots just 2 in (5 cm) across when mature, this variety is often sown at high density to restrict the size still further and make pulling in bunches possible. The roots are deep orange, with an excellent, sweet flavor.

	suitable for containers
	early spring to late summer
	poor resistance
	hardy
	late spring to late fall

'Purple Haze'

A new variety with striking purple skin, 'Purple Haze' has bright orange, tender, crunchy flesh. To preserve the skin's color it is best to eat the roots raw or only cook them lightly. Given protection, the roots can overwinter in the soil.

	suitable for containers
	early spring to early summer
	poor resistance
	hardy
	early summer to late winter

'Cosmic Purple'

The roots of this variety are 7 in (18 cm) long and purple-skinned, with coreless orange flesh and a high sugar content that gives them a sweet flavor. The attractive color is retained after cooking. Seed can be sown under cloches from early spring.

 suitable for containers
 late spring to midsummer
 poor resistance
 hardy
 late summer to mid-fall

'Danvers 126'

The deep orange roots of this improved version of 'Danvers Half Long' reach about 6–8 in (15–20 cm) long and are blunt or slightly tapered, nearly coreless, sweet, and crunchy. It is vigorous and heavy-cropping, and tolerant of different soil types.

 suitable for containers
mid-spring to early summer
poor resistance
hardy
early summer to mid-fall

'Kingston'

This new 'Autumn King' hybrid produces large, pointed roots with a strong, attractive color and very good flavor. It is easy to grow, high-yielding, and has strong tops that make the roots easy to lift. It also stores well over winter.

 unsuitable for containers
late spring to midsummer
poor resistance
hardy
late summer to late fall

'Berlicum'

Renowned for the excellent flavor of its deep orange carrots, 'Berlicum' also has the advantage of keeping well over winter. The roots are slender, up to 8 in (20 cm) long and with small cores; they are not prone to woodiness.

- unsuitable for containers
- mid-spring to early summer
- poor resistance
- hardy
- early fall to mid-spring

'Kuroda Long'

Popular in Asia, this orange-red carrot stores well and is a preferred choice for juicing due to its high moisture content. Each cylindrical root is 8 in (20 cm) long and weighs up to 1 lb (450 g). Plants show resistance to alternaria leaf blight.

- unsuitable for containers
- mid-spring to early summer
- some resistance
- hardy biennial
- late summer to fall

'Ulysses'

This variety produces top-quality, deep orange, cylindrical roots 7–8 in (18–20 cm) long, with strong tops. It is resistant to splitting and bolting and will overwinter well in the ground or storage. Sow under protection in late winter or early spring for earlier crops.

- unsuitable for containers
- mid- to late spring
- good resistance
- hardy
- midsummer to mid-fall

'Chantenay Red Cored'

Also known as 'Chantenay Red Core', this old variety produces blunt, deep orange roots that reach 6 in (15 cm) long, and are now often pulled at about 3–4 in (7.5–10 cm) for use as very sweet-flavored baby carrots. It is tolerant of heavy soils and stores well.

 suitable for containers
 early spring to early summer
poor resistance
hardy
early summer to late fall

'Purple Dragon'

This unusual purple-skinned carrot, also known as 'Dragon', has an uncommon flavor described by some as wild and spicy, and an very high antioxidant content. Tapered roots grow to 8 in (20 cm), and reveal an orange interior and bright yellow core when sliced.

unsuitable for containers
mid-spring to early summer
no resistance
hardy biennial
late summer to fall

'Yellowstone'

Canary yellow and 9–10 in (23–25 cm) long, the roots of this variety are distinctive and retain their color after cooking. The flavor is mild, and is sweetest when they are eaten raw. Sow under protection in mid- to late winter for earlier crops.

 unsuitable for containers
 early spring to early summer
 poor resistance
hardy
 midsummer to early winter

PARSNIPS *Pastinaca sativa*

Sweet, delicious parsnips are excellent cooked in soups or stews, or roasted like potatoes. Although they are fairly slow to germinate, once established, they are a relatively low maintenance crop, and will reliably bear roots as long as they are sufficiently watered and have enough space. Roots are available in different shapes, sizes, and even colors, so try some unusual varieties.

	SPRING	SUMMER	FALL	WINTER
SOW				
HARVEST				

SOWING

Parsnips thrive in an open, sunny position, in light, sandy soil, with a slightly acidic pH of 6.5. They come in a range of shapes and sizes, so make sure that your soil is deep enough for whichever type you choose. Dig well-rotted manure into the soil the previous fall, and ensure that it is not too compacted.

Wait until mid- to late spring before sowing any seed. Sow directly into the soil about .75 in (2 cm) deep, either thinly along the row, or with two or three seeds together, since parsnips often germinate unreliably. Once the seedlings are established, thin to 4–6 in (10–14 cm) apart for medium roots, and 12 in (20 cm) for large.

Sow thinly to increase chances of success.

CROP CARE

Water your seeds regularly while they are germinating, then only water the developing roots if the ground is very dry. Roots may split if they are allowed to dry out and are then watered. Parsnips do not normally need feeding, but give them a liquid feed if growth is poor. Weed your parsnips carefully until they are established.

HARVESTING

Parsnips can be harvested in the summer when young or left in the ground until the first frosts, which is said to improve flavor.

STORING

Spread moist sand in the bottom of a wooden box, and place a layer of parsnips on top, ensuring that they are not touching. Cover with sand and store in a cool, dry place. The sand will prevent the roots from shriveling or rotting. Alternatively, parsnips can be left in the ground until you need them. Cover with a layer of straw if the weather turns cold.

PESTS AND DISEASES

Parsnips are vulnerable to pests such as carrot fly and celery root miner. Female carrot flies lay eggs in the soil near to plants, which hatch and tunnel into the roots, rotting them. Use fine mesh to deter them (see carrots pp.184-5). There is no cure, so dig up affected roots. Celery leaf miner causes brown spots on leaves, but may not be fatal if prompt action is taken.

Diseases include parsnip canker and downy mildew. There is no cure for parsnip canker, which causes roots to rot, so choose resistant varieties.

'Gladiator'

With fast-maturing, tapering roots with smooth, white skin and a fine, sweet flavor, this consistently high-quality F1 hybrid variety is popular for both exhibition purposes and the table. It is resistant to canker and it is easy to clean for cooking.

- unsuitable for containers
- early to late spring
- good resistance
- hardy
- early fall to early spring

'Cobham Improved Marrow'

Medium-sized roots with a tapering, elegant shape and smooth white skin make this a good variety for exhibition; they also have a fine, sweet flavor. They mature in 32 to 36 weeks and are resistant to canker.

- unsuitable for containers
- late winter to late spring
- good resistance
- hardy
- early fall to mid-spring

'Hollow Crown'

This popular 19th-century variety has tapering roots up to 12 in (30 cm) long and 3 in (7.5 cm) in diameter, with a hollow crown and sweet, mellow-flavored flesh. It is very high-yielding and is resistant to canker.

- unsuitable for containers
- late winter to mid-spring
- good resistance
- hardy
- early fall to late winter

'Albion'

This variety has uniformly long, smooth, tapering roots with whiter skin than most parsnips. The flavor is very sweet, becoming more so after the first frosts. It is an F1 hybrid, bred for resistance to canker and other diseases.

🪣	unsuitable for containers
🥄	late winter to mid-spring
🐛	good resistance
❄	hardy
🔒	early fall to late winter

'Javelin'

An F1 hybrid variety giving a high yield, 'Javelin' produces long, slender, tapering roots with smooth, easy-to-wash skins and a good flavor. Their uniformity makes the roots good for the show bench, too. It is resistant to pests and diseases.

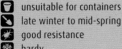

🪣	unsuitable for containers
🥄	late winter to mid-spring
🐛	good resistance
❄	hardy
🔒	mid-fall to late winter

'Lancer'

With short, slender, wedge-shaped roots, this variety is ideal for planting in small plots and for use as a baby vegetable. The roots have smooth, white skins and good-flavored flesh. 'Lancer' is very hardy and is resistant to canker.

🪣	unsuitable for containers
🥄	late winter to early summer
🐛	good resistance
❄	hardy
🔒	early summer to late fall

'Countess'

This variety has smooth, creamy-skinned, conical roots with shallow crowns that can be lifted as late as mid-spring with no loss of quality. They mature about 32 to 36 weeks after sowing, with increasing sweetness over time. 'Countess' is a hybrid, and is vigorous and disease-resistant.

- unsuitable for containers
- early to late spring
- good resistance
- hardy
- mid-fall to mid-spring

'Panache'

A new and vigorous hybrid variety, 'Panache' has smooth, white-skinned roots with creamy, sweet-flavored flesh; they are uniformly large and wedge-shaped, with shallow crowns. This variety is very resistant to canker and has good storage capabilities.

- unsuitable for containers
- mid-spring to early summer
- good resistance
- hardy
- early fall to late winter

'Archer'

A strong-growing variety, easy to germinate, with uniform tapering, long, white roots and smooth, unblemished skin, 'Archer' is an excellent variety for exhibition displays as well as for the table. It is best harvested before midwinter.

- unsuitable for containers
- late winter to late spring
- poor resistance
- hardy
- early fall to late winter

'White Gem'

This high-yielding variety has comparatively short roots, making it suitable for shallow soils. It is tolerant of most soil types and has good resistance to canker. The roots are broad-shouldered, with a smooth, white skin and excellent flavor.

 unsuitable for containers
 late winter to late spring
 good resistance
hardy
early fall to mid-spring

'Harris Model'

'Harris Model' has been popular with gardeners for years. Plants produce smooth, white roots, 12 in (30 cm) in length and 3.5 in (9 cm) at the shoulder. One or two large roots left in the ground over winter will produce seed the following spring.

 unsuitable for containers
 early to mid-spring
good resistance
hardy
 mid-fall to early spring

'All American'

Like all parsnips, 'All American' should be left in the ground for two to four weeks after the temperatures dip below freezing. When mulched with straw, the 12-in (30-cm) tapered white roots can be harvested through winter. Flavor is sweet and nutty.

 unsuitable for containers
 early to mid-spring
good resistance
hardy
 mid-fall to early spring

BEETS *Beta vulgaris*

Beets are a highly underrated vegetable—being not only simple to grow, but also a delicious, versatile culinary crop; grow roots for pickling or eating fresh in salads, and harvest the bright, beautiful leaves when young to be eaten raw or cooked like spinach. Beets come in a multitude of sizes, shapes, and colors, from the standard purple globes, to tiny baby beets, in a range of colors from orange or white, to pink-and-white striped.

	SPRING	SUMMER	FALL	WINTER
SOW				
HARVEST				

SOWING

Beets will grow almost anywhere, but they prefer a sunny, open site and light, sandy soil, with a pH of around 6.5–7. It can sometimes be difficult to encourage beet seeds to germinate, so soak them in warm water for about an hour before planting—this will remove any traces of germination inhibitor.

Sow early, bolt-resistant seed under cover of a cloche or cold frame while there's still risk of frost, or directly into the ground between late spring and summer. Sow standard-sized beets 4 in (10 cm) apart, and smaller varieties about 2 in (5 cm) apart, at a depth of 1 in (2.5 cm), with 6 in (15 cm) between rows. Thin seedlings, if necessary.

Thin out seedlings as they develop.

CROP CARE

Protect seedlings and young plants against frosts or pests, as necessary. Once established, water in moderation; too much water will encourage leafy growth but no root, while too little will turn the root woody. Spray with a foliar, seaweed-based fertilizer once or twice during growth to boost levels of manganese and boron in the soil.

HARVESTING AND STORING

Begin to harvest roots when they are about 2 in (5 cm) wide. Spring-sown beets will be ready in summer; summer-sown beets in fall. The longer you leave the roots in the ground, the larger they will become, so thinning them as you harvest will encourage remaining crops to grow bigger. Beets can be overwintered by leaving them in the ground and covering with a 6 in (15 cm) layer of straw. Alternatively, pull up the roots, twist off the leaves, and store in a box of moist sand in a cool, dark place.

PESTS AND DISEASES

Beets are usually relatively trouble-free, but may fall victim to aphids or cutworms. Seedlings may be at risk of damping off; protect against this by maintaining good garden hygiene and giving plants enough light and space.

Beet leaf infested with aphids.

'Red Ace'

This hybrid, globe variety produces high-quality, oval roots that are dark red in color with red, ringless flesh, and an excellent flavor. The roots grow well in all soils, even dry conditions, and are a favorite with exhibition growers.

	suitable for containers
	early spring
	good resistance
	hardy
	midsummer to late fall

'Early Wonder'

Considered the best beet for greens, 'Early Wonder' tops reach 16–18 in (40–46 cm) in height, and can be substituted for spinach or chard in recipes. The dark red 3-in (7.5-cm) roots are also flavorful, and reach a harvestable size in as little as 45 days.

	suitable for containers
	mid- to late spring; late summer
	some resistance
	fairly hardy
	summer and fall

'Kestrel'

This fast-maturing globe variety reliably produces good-quality, smooth, round, dark-red beets. The sweet flavor of the deep red flesh is particularly good when the roots are harvested young. It has good resistance to disease and bolting.

	suitable for containers
	early spring to mid-summer
	good resistance
	hardy
	midsummer to late fall

'Chioggia'

A striking globe variety from Italy, its large, round, red roots mature very early in the season, and when sliced, the flesh reveals attractive red and white rings that fade to light pink when cooked. The young leaves can be cooked like spinach.

 suitable for containers
early spring to midsummer
good resistance
fairly hardy
late spring to late summer

'Pronto'

This globe variety is bolt-resistant and can be sown early in the season and successively throughout the summer. Roots are round, purple, and smooth-skinned, and have the sweet flavor of baby beets. The leaves are ideal for picking for salads.

 suitable for containers
early spring to midsummer
good resistance
hardy
midsummer to late fall

'Albino'

This heirloom may lack the deep red color of the typical beet, but not the sweet flavor. The green, white-stemmed tops can be harvested for salad greens, and the smooth white roots, which are ready in 50 days, are delicious steamed or grated raw in salads.

 suitable for containers
mid- to late spring; late summer
some resistance
fairly hardy
summer and fall

'Moneta'

This globe variety can be sown early without the risk of bolting. Each seed reliably produces one plant (beets normally produce up to four plants per seed), so less thinning out will be required. The uniform, round, and smooth-skinned roots have crimson flesh with an excellent flavor.

🪣	suitable for containers
🌱	early spring
✳	good resistance
❄	hardy
🔒	midsummer to late fall

'Cylindra'

This late-ripening variety produces sturdy, dark-red, long cylindrical roots that are perfect for slicing. They keep their sweet flavor all season and store well for a long period once harvested. They are slow to bolt and have good disease resistance.

🪣	suitable for containers
🌱	early spring
✳	good resistance
❄	fairly hardy
🔒	mid- to late summer

'Mr Crosby's Egyptian'

This is one of the earliest maturing, larger beet varieties and has good resistance to bolting. A rapid grower, it produces deep-red, smooth, rounded, but slightly flattened, roots with an excellent flavor. The beets can be lifted young or when mature.

🪣	suitable for containers
🌱	early spring
✳	good resistance
❄	fairly hardy
🔒	late spring to late summer

'Action'

This variety reliably produces good crops of well-flavored, round, baby roots with a smooth skin. The red-colored flesh has no rings and is tender when young. The 'Action' variety is ideal for growing in containers or growbags.

- suitable for containers
- early spring to midsummer
- good resistance
- hardy
- midsummer to late fall

'Touchstone Gold'

Smooth, orange-skinned, uniform globes are vivid gold inside, and have a sweet, mild flavor. 'Touchstone' is easy to grow and the roots, which can be harvested at a mature 4-in (10-cm) diameter or as babies, retain their vibrant color when cooked.

- suitable for containers
- mid- to late spring; late summer
- good resistance
- fairly hardy
- summer and fall

'Merlin'

'Merlin' is recommended for its hybrid vigor, even when planted densely, and its resistance to downy mildew and root rot. The dark red roots, notable for their exceptionally high sugar content, are ready to harvest in 55 days.

- suitable for containers
- mid- to late spring; late summer
- good resistance
- fairly hardy
- summer and fall

'Solo'

'Solo' is a British variety that is easy to grow and requires no thinning. It produces good yields of uniform, round, and medium-sized beets that have a smooth, red skin and sweet flesh. This variety is an excellent choice for growing as baby beets.

🪣	suitable for containers
🌱	early spring to late summer
✳️	good resistance
❄️	hardy
🔒	midsummer to late fall

'Detroit Dark Red'

Introduced in 1892, 'Detroit Dark Red' is still very popular among home gardeners. The uniform blood-red roots are tender and quite tasty, and the young leafy greens are good in salads. Plants are resistant to downy mildew.

🪣	suitable for containers
🌱	mid- to late spring; late summer
✳️	good resistance
❄️	fairly hardy
🔒	summer and fall

'Boro'

This good-quality, globe variety produces crops that have a dark-red, smooth skin. They can be harvested early and used as baby beets or allowed to mature. Seeds sown later in the growing season can be lifted in mid-fall to store.

🪣	suitable for containers
🌱	early spring to mid-summer
✳️	good resistance
❄️	fairly hardy
🔒	midsummer to fall

'Alto'

A very popular, early-maturing hybrid, 'Alto' produces good crops that have uniform and cylindrical roots, which are perfect for slicing. Under the smooth, red skin is a ringless, red flesh, known for its sweet flavor. Hardy, it benefits from disease resistance.

 suitable for containers
 early spring
 good resistance
hardy
early summer to late fall

'Burpee's Golden'

This unusual variety has orange flesh that turns yellow when cooked, and doesn't bleed and stain when cut. The beets have an outstanding flavor and are best harvested when small. The spinachlike leaves can be steamed or boiled.

 suitable for containers
 early spring to midsummer
 good resistance
fairly hardy
early summer to mid-fall

'Forono'

A high-yielding beet with long, deep-red, cylindrical roots, 'Forono' has an outstanding flavor, which is at its best when the beets are eaten young and tender. Sow slightly later than other varieties to prevent bolting. The roots store well.

 suitable for containers
mid-spring
 good resistance
 fairly hardy
 late summer to late fall

SWEET POTATOES *Ipomoea batatas*

Sweet potatoes are not related to potatoes at all but are actually members of the bindweed family. Like potatoes, though, their orange or white flesh is delicious roasted, baked, or mashed. They originate from tropical or subtropical climates so will only produce a good crop during a very warm summer, or if grown in a greenhouse. Raise your own seeds under cover and then plant out, or, alternatively, buy rooted cuttings called "slips."

	SPRING	SUMMER	FALL	WINTER
SOW/PLANT				
HARVEST				

SOWING & PLANTING

Sweet potatoes need a warm, sheltered site, with sandy, highly fertile soil and a pH range of 5.5–6.5. Sow indoors in trays or pots at a depth of 1 in (2.5 cm) in early to mid-spring. Harden off and transplant once the young plants reach a height of about 4–6 in (10–15 cm). If growing from slips, plant out in late spring.

Create a 12 in (30 cm) high ridge in the soil and plant seedlings or slips at least 10–12 in (25–30 cm) apart; plant slips 2–3 in (5–8 cm) deep. Bear in mind that sweet potatoes grow very large and will need plenty of space—at least 30 in (75 cm) between rows. Consider trimming foliage or training it up wire supports to keep your plot looking neat.

Trim the foliage to keep it under control.

CROP CARE

Sweet potatoes require a lot of water, especially during their early growth period. Consider sinking the tops of cut-off plastic bottles upside down into the soil around your crops, since pouring water into these will ensure that it reaches right down to the roots. Feed your sweet potatoes with a balanced fertilizer every two to three weeks.

HARVESTING

Pick the leaves as you require them—they can be cooked and eaten like spinach. The tubers should be ready to harvest from early fall, and you should finish lifting them before the first frosts. Take care not to split or damage the sweet potatoes when digging them up, since the skins are delicate.

STORING

Roots can be stored inside for several months, but they will need to be "cured" first; leave in the sunshine for four to seven days to toughen their skins.

PESTS AND DISEASES

Red spider mite, aphids, and whitefly may affect your crops, as may other general fungal diseases and viruses. Practice good garden hygiene to minimize the risks, and check plants regularly for symptoms. If these spread, treat accordingly.

Mottling may indicate red spider mite.

'Centennial'

Uniformly cylindrical roots with copper skin and orange flesh are produced in abundance and are ready to harvest about 120 days after planting, or 100 days for smaller, tender roots. 'Centennial' is suitable for heavy soils and is resistant to viral disease.

- unsuitable for containers
- mid-spring to early summer
- good resistance
- not hardy
- mid-fall

'Carolina Ruby'

This excellent producer bred by North Carolina Agricultural Research Service is resistant to fusarium wilt and soil rot, but susceptible to root knot nematode. Garnet-colored roots mature in about 90 days. The moist, tasty flesh is an attractive bright orange.

- unsuitable for containers
- late spring
- some resistance
- not hardy
- late summer to early fall

'Hernandez'

Red-orange skinned 'Hernandez' is a good choice for both northern and southern gardens. Plants exhibit intermediate resistance to bacterial and fungal diseases, as well as Southern root knot nematodes. The orange-fleshed roots are very moist when cooked.

- unsuitable for containers
- late spring
- some resistance
- not hardy
- late summer to early fall

'Jewel'

This variety offers above-average yields, producing medium-sized, orange-skinned roots with sweet, moist, light-orange flesh. It has an excellent flavor and soft texture. It is resistant to cracking and root knot nematodes, but is intolerant of cold, wet soil.

- unsuitable for containers
- mid-spring to early summer
- some resistance
- not hardy
- mid-fall

'Beauregard'

This vigorous variety is one of the fastest to mature, at 90 to 95 days, and is high-yielding. The roots have a red-coppery skin and moist, sweet, soft orange flesh. They are resistant to cracking, nematodes, and pox and they store well after harvesting.

- unsuitable for containers
- mid-spring to early summer
- good resistance
- not hardy
- mid-fall

'Vardaman'

Released by the Mississippi Agricultural Extension Service in 1981, 'Vardaman' is known for producing small, deep orange roots with outstanding flavor. The plant grows in a compact bush form and has attractive foliage, making it an excellent choice for the ornamental garden.

- unsuitable for containers
- late spring
- some resistance
- not hardy
- late summer to early fall

'Nancy Hall'

This heirloom variety is a favorite of gardeners because of the sweet flavor and firm texture of its yellow flesh. The pale-colored roots do not have the disease resistance of the newer varieties, and are generally smaller. They keep well.

- unsuitable for containers
- late spring
- poor resistance
- not hardy
- late summer to early fall

'Vineless Porto Rico'

This vineless, or bush, variety is a favorite of gardeners with limited space. 'Porto Rico' roots have copper skin and reddish-orange flesh with a rich flavor and a smooth texture. An older variety, it is susceptible to fusarium wilt and Southern root knot nematodes.

- unsuitable for containers
- late spring
- poor resistance
- not hardy
- late summer to early fall

'O'Henry'

Ready to lift in around 100 days, the prolific roots of 'O'Henry' have creamy colored flesh and skin. The tubers have a drier texture than other varieties, but their flavor is sweet and delicious. The roots develop in a cluster beneath the plant, allowing easy picking.

- unsuitable for containers
- late spring
- some resistance
- not hardy
- late summer to early fall

'White Yam'

Also called 'White Triumph', this heirloom variety is one of the oldest available sweet potatoes. Vines produce good yields of tan-skinned, white-fleshed roots that sweeten with storage, and have a drier, firmer texture than orange-fleshed varieties.

- unsuitable for containers
- late spring
- some resistance
- not hardy
- late summer to early fall

'Violetta'

This vining heirloom variety produces above-average yields of bright-purple roots with white flesh. 'Violetta' roots mature earlier than most sweet potatoes and are very flavorful, but vines lack the disease resistance of recently released varieties.

- unsuitable for containers
- late spring
- poor resistance
- not hardy
- late summer to early fall

'T65'

This reliable, vigorous sweet potato is known to produce very large yields. Its large reddish-pink tubers have white-golden flesh, with a good flavor and a pleasant, creamy texture. They are excellent for culinary use.

- unsuitable for containers
- late spring
- some resistance
- not hardy
- late summer to early fall

'Allgold'

High-yielding 'Allgold', which was developed in Oklahoma in 1952, produces moist, orange-fleshed roots that store well. The vigorous variety resists soil rot and internal cork, but is susceptible to root knot nematodes, scurf, and black rot.

- unsuitable for containers
- late spring
- some resistance
- not hardy
- late summer to early fall

'Nemagold'

A variety from Oklahoma, 'Nemagold' has dark orange skin and dry orange flesh that is high in beta carotene. It is resistant to root knot nematode and black rot, which makes it a choice for and favorite of the organic gardener.

- unsuitable for containers
- mid-spring to early summer
- some resistance
- not hardy
- mid-fall

'Georgia Jet'

A reliable heavy-cropping and early-maturing variety, 'Georgia Jet' has deep purplish-red skin and deep orange, moist flesh with an excellent flavor. Ready to harvest 90 days after planting, the roots will store well in a warm place at the end of the season.

- unsuitable for containers
- mid-spring to early summer
- poor resistance
- not hardy
- mid-fall

'Covington'

This variety is a favorite among growers in the South because of its flavorful orange flesh, consistently good yields, and resistance to fusarium wilt, root knot nematodes, and bacterial rot. The reddish-skinned roots are high in fiber and beta carotene.

- unsuitable for containers
- late spring
- good resistance
- not hardy
- late summer to early fall

RUTABAGAS *Brassica napus* Napobrassica Group

Known as "Swedish turnips" or "Swedes" in England, turnips or "neeps" in Scotland, and rutabagas in the United States, rutabagas are a staple of many soups, stews, and casseroles. Their sweet orange or yellow flesh is also delicious mashed. This very hardy root vegetable is actually a member of the brassica family and is well worth growing, despite its slow growth and the number of pests and diseases that can affect crops.

	SPRING	SUMMER	FALL	WINTER
SOW/PLANT				
HARVEST				

SOWING

Prepare your plot the previous fall by digging in well-rotted manure or compost. Rutabagas like a sunny position in a light soil with a pH above 6.8. Relatively slow-growing, they can take up to six months before they are ready to harvest, so sow as soon as the soil has warmed up, and protect with fleece, cold frames, or cloches if the weather turns cold.

Sow in pots and transplant or sow directly into shallow drills that are .75 in (2 cm) deep, and at least 15 in (38 cm) apart. Once the seedlings have established, thin to about 9 in (23 cm) apart.

CROP CARE

Weed and water regularly and be vigilant against pests.

Cut away the leafy stems before storing.

HARVESTING

Rutabagas should be ready to harvest in fall or early winter when they are about 4–6 in (10–15 cm) in diameter. They can be left in the ground for as long as needed, even over winter, although bear in mind that the longer they are left, the greater the risk that they will turn woody and will need a protective layer of straw if the weather turns cold.

STORING IN A CLAMP

Rutabagas can be left in the ground over winter or, when harvested, stored in boxes packed with moist sand. Traditionally, however, rutabagas are stored in "clamps." To make a clamp, spread a layer of straw 8 in (20 cm) thick on the ground in a sheltered spot. Arrange your rutabagas in a pyramid, twice as wide as tall, with the largest at the bottom and the necks facing outward. Cover with an 8 in (20 cm) layer of straw, and, if the weather is particularly cold, a layer of soil as well. Pack down, and check occasionally for signs of pests or damage.

PESTS AND DISEASES

Rutabagas are prone to the pests and diseases that afflict members of the cabbage family: cabbage root fly, clubroot, flea beetle, mealy cabbage aphids, and mildew (see pp.246-7). Try using fine netting to deter cabbage root fly and flea beetles.

Aphids cause white blisters on leaves.

'Brora'

This popular, fast-growing variety develops an attractive reddish-purple skin. The fine-grained, creamy yellow flesh has a good flavor and no bitterness. It is resistant to clubroot and powdery mildew, has good winter hardiness, and stores well.

- suitable for containers
- early summer
- good resistance
- hardy
- early fall

'Marian'

This old favorite bears heavy crops of uniform, purple, globe-shaped roots with cream-colored bases. The yellow flesh is of a fine texture and an excellent flavor. This variety is resistant to both clubroot and powdery mildew.

- suitable for containers
- early summer
- good resistance
- hardy
- early fall

'Laurentian'

An improved "purple top" variety, 'Laurentian' produces high yields of round, 4–6-in (10–15-cm) creamy yellow roots with purple shoulders. Harvested after frost, the sweet, mild flesh is excellent roasted, and adds a rich flavor to soups and stews.

- suitable for containers
- early to midsummer
- some resistance
- hardy
- mid- to late fall

'Helenor'

This large, purple, globe-shaped variety has a cream-colored base and a deep yellow flesh that has a smooth texture and sweet flavor. 'Helenor' is resistant to mildew, has excellent winter hardiness, and stores well once it has been harvested.

- suitable for containers
- early summer
- good resistance
- hardy
- early fall

'American Purple Top'

Best planted when they can mature in the cool fall weather, 'American Purple Top' produces large, firm, yellow roots with purple crowns. The roots store well for winter use, and the sweet, mild flesh turns a bright orange when cooked.

- suitable for containers
- early to midsummer
- some resistance
- hardy
- mid- to late fall

'Joan'

'Joan', a "purple top" type rutabaga, shows resistance to clubroot and produces very uniform large round roots. The smooth-textured yellow flesh gets sweeter after frost, and is excellent mashed with potatoes or added to soups.

- suitable for containers
- early to midsummer
- good resistance
- hardy
- mid- to late fall

RADISHES *Raphanus sativus*

You may be surprised to discover that there are hundreds of different types of radish, not just the familiar small, red salad type. If you want some variety, try the large, white Oriental mooli (or daikon) radishes that can grow as long as 24 in (60 cm) and weigh up to 4.5 lb (2 kg), or grow winter radishes in rainbow shades of black, purple, yellow, or green, and eat these raw, or cook in the same way as rutabagas or turnips.

	SPRING		SUMMER		FALL		WINTER	
SOW								
HARVEST								

SOWING

Radishes are a versatile crop and will grow in almost any location—they will tolerate partial shade, and are happy interplanted with other crops or grown in containers—but they dislike soil that has been recently manured. Radishes can be grown strategically to provide a year-round crop; very early radishes can be sown indoors before planting out; summer radishes should be sown directly in the ground in early spring; and winter radishes in mid- to late summer. By sowing a few seeds every few weeks you can achieve a continuous harvest.

Sow at a depth of .5 in (1 cm) in rows or blocks, thinning summer radishes to 1 in (2.5 cm) apart, and

Interplant with slow-growing crops.

winter radishes to 6 in (15 cm) apart once crops are established.

CROP CARE

Water regularly, but be careful not to overwater or you will simply encourage too much leafy growth.

HARVESTING

Summer radishes grow very quickly and some may be ready to eat in as little as one month.

Harvest promptly, since they tend to bolt and become woody. Winter radishes can be harvested from fall until the following spring. Their seed pods are also edible, so leave the roots in the ground over winter and they will produce a flowering stem and juicy seed pods.

STORING

As with other root crops, radishes can be stored in boxes packed with moist sand. Alternatively, winter radishes can be left in the ground until the middle of winter, although they made need protection from hard frosts.

PESTS AND DISEASES

Try to prevent flea beetles, slugs, and snails from targeting radish leaves by using fine netting around plants. Practice strict crop rotation to help prevent diseases such as clubroot, which is an incurable fungus that can persist in the soil for up to 20 years.

Flea beetles create ragged leaf holes.

'Saxa 2'

An early variety with roots that mature within just three weeks of sowing outdoors, 'Saxa' can also be sown under glass or cloches for an even earlier crop. The round roots are bright red, with crisp, mild, white flesh.

🪣	unsuitable for containers
🕤	late winter to midsummer
🕷	poor resistance
❄	hardy
🔒	late spring to early fall

'Purple Plum'

A striking variety with purple skin and crisp, white, sweet, and mild flesh, this radish tolerates heat well. It is slow to develop pithiness and is hardy, adaptable, and fast-maturing. It's good in containers as well as in the vegetable bed.

🪣	suitable for containers
🕤	late winter to early fall
🕷	poor resistance
❄	hardy
🔒	late spring to mid-fall

'Lady Slipper'

'Lady Slipper' radishes are plump and elongated, similar in shape to 'French breakfast' types, but their coloring is a solid pink bordering on magenta. The white flesh is crisp, mild, and sweet, and the roots are ready to harvest 27 days after sowing.

🪣	suitable for containers
🕤	spring; late summer
🕷	poor resistance
❄	fairly hardy
🔒	mid-spring to early summer; fall

'Amethyst'

Shiny, deep purple skins and crisp white flesh make this new variety attractive for its appearance as well as its flavor. The roots retain their crispness well and the strong tops allow roots to be pulled easily from the ground.

 suitable for containers
 early spring to early fall
some resistance
hardy
late spring to midwinter

'Giant of Sicily'

An heirloom radish from Sicily, this variety has bright red-skinned roots up to 2 in (5 cm) across with tender, crisp white flesh with a good flavor. Roots mature 45 days after sowing. It is easy to grow and shows some resistance to clubroot.

 unsuitable for containers
 early spring to early fall
good resistance
hardy
late spring to mid-fall

'White Icicle'

Also known as 'Lady Fingers', this 16th-century Italian variety has smooth, tapering roots 4–5 in (10–13 cm) long, with crisp, mild flesh. It is at its best harvested 30 days after sowing, but retains its mildness in maturity and is slow to become pithy.

 unsuitable for containers
 early spring to early fall
 poor resistance
 hardy
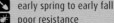 mid-spring to mid-fall

'Scarlet Globe'

Bright red, round roots with crisp, white, mild flesh are produced on an adaptable plant that will do well even in poor soils. It can be grown under cloches for early cropping; roots will be ready to pull in four to six weeks.

🪣	unsuitable for containers
🌱	late winter to early fall
🕷	poor resistance
❄	hardy
🔒	early spring to mid-fall

'Munchener Bier'

This radish is grown for its 3-in (7.5-cm) green pods as well as for its turniplike white roots, both of which are good in salads and stir-fries. Sow in spring for the pods, or summer and fall for the roots.

🪣	unsuitable for containers
🌱	early spring to early fall
🕷	poor resistance
❄	hardy
🔒	late spring to late fall

'Pink Beauty'

Even when large, the roots of 'Pink Beauty' retain their sweet, mild flavor and resist the onset of pithiness longer than most varieties. They are round, with rose-pink skins and crisp white flesh. This variety is also slow to bolt.

🪣	unsuitable for containers
🌱	late winter to early fall
🕷	poor resistance
❄	hardy
🔒	late spring to mid-fall

'French Breakfast'

Elongated, bright-scarlet roots with white tips identify this classic variety. It is one of the fast-growing radishes, but also one of the quickest to turn pithy. The flavor is mild and sweet when young, growing hotter as the roots mature.

 suitable for containers
 late winter to early fall
 poor resistance
❄ hardy
🔒 late spring to mid-fall

'Shunkyo Semi-Long'

Originating in northern China, this unusual, slow-bolting radish produces 4–5-in (10–13-cm) cylindrical roots with deep pink skin and crisp white flesh that is hot and sweet. The pink stems and lobeless green leaves can be used in salads and stir-fries.

 suitable for containers
spring; late summer
none
fairly hardy
mid-spring to early summer; fall

'Minowase Summer Cross'

The white tapering roots of this daikon radish have a crisp texture and mild, sweet flavor. They grow up to 20 in (50 cm) long and can be used raw or cooked. Its good resistance to viruses, fusarium, and heat are added advantages.

 unsuitable for containers
early to late summer
good resistance
hardy
mid to late fall

'Cherry Belle'

This early, fast-growing variety is cherry-shaped, with a bright red skin and mild-flavored, crisp, white flesh that is slow to become pithy in maturity. Sow under cloches for an early crop; the roots are ready to pull only 24 days later.

🪣	unsuitable for containers
🌱	early spring to early summer
🐛	some resistance
❄️	hardy
🔓	mid-spring to midsummer

'Daikon Radish'

The white cylindrical roots of this daikon radish grow up to 15 in (38 cm) long and 2 in (5 cm) in diameter. Roots have crisp, fine-textured flesh with a mild flavor, which is good for cooking or for salads. This variety is slow to bolt and stores well.

🪣	unsuitable for containers
🌱	early to late summer
🐛	poor resistance
❄️	hardy
🔓	late summer to late fall

'Cherriette Hybrid'

This hybrid radish produces handsome 2-in (5-cm) globes with scarlet skin and white flesh. Ready to harvest 3 to 4 weeks after sowing, the roots can be left in the ground longer without developing pithiness. 'Cherriette' is well adapted to fall growing.

🪣	suitable for containers
🌱	spring; late summer
🐛	none
❄️	fairly hardy
🔓	mid-spring to early summer; fall

'China Rose'

The oblong roots of this winter variety have pinkish-red skin and white flesh with a hot, pungent flavor. Best harvested when they are 4–6 in (10–15 cm) long, they keep well if stored in dry sand. The leaves are also good to eat.

 unsuitable for containers
 early to midsummer
 poor resistance
❄ hardy
🔒 late summer to mid-fall

'Long Black Spanish'

Also known as 'Noir Gros Long D'Hiver', this winter radish has black skin and white flesh. Roots can reach a length of 8 in (20 cm) and are more pungent than round types. They can be left in the ground until needed, or stored in sand.

 unsuitable for containers
 early summer to early fall
poor resistance
hardy
 early fall to midwinter

'Mantanghong'

This Chinese-type winter radish has greenish-white skin and crisp bright magenta flesh. It tastes sweet and slightly nutty and is good in salads or as a winter vegetable. They can grow up to 14 in (36 cm) long and may be left in the ground until needed.

 unsuitable for containers
early to late summer
poor resistance
hardy
 early fall to midwinter
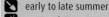

TURNIPS *Brassica campestris* Rapifera Group

Grown like root vegetables but members of the brassica family, turnips are an often overlooked crop. Harvested young, their roots have a delicious nutty flavor and are excellent cooked or eaten raw. Also try harvesting the spicy young leaves, or "turnip tops," and cook as spring greens. There are many unusual varieties that are well worth trying, in a variety of striking colors, such as black, purple, and white.

	SPRING	SUMMER	FALL	WINTER
SOW/PLANT				
HARVEST				

SOWING

Turnips will grow well in most soils, but they require high levels of nitrogen and a pH of between 5.5–7.5. Dig in some well-rotted manure or compost the fall before planting.

Sow four seeds to a cell in module trays and transplant each group when seedlings have grown two or three true leaves each. Protect seedlings from frost. Alternatively, sow seeds directly into the ground in early spring; they are less likely to germinate in later months when the weather warms up. To avoid a glut, sow successively every few weeks. Scatter seeds thinly along rows 9–12 in (23–30 cm) apart, or in blocks with 6 in (15 cm) spacing. Cover with .75 in (2 cm) of soil

Plant out module-grown crops in spring.

and water in. Thin seedlings to 4–6 in (10–15 cm) apart before they are more than 1 in (2.5 cm) tall. For turnip tops, sow in late summer, early fall, or early spring.

CROP CARE

Keep plants weeded and well-watered, especially during the summer, to prevent them from bolting. Turnips should not need an additional feed during growth.

HARVESTING

Early turnips will be ready to harvest within about five to six weeks, and larger maincrop varieties in about 10. Harvest by late fall, since the roots risk becoming woody if left in the ground for too long. Pick the "turnip tops" when leaves are still young, about 5–6 in (13–15 cm) tall If kept well-watered,the tops will usually crop a couple of times.

STORING

Turnips have a relatively high water content and do not store well. Harvest as needed and use them as soon as possible.

PESTS AND DISEASES

Like rutabagas, turnips are members of the brassica family and fall prey to the same pests and diseases (see pp.246–7). Sow seeds under fine mesh to prevent attack from cabbage root fly and flea beetles. Also watch out for diseases such as clubroot and downy mildew.

Clubroot stunts growth and kills crops.

'Golden Ball'

A dwarf variety popular since the 19th century, this very hardy turnip has deep yellow roots with soft flesh and a sweet flavor. Round while young, they flatten a little at their mature size of 3–4 in (7.5–10 cm). They store particularly well.

- unsuitable for containers
- late spring to late summer
- poor resistance
- hardy
- midsummer to late fall

'Oasis'

Eaten raw, this unusual turnip has a flavor like that of a melon; cooked, it tastes like a turnip, but with a more delicate flavor. The conical white roots mature fast and can be picked at any size. It has good resistance to viruses.

- unsuitable for containers
- mid-spring to midsummer
- good resistance
- hardy
- late spring to early fall

'Tokyo Cross'

This early, fast-growing variety is often harvested at about 1 in (2.5 cm) in diameter, when it can be eaten raw and tastes not unlike a radish. Equally, it can be left in the ground to mature and has smooth, sweet flesh when cooked.

- unsuitable for containers
- mid-spring to midsummer
- some resistance
- hardy
- late spring to mid-fall

'Purple Top Milan'

This 19th-century turnip has flattened roots, which are purple at the top and white below ground. It is useful for early crops when sown under protection of cloches. It does not store well and is best pulled when the roots are 2–3 in (5–7.5 cm) across.

 unsuitable for containers
 late spring to midsummer
poor resistance
hardy
midsummer to early fall

'Snowball'

A fast-growing variety, 'Snowball' can be brought to harvesting point even earlier by sowing under cloches. It has white globes and the tender flesh has a mild and sweet flavor. They can be pulled at six to eight weeks for use as baby vegetables.

 unsuitable for containers
early spring to midsummer
poor resistance
hardy
late spring to mid-fall

'Hakurei'

These smooth, white "salad turnips" are best when harvested slightly larger than radishes, at 30–40 days. Repeat sowings will yield a continuous supply of the sweet flavored, crisp roots for as long as the weather stays cool. They are delicious raw or cooked.

 suitable for containers
early spring to late summer
some resistance
fairly hardy
late spring to fall

'Atlantic'

The 'Atlantic' variety crops over a long period, producing flattened, round, white roots with purple crowns, which can be harvested from the time they reach golf ball size. The upright leaves can be cooked as a green vegetable and will resprout after cutting.

- suitable for containers
- early spring to late summer
- some resistance
- hardy
- late spring to early winter

'Shogoin'

Grown as much for its mild green tops as for its round white roots, 'Shogoin' produces leaves suitable for braising in 30 days. Roots will grow quite large, but are at their most flavorful when harvested at 2–3 in (5–7.5 cm) in diameter.

- suitable for containers
- spring and late summer
- some resistance
- fairly hardy
- early to midsummer and fall

'White Egg'

This fast-growing turnip has been popular for more than 100 years. Egg-shaped roots have fine-grained, mild white flesh with green shoulders, and can be harvested in 45–60 days; the tall tops are good for greens. 'White Egg' is a good storage variety.

- suitable for containers
- spring and late summer
- some resistance
- fairly hardy
- early to midsummer and fall

'Blanc de Croissy'

This old and easy-to-grow French-bred variety produces unusual, oblong, white roots that have a sweet, pungent flavor and crisp texture. They grow up to 6 in (15 cm) long and 1.5 in (4 cm) across, maturing 45 to 60 days after sowing.

 unsuitable for containers
late winter to early summer
poor resistance
hardy
mid-spring to late summer

'Tiny Pal'

The roots of 'Tiny Pal' are the size of golf balls, round and white with a good flavor. They grow very fast, and making staggered, successional sowings will produce crops over a long harvesting period. They will do well in a container.

suitable for containers
early spring to late summer
some resistance
hardy
late spring to mid-fall

'Purple Top White Globe'

This heirloom is the classic turnip, purple above ground where the roots are exposed to sun, and white below. The crisp, fine-grained roots are best when 3–4 in (7.5–10 cm) across. Young greens are tasty braised or stir-fried.

suitable for containers
spring and late summer
some resistance
fairly hardy
early to midsummer and fall

SALSIFY AND SCORZONERA

Tragopogon porrifolius and *Scorzonera hispanica*

Salsify and scorzonera, sometimes called black salsify, are root crops that are relatively uncommon but well worth growing if you have the space. Similar in texture to a parsnip but with an oysterlike flavor, salsify can be cooked in stews or soups, and the young leaves can be used in salads. Scorzonera is similar, but has black skin and larger leaves.

	SPRING	SUMMER	FALL	WINTER
SOW				
HARVEST				

SOWING

Both salsify and scorzonera will develop long, tapering roots, so ensure that you sow them in deep, light soil where there are no root-obstructing stones. Both crops prefer a pH range of 6–7.5 and an open, sunny position. It is important to use fresh salsify seed every year, since old seed declines in quality and is unlikely to germinate.

Sow seed directly into the ground in mid- to late spring, as soon as the soil warms up. Sow thinly in drills at a depth of .5 in (1 cm), allowing both salsify and scorzonera 6–12 in (15–30 cm) between rows. Scorzonera can also be sown in late summer to be harvested the following fall; it is slow-growing and

Keep the leafy crops well-weeded.

can be left in the ground for up to 18 months, if necessary. Both crops can be overwintered.

CROP CARE

Keep plants well-watered and ensure that they are kept free from weeds; either apply a mulch, such as black plastic sheeting, to suppress them, or weed by hand. Using a hoe may damage the roots.

HARVESTING

Both crops can be harvested for their roots or leaves. When roots have reached the desired size, dig them out carefully, since they can be quite brittle; scorzonera roots are prone to "bleed" if damaged.

If roots are left in the ground over winter they will sprout again in spring. Cover the plants with a layer of straw or leaves to blanch new growth. Salsify produces tasty shoots and will resprout two or three times. Blanched scorzonera leaves should be cut when they reach 4 in (10 cm) long, and flowerbuds can also be harvested and eaten.

PESTS AND DISEASES

Both salsify and scorzonera have excellent general pest and disease resistance, but are sometimes prone to white blister disease. This fungus causes white patches to appear on the underside of leaves and creates yellowish patches on the top, causing leaves and flowers to become misshapen. Ensuring that plants are well ventilated, with enough air and space, will help to prevent the spread of this disease. Practice crop rotation to prevent a buildup in the soil. Resistant varieties are available.

'Sandwich Island Mammoth'

This heirloom variety, also called 'Mammoth Sandwich Island', bears some of the finest-tasting salsify. The long, white roots have a sweet, tender flesh with an outstanding oysterlike flavor. This variety keeps well, and can be overwintered in soil until spring.

- 🪣 suitable for containers
- 🌱 mid-spring
- ✳ good resistance
- ❄ hardy
- 🔒 mid-fall to mid-spring

'Fiore Blu'

This European variety produces long, golden, fleshy roots, and blue flowers in its second year. Like parsnips, salsify seeds lose their viability quickly, so fresh seed is required for good germination. Harvest roots after the weather turns cool.

- 🪣 unsuitable for containers
- 🌱 early to mid-spring
- ✳ good resistance
- ❄ hardy
- 🔒 mid- to late fall

'Hoffmans Schwarze Pfahl'

This selection is known for producing long, black-skinned roots with white, flavorful flesh. Spring-planted and fall-harvested, perennial scorzonera can be left in the ground for a second year without loss of quality.

- 🪣 unsuitable for containers
- 🌱 early to late spring
- ✳ good resistance
- ❄ hardy
- 🔒 mid- to late fall

'Long Black Maxima'

This modern introduction of scorzonera produces long, black-skinned roots that have a delicate flavor. This variety produces heavy yields and also has good resistance to bolting. The roots can be harvested in fall or left to overwinter in the ground.

 unsuitable for containers
 mid-spring
 good resistance
 hardy
 mid-fall to mid-spring

'Russian Giant'

Also known as 'Geante Noire de Russie', this is the most popular and widely available of scorzonera varieties. The long, slender, black roots have a white flesh and a delicate flavor. The leaves can also be used in salads.

 unsuitable for containers
mid-spring
good resistance
hardy
mid-fall to mid-spring

'Belstar Super'

This perennial scorzonera is grown for its long, straight, 9–11-in (23–28-cm) black-skinned, white-fleshed roots that are eaten boiled, baked, or in soups and stews. 'Belstar Super' is a vigorous, early-maturing strain that is free of side roots.

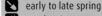 unsuitable for containers
 early to late spring
 good resistance
hardy
mid- to late fall

JERUSALEM ARTICHOKES
Helianthus tuberosus

A relative of the sunflower, Jerusalem artichokes are tall and stately plants that can produce bright yellow sunflowerlike blooms. The knobbled tubers develop in the soil among the roots, and can be eaten raw or cooked, but beware—they are notorious for producing flatulence. Don't be put off, since the tubers are a delicious vegetable.

	SPRING	SUMMER	FALL	WINTER
PLANT				
HARVEST				

PLANTING TUBERS

Jerusalem artichokes will grow almost anywhere as long as the soil is not waterlogged, but they prefer alkaline conditions so add lime to the soil if its pH is below 5. Plants can grow to about 10 ft (3 m) tall, so site them carefully—they could be grown to form natural screens or windbreaks. Either obtain tubers fresh from a greengrocer, or use saved tubers from previous years. Apply a medium-fertility soil improver before planting to encourage larger tubers.

Plant when the soil has warmed up in early spring. Dig a drill 4–6 in (10–15 cm) deep and place tubers along it at intervals of 12–18 in (30–45 cm), before covering over with soil.

The vibrant flowers add a splash of color.

CROP CARE

Weed well, and water during dry spells. Plants will need to be earthed up as they grow, with about 1.5–4 in (4–10 cm) of soil, and then supported with canes or wires. This provides the tall stems with stability, which is especially useful if they are planted in an exposed or windy position. In mid- to late summer cut the plant down to 5 ft (1.5 m),

and remove any flowers. This will encourage the plant to divert its energy and attention into producing tubers. Remove any yellowing foliage in fall, and cut the stem back to about 4 in (10 cm) above ground level.

HARVESTING

Jerusalem artichoke tubers should be left in the ground and harvested as required—they don't keep very well once lifted. Ensure that all tubers are removed from the ground at the end of the season, since they will grow again the following year, and may become invasive.

PESTS AND DISEASES

Jerusalem artichokes are generally quite problem-free, but they may come under attack from slugs and snails. To deter these, use pellets, place beer traps around your plot, and lay a ring of sharp gravel, crushed eggshells, or copper tape as a barrier.

More rarely, white blister may affect crops. It causes whitish patches on the underside of leaves with yellow patches on the top. There is no cure for this fungus, so remove and destroy any affected plants, improve ventilation, and practice crop rotation.

'Common'

This variety of Jerusalem artichoke has knobbled, irregular-shaped tubers and a pale purple-brown skin that needs peeling before cooking. Despite this extra preparation, its flavor is as good as that of the other varieties.

- unsuitable for containers
- early spring
- good resistance
- hardy
- mid-fall to mid-spring

'Fuseau'

This is perhaps the most popular variety, because of its large, smooth-skinned tubers, which are easier to peel than other, more knobbled types. The white flesh has a nutty flavor and is good roasted, boiled, or baked.

- unsuitable for containers
- early spring
- good resistance
- hardy
- mid-fall to mid-spring

'Red Fuseau'

This Jerusalem artichoke (also called sunchoke) produces long, red-skinned tubers with a sweet, nutty taste, and a texture similar to water chestnuts. The tubers are relatively free of knobs, so easier to clean than other varieties. Harvest after the first frost.

- unsuitable for containers
- early spring
- good resistance
- hardy
- mid- to late fall

'Stampede'

Recommended for areas with early frosts, 'Stampede' flowers and matures a month earlier than other varieties. Plants are 6–8 ft (1.8–2.4 m) tall, and the tubers are white and rounded and can weigh as much as 8oz (225 g) each.

- unsuitable for containers
- early spring
- good resistance
- hardy
- mid- to late fall

'Fuseau'

Brassicas and Leafy Vegetables

- Cabbages
- Brussels sprouts
- Cauliflower
- Broccoli
- Kale
- Spinach
- Swiss chard
- Kohlrabi
- Bok choy
- Chinese cabbage

CABBAGES *Brassica oleracea* Capitata Group

Cabbages are usually classified according to when they are
harvested, and by planting a number of different varieties you can
ensure a year-round supply. Spring and summer cabbages are round
or pointed in shape, and need to be eaten soon after picking. Fall
and winter cabbages are generally larger in size, with denser heads,
and are hardy. They can be stored for months once harvested.

	SPRING	SUMMER	FALL	WINTER
SOW/PLANT				
HARVEST				

SOWING

Dig in well-rotted manure or
compost in the fall before
planting, and add some lime to
the soil in winter if its pH is less
than 6.8. Most importantly, the
soil needs to be firm, since some
cabbages will grow very heavy
and their roots will need to
support their weight. Ensure
that you have a crop rotation
system in place, since cabbages
should not be planted where
brassicas have been grown
within the last three years.

Although summer and winter
cabbages need to be sowed at
different times of year, the
method is still the same. Sow
in pots or modules at a depth of
.75 in (2 cm). Sow summer, fall,
and red cabbages in early spring.

Thin seedlings to give them room to grow.

Sow winter cabbages in mid-
to late spring, and sow spring
cabbages in summer, ready for
harvesting the following year.

PLANTING OUT

Plant out your seedlings when
they have four true leaves. Plant
in rows 16–24 in (40–60 cm) apart,
with 12–18 in (30–45 cm) between
plants. Dig holes about 6 in (15 cm)
deep, and water before gently

placing the seedlings. Fit your seedlings with a brassica collar (see right) to deter cabbage root fly, which will attack the plants' roots. At all stages of growth, cabbages will be irresistible to birds and cabbage white butterflies, so put mesh or netting over your crop.

Net cabbages to deter butterflies.

CROP CARE

Weed seedlings thoroughly. Water regularly, daily, if necessary, when young, and then once a week when plants are more established. As cabbages grow, you will need to earth up the soil around them to support the weight of their growing heads. Trim off any dead outer leaves. Apply a high-nitrogen fertilizer or organic liquid feed to summer-sown cabbages in winter; feed fall-sown cabbages in spring.

HARVESTING

Spring or early summer cabbages can be harvested when they are still loose and leafy, before their leaves develop into a firm head; these are known as "spring

DISEASES

Cabbages are under threat from diseases such as downy and powdery mildew and white blister, but there are few as serious as clubroot—a disease to which all brassicas are prone. This fungus attacks the plants' roots, rotting and eventually killing them. There is no cure—so good garden hygiene, crop rotation, and digging up and destroying infected plants are absolutely essential.

Plants cannot be cured of clubroot. It can persist in the soil for up to 20 years.

greens." Once cut, you might be able to persuade the remaining stumps to produce a second crop: with a sharp knife, make a cross-cut pattern on the stalk and water as normal. Alternatively, wait for your cabbages to develop dense hearts, and then cut the head from the roots with a sharp knife. Use spring and summer types as soon as possible after harvesting, since they don't keep well.

Harvest fall and winter cabbages as needed. Winter cabbages are frost-hardy and slow to bolt—they can be left in the ground over winter, so there is no rush to harvest them. As with spring and summer cabbages, cut the heads from the roots with a sharp knife, or dig the entire cabbage up. To reduce the risk of diseases persisting in the soil, dig up all remaining roots shortly after harvesting.

STORING

Fall and winter cabbages can be stored for months if they are harvested before the first frosts, but ensure that they are cut with at least a 6 in (15 cm) stem. Hang them in net bags in a cool dark place, or lay them on wooden slats and cover them with straw or newspaper, to protect them if the weather turns cold.

PESTS

You may find your cabbages under threat from a range of pests, and may have to use more than one different measure during the crop's growth. When seedlings are young or first planted out, use a collar to prevent cabbage root flies from laying eggs next to the vulnerable plants. You can make your own using a small square of cardboard or carpet underlay.

Consider using a cloche or the cut off top of a plastic bottle for protection against other pests such as cabbage caterpillars and mealy cabbage aphids, although these may also be a problem at later stages of growth. Use netting to keep birds and cabbage white butterflies away. Construct a wooden or wire frame over your plants and attach the netting to it.

Cabbage white butterfly caterpillars will swarm on a cabbage, stripping its leaves. Pick the caterpillars off by hand. If necessary, spray with an insecticide.

'Ruby Ball'

This ruby-red summer variety is an excellent cabbage. Quick to grow from a spring sowing, it produces a dense, compact head with colorful, tasty leaves; add vinegar to the water when cooking to retain the color. It can also be used in salads and coleslaw.

- unsuitable for containers
- mid-spring
- poor resistance
- fairly hardy
- late summer to fall

'Integro'

This excellent, quick-growing, tasty cabbage produces a rosette of large, red-veined, grayish, outer leaves. Tucked down, right in the center, is a tight crisp ball of shiny, ruby red, making it ideal for colorful salads, coleslaw, and pickling.

- unsuitable for containers
- mid-spring
- poor resistance
- fairly hardy
- late summer to fall

'Red Jewel'

A top choice, this hardy variety produces large, tightly packed, round, purple-red heads, set off by their wide rosettes of leaves. Sow it in mid-spring for cutting from mid-fall, or leave it in the ground over winter for harvesting when it is required.

- unsuitable for containers
- mid-spring
- poor resistance
- hardy
- early to mid-fall

'Red Express'

This compact variety is earlier to mature than most, bearing small, dense heads in around 60–70 days; they are uniform in size. The crisp, deep red-purple leaves have an excellent flavor and are delicious cooked or eaten raw in salads.

- unsuitable for containers
- mid-spring
- some resistance
- hardy
- midsummer

'Ruby Perfection'

A good choice for containers and small plots because of its upright growth, 'Ruby Perfection' puts on quick growth from a spring sowing. The tight, round, red heads can be harvested from late summer and are excellent used in salads or risottos.

 suitable for containers
 mid-spring
poor resistance
fairly hardy
late summer to fall

'Super Red 80'

Round, rich burgundy heads weighing about 4 lb (1.8 kg) are produced about 80 days after transplanting. Resistant to tip burn and rot, and protected by thick, tough wrappers, the leaves have a pleasantly peppery taste, and hold up well in heat and chill.

 unsuitable for containers
mid-spring to midsummer
some resistance
fairly hardy
 midsummer to mid-fall

'Red Drumhead'

This variety is a good choice for small gardens due to its compact size, and for the kitchen because of its dark red, solid, round heads. It is good for adding color to salads, or used finely shredded in risottos and sautées. Sow in mid-spring for a fall harvest.

 unsuitable for containers
mid-spring
poor resistance
fairly hardy
early to mid-fall

'Duncan'

This versatile cabbage has a range of sowing options: sow in late summer for a spring crop; sow in early summer for a fall crop; or sow in late summer for a late fall crop of heartless leafy greens. It has excellent flavor and won't split when left in the ground.

- unsuitable for containers
- early to late summer
- some resistance
- hardy
- spring to late fall

'Tundra'

This excellent, sweet-tasting, and frost-hardy, Savoy cabbage is sown in late spring and is ready for cutting from fall to mid-spring the following year. The solid, dark-green cabbages keep well when left in the cold ground.

- unsuitable for containers
- late spring
- some resistance
- hardy
- mid-fall to mid-spring

'Durham Early'

This very popular and tasty cabbage has a pointed, firm shape. It is worth growing for fresh spring crops from a fall sowing. It can also be grown to produce tasty end-of-winter and early-spring greens, if cabbages are closely planted the previous summer.

 unsuitable for containers
mid- to late summer
poor resistance
hardy
mid- to late spring

'Early Jersey Wakefield'

Regarded by many gardeners as one of the tastiest cabbages, 'Early Jersey Wakefield' dates back to the mid-19th century. Compact plants produce solid, conical heads that average 2–3 lb (1–1.5kg), and mature 60 to 65 days from transplanting.

 unsuitable for containers
mid-spring to midsummer
poor resistance
fairly hardy
midsummer to mid-fall

'Parel'

This extra-early hybrid matures its solid and juicy, 6-in (15-cm) heads 45 to 50 days after transplanting. Mild, sweet flavor, good split resistance, and compact size make 'Parel' a good choice for a spring or fall home garden crop.

 unsuitable for containers
mid-spring; late summer
poor resistance
fairly hardy
midsummer; mid-fall

'Charmant'

This hybrid is well-suited to close plantings and forms dense, blue-green heads that are ready to harvest about 65 days after they are transplanted. This cabbage holds well in the field without splitting, and is resistance to fusarium yellows.

 unsuitable for containers
 mid-spring; midsummer
 some resistance
 fairly hardy
 midsummer; mid-fall

'Wheeler's Imperial'

Grown for at least 100 years, this compact dwarf variety produces dark-green, dense heads in fall from a spring sowing. With few outer leaves, plants can be set just 12 in (30 cm) apart. Closer planting in late summer will generate an abundance of fresh spring greens.

 unsuitable for containers
 mid-spring
 poor resistance
 hardy
 early fall

'Gonzales'

With softball-shaped heads of just 1 lb (450 g) at maturity, 'Gonzales' can be planted 8 in (20 cm) apart to yield a plentiful harvest in a small bed. Ready 55 to 60 days after transplanting, the mini-cabbages resist splitting, and have a sweet flavor.

 unsuitable for containers
 mid-spring; midsummer
 some resistance
 fairly hardy
 early to midsummer; mid-fall

'Savoy Express Baby'

One petite, yellow-green head of 'Savoy Express' is the right size for a single meal. The sweet flavor of this attractive, crinkled hybrid, combined with its extra early ripening time, earned it an All-America Selections award in 2000.

 unsuitable for containers
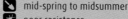 mid-spring to midsummer
 poor resistance
 fairly hardy
 early summer to fall

'Wheeler's Imperial'

'Stonehead'

This variety gets its name from the solid, round, packed-tight, crisp heads growing on short, thick stalks. It is an ideal choice for small gardens, as cabbages can be planted just 12 in (30 cm) apart. Sow in early spring for cropping after midsummer, or sow later for a fall crop.

 unsuitable for containers
early to late spring
some resistance
fairly hardy
midsummer to fall

'Hispi'

This compact variety is an excellent cabbage for a small garden. It can be sown year round: sow in the winter greenhouse for a tasty early summer crop, or in mid-spring for a midsummer harvest. It can be left in the ground without splitting.

 unsuitable for containers
 mid-spring
some resistance
fairly hardy
  late summer to early fall

'Minicole'

This variety produces small, crisp, tightly packed, greenish-white heads that are ideal for a small garden. They grow quickly from spring to fall, and can be left standing for up to four months without deteriorating. They are ideal for use in salads and coleslaws.

- unsuitable for containers
- late spring
- some resistance
- hardy
- early fall to early winter

'Famosa'

This quick-growing, fast-maturing, F1 Savoy type is grown for its compact, solid heads which are ready for cutting from late summer. It produces an excellent show of attractive, fresh green, crinkly leaves that are packed with flavor.

- unsuitable for containers
- mid-spring
- poor resistance
- fairly hardy
- late sumer to early fall

'Brunswick'

This large, quick-growing variety dates back to the 1870s and even earlier. It produces dense, solid, 9-in (23-cm) wide heads, each weighing up to 9 lb (4 kg). The cabbages are borne in the center of a wide ruff of green outer leaves.

- unsuitable for containers
- mid-spring
- poor resistance
- fairly hardy
- late summer to early fall

'Winningstadt'

This dual-purpose, pointy-headed cabbage is an old variety, dating to the mid-19th century. The cabbages have a sweet flavor, and can be grown for a fall crop of solid hearts when sown in spring, or alternatively, leafy greens, if sown in late summer.

	unsuitable for containers
	mid- to late spring
	poor resistance
	fairly hardy
	early to late fall

'Alcosa'

This early producer of coconut-sized, 2–4-lb (1–1.8-kg) crinkled heads is resistant to tip burn. Delicious raw or cooked, the dense, attractively savoyed heads mature 72 days from transplanting, with flavor improving in cold weather.

	unsuitable for containers
	mid-spring; midsummer
	some resistance
	fairly hardy
	midsummer; mid-fall

'Derby Day'

One of the best early ballhead types, this variety is ready for harvesting several weeks before midsummer. It grows quickly, producing light green, tasty heads with very good resistance to bolting. They can be sautéed, steamed, or shredded in salads.

	unsuitable for containers
	mid-spring
	some resistance
	fairly hardy
	mid- to late summer

'Farao F1'

This short-season hybrid yields dense, round, deep-green heads that are larger than most, reaching up to 3.5 lb (1.6 kg) or more. They have a crisp, peppery sweet taste. The plants are resistant to tip burn and thrips, and hold well in summer heat.

- unsuitable for containers
- mid-spring to midsummer
- good resistance
- fairly hardy
- midsummer to mid-fall

'Caraflex Pointed-Head'

This hybrid produces small, pointed, and very uniform heads with tight wrapper leaves that protect the tender insides from insects. Weighing less than 2 lb (1 kg), 'Caraflex' has crunch and sweetness, and stores well. It is resistant to fungal fusarium yellows.

- unsuitable for containers
- mid-spring to midsummer
- good resistance
- fairly hardy
- midsummer to mid-fall

'January King'

This very attractive, crispy, crunchy, ballheaded winter variety reliably reddens up in the cold. It is excellent when gently sautéed or used in stir-fries or risottos. A late-spring sowing gives a crop ready for harvest from late fall into midwinter.

- unsuitable for containers
- late spring
- some resistance
- hardy
- late fall to midwinter

'Danish Ballhead'

"Danish Ballhead' is a dependable, old-time favorite and has been known as a standard storage variety since it was first introduced over a century ago. The late-maturing, round, bluish-green heads are heavy, and can weigh up to 7 lb (3 kg).

- 🪣 unsuitable for containers
- 🗡 spring to early summer
- 🐛 poor resistance
- ❄ fairly hardy
- 🔒 mid- to late fall

'Celtic'

One of the best winter cabbages, this F1 hybrid is produced from a cross between winter-white and Savoy types. The round, hard heads can stand outside for months over winter without danger of splitting. They are excellent in soups and stews.

- 🪣 unsuitable for containers
- 🗡 late spring
- 🐛 some resistance
- ❄ hardy
- 🔒 late fall to midwinter

'Kaitlin'

A late-season hybrid that was bred especially for sauerkraut, 'Kaitlin' produces large, dense cabbages that contain a good yield of very white dry matter with a high vitamin C content. The heads store moderately well, until December and January.

- 🪣 unsuitable for containers
- 🗡 mid- to late summer
- 🐛 some resistance
- ❄ fairly hardy
- 🔒 mid- to late fall

'Premium Late Flat Dutch'

This German heirloom produces huge, flattened oval heads that can weigh 15 lb (6.8 kg) and keep well into the winter. It grows slowly, requiring 3 to 4 months to mature, and is considered one of the best late-season cabbages.

- 🪣 unsuitable for containers
- 🗡 spring to early summer
- 🐛 poor resistance
- ❄ fairly hardy
- 🔒 mid- to late fall

'Celtic'

BRUSSELS SPROUTS

Brassica oleracea Gemmifera Group

Love them or hate them, this distinctive tasting vegetable resists indifference. Sprouts have a delicious, sweet, nutty taste when picked and cooked young, and their flavor is enhanced if harvested after a frost. Try growing one of the more unusual purple or red types and interplant with fast-growing crops like lettuces, to make the most of your space.

	SPRING	SUMMER	FALL	WINTER
SOW/PLANT				
HARVEST				

SOWING

Sprouts need a soil with a pH of at least 6.8, so apply some lime if necessary. Dig in some well-rotted manure or compost in the fall before planting, and ensure that the soil is firm—the plants will grow quite heavy and need to support their own weight. Make sure that you have rotated your crops and that you are not planting sprouts where brassicas have been grown in the last three years.

Sow seeds in trays or modules at a depth of .75 in (2 cm), or sow directly into the ground and protect with a cloche or fleece against frost. After about four or five weeks the seedlings should be ready to plant out. For fall or late winter crops, plant seedlings

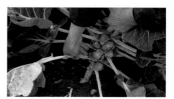

Harvest sprouts from the bottom upward.

in early or mid-spring; for late summer–early fall crops, sow seeds under cover in winter and plant out in spring. Space large plants 24 in (60 cm) apart, and dwarf varieties 18 in (45 cm). Plant them deeply, with the lowest leaves touching the soil.

CROP CARE

Fit a brassica collar around the seedlings to deter cabbage root

fly, and cover with netting. Keep plants weeded and well-watered, and earth up around the stems to provide extra support. Feed with a nitrogenous fertilizer or organic liquid feed in summer.

HARVESTING AND STORING

Harvest sprouts from the bottom of the plant first, and either cut them off with a knife, or snap them off. You could also dig up the whole plant, hang the stem in cool, frost-free place, or stand in a bucket of water, and pick sprouts from it as you need them. The youngest leaves can be picked and eaten as spring greens.

PESTS AND DISEASES

Covering your Brussels sprouts with netting and giving them a brassica collar will minimize the risk of birds, butterflies, and cabbage root fly, which should be controlled as much as possible. The flies attack plant roots and leave them to rot; see pages 246–7 for ways to deal with them. Brussels sprouts are also prone to mealy cabbage aphids and whitefly, which target leaves and will cause them to shrivel. Remove any insects or eggs that you find and spray infected plants with insecticidal soap.

'Diablo'

This variety produces sweet-tasting sprouts that are of uniform size and, since all mature at the same time, the whole crop can be picked in one harvest, if required. 'Diablo' grows vigorously and is resistant to the fungal disease fusarium wilt.

 unsuitable for containers
early to mid-spring
some resistance
hardy
fall to winter

'Nautic'

Although generally regarded as a midseason variety, this sprout often continues to provide crops into late winter. It produces smooth, round buttons with a good flavor. The variety is resistant to white blister, ring spot, and powdery mildew.

unsuitable for containers
early to late spring
excellent resistance
hardy
fall to winter

'Clodius'

The firm, tasty sprouts produced by this variety can be harvested right through the winter, since it stands up exceptionally well to cold weather. It also has an excellent record for resistance to disease, in particular, to powdery mildew and ring spot.

unsuitable for containers
late spring
excellent resistance
hardy
winter

'Rubine'

Also called 'Red Rubine', the small purple-red sprouts of this striking plant are both decorative and good to eat. They have a nutty flavor and keep their color during cooking if steamed rather than boiled. This variety crops early but its season may extend through to late winter.

 unsuitable for containers
 early to mid-spring
 poor resistance
 hardy
late fall to midwinter

'Long Island Improved'

This heirloom variety produces very high yields, despite its compact size. Its dependability has made it a long-standing garden favorite. The firm, round, dark green sprouts grow closely packed together on the stem, and have a particularly fine flavor.

unsuitable for containers
early spring to summer
poor resistance
hardy
fall to winter

'Igor'

The tightly wrapped, dark green sprouts of this heavy-cropping variety have an excellent flavor. They can be harvested in succession as needed, but will also last well on this very frost-tolerant plant for picking as a single harvest.

unsuitable for containers
early to mid-spring
some resistance
hardy
late fall to winter

'Falstaff'

The color of this gourmet variety develops as the plant matures, from green to rich purple-red when the plant is touched by frost, and is retained during light cooking. 'Falstaff' matures slowly, bearing sprouts that are milder and nuttier in flavor than many other types.

🪣	unsuitable for containers
🌱	early to mid-spring
🕷	poor resistance
❄	hardy
🔒	fall to winter

'Jade Cross'

This variety has gotten high marks in the South, where others fail to produce. Maturing in 87–100 days, the 1.5-in (4-cm) dark green sprouts are spaced closely on 30-in (75-cm) stems. 'Jade Cross' F1 hybrids are bred for resistance to fusarium yellows and gray mold.

🪣	suitable for containers
🌱	mid-spring to early summer
🕷	good resistance
❄	hardy
🔒	early to late fall

'Gustus'

An early maturing F1 hybrid, 'Gustus' produces smooth, medium-sized, dark green sprouts in 99 days, beginning in early fall. Plants are sturdy and resistant to rots that affect some varieties in heavy rains. Sprouts are uniform and high quality.

🪣	suitable for containers
🌱	mid-spring to early summer
🕷	some resistance
❄	hardy
🔒	early to late fall

'Red Delicious'

The purple-red sprouts of this unusual cultivar hold their color better during cooking than some of the older red varieties. They have a mild flavor. Well formed, these sprouts look attractive on the stem, adding welcome interest to a winter garden.

 unsuitable for containers
 spring
 poor resistance
hardy
winter

'Tasty Nuggets Hybrid'

Small 1–1.5-inch (2.5–4-cm) sprouts begin maturing just 78 days after planting. The vigorous hybrid plants grow 3–4 ft (1–1.2 m) tall, and the tender sprouts are mildly sweet. Like all Brussels sprouts, flavor is improved by a few light frosts.

unsuitable for containers
mid-spring to early summer
some resistance
hardy
early to late fall

'Catskill'

This open-pollinated variety was introduced in 1941 and, though not a good producer in warmer climates, it remains a favorite in cold-winter regions. Compact plants reach about 2 ft (60 cm) and produce high yields of 1.5-in (4-cm) sprouts in 90–110 days.

suitable for containers
mid-spring
poor resistance
hardy
mid- to late fall

CAULIFLOWER *Brassica oleracea* Botrytis Group

Cauliflowers require an investment of both time and space, since they can stay in the ground for up to a year, taking up a relatively large amount of ground. If you keep them well-watered and can persuade them not to bolt, they will produce striking white, purple, or even lime-green heads, or "curds." With careful planning, you can ensure a delicious crop, which can be cooked or eaten raw in salads, all year round.

	SPRING	SUMMER	FALL	WINTER
SOW/PLANT				
HARVEST				

SOWING

Cauliflowers prefer fertile soil with a pH of no less than 6.8, so add lime to the soil, if necessary. Fully grown heads, or "curds," will eventually become quite heavy, so cauliflowers need a firm soil to support them. Ensure that crops are rotated, and do not plant cauliflower where any brassicas have been grown in the last three years.

Cauliflowers can be grown to produce a year-round harvest: sow seeds in fall or winter to produce an early summer crop; sow in spring for a summer and fall crop; sow in late spring for a winter or spring crop.

Sow in pots or module trays at a depth of .75 in (2 cm) and keep indoors or under a cloche or cold

Use a cloche to protect young seedlings.

frame to protect from frost and to encourage germination.

PLANTING

Do not let seedlings grow taller than 2 in (5 cm) before you plant them out, or you will risk damaging the roots; this might encourage plants to bolt.

Cauliflowers need space to grow, and generally the later you plant them, the more space they

need. Leave about 24 in (60 cm) between summer and fall cauliflowers, and 28 in (70 cm) between winter and spring varieties. If you wish to grow miniature cauliflowers, choose fast-growing early summer varieties and plant seedlings about 6 in (15 cm) apart. The crowded environment will cause growth to be stunted, producing heads that are approximately 1.5–3 in (4–8 cm) in width.

At this height, seedlings are ready to plant.

CROP CARE

Young seedlings are a tempting delicacy for pests, so fit brassica collars (see pests and diseases box, below) to deter cabbage root fly, and use netting to prevent birds and butterflies from getting at crops. Keep cauliflowers free from weeds, but most importantly, keep them well-watered; they are thirsty crops that require a lot of water during growth. Without sufficient water, they may bolt or produce small, premature heads. Give winter and spring cauliflowers an organic liquid feed or nitrogenous fertilizer in late winter or early

PESTS AND DISEASES

Cauliflowers are prone to the pests and diseases that trouble all brassicas, so take the same precautions as for cabbages (see pp.246-7): place brassica collars around the stems of vulnerable seedlings, net plants against attack from birds, and as best you can, guard against clubroot as this disease in incurable and can persist in the soil for decades. Cauliflowers are also prone to boron and magnesium deficiencies.

Construct a frame out of bamboo canes and fasten your netting to it.

spring. Mulching around the plants during summer will also encourage steady growth.

Cauliflowers will need protection from discoloration by the sun, which can turn their curds yellow. To prevent this, use the leaves to form a shield over the curd (see tip box, right). This method can also be used to provide protection from the cold in winter. Firm the soil around the plants to give them extra support and protection in frosty and windy weather.

HARVESTING AND STORING

Harvest cauliflowers when the curds are firm—if left in the ground, the flower buds will open and the cauliflower will deteriorate. If you are not harvesting for immediate use, cut the heads from the roots, leaving some of the outer leaves on the curd. This will help to protect it from damage and keep it humid. Store summer cauliflowers by hanging them in a cool, dark place, and spray them with water occasionally. They will last for up to three weeks. Fall and winter cauliflowers store for longer.

Miniature cauliflowers don't keep, so should be harvested and eaten as soon as possible.

TIP BLANCHING

Tying the cauliflowers' leaves so that they cover the curds forming a "shield" is usually done in summer as it prevents the sun from reaching the curds and turning them yellow. However, it will also help to protect cauliflowers from frost in winter, since the leaves act as a layer of effective insulation.

Once plants are large enough, simply wrap the leaves inward, making sure to cover the curd completely, and fix in place with garden string or soft twine. Ensure that plants are dry or you may encourage the cauliflower to rot. Some varieties are self-blanching, and their inner leaves will naturally fold inward. They may still benefit from protection in winter.

Ensure that no light can reach the cauliflower curds, since this would cause them to discolor. Keep the string in place until you are ready to harvest.

'Mayflower'

A very early-cropping variety, 'Mayflower' is ready to be harvested ahead of most other summer cauliflower varieties. It produces medium-to-large heads with pure white, beautifully shaped curds that are resistant to discoloration in hot weather. It has an excellent flavor.

- unsuitable for containers
- late winter
- some resistance
- not hardy
- early summer

'Fremont F1'

Vigorous, self-blanching plants produce large leaves that wrap around impressive 2-lb (1-kg) heads. Popular with home gardeners and commercial growers, this hybrid is a strong midseason performer, harvested 65 to 75 days after planting.

- unsuitable for containers
- mid-spring and midsummer
- some resistance
- fairly hardy
- early summer and fall

'Giant of Naples'

This impressive Italian heirloom takes all season to mature into large, tight, white heads that can weigh over 3 lb (1.4 kg). Plants are vigorous, with a good leaf cover, but not self-blanching. Tie leaves over the heads to preserve their white color.

- unsuitable for containers
- mid-spring
- poor resistance
- fairly hardy
- fall

'Violet Queen'

A prolific cropper, this variety
has a beautiful, vibrant purple
head that turns green when
cooked. It is a reliable plant
for late summer and fall
harvesting. In areas where
heavy frosts are unlikely, it
can also be overwintered for
harvesting the following spring.

- unsuitable for containers
- spring
- poor resistance
- fairly hardy
- spring to fall

'Galleon'

A hardy variety that is also
known for its superb flavor,
'Galleon' has a long maturing
period. After spring or summer
plantings, it overwinters well
and the firm, white heads are
ready for harvesting the
following spring.

- unsuitable for containers
- late spring to early summer
- some resistance
- hardy
- spring

'Amazing'

This variety has some impressive
qualities: the enormous, ivory-
white heads can grow up to 10 in
(25 cm) and are densely packed.
It will last for an exceptionally
long period in the ground
without losing its excellent
flavor or texture.

- unsuitable for containers
- early spring to late summer
- poor resistance
- not hardy
- late spting to fall

'Clapton'

'Clapton' is hailed as the first cauliflower with resistance to clubroot. It is a sturdy plant, with a dense, white head that is well protected by the leaves. The 'Clapton' variety can be sown over two to three months to produce a succession of crops.

🪣	unsuitable for containers
🌱	spring to early summer
✳️	good resistance
❄️	not hardy
🔒	late summer to late fall

'Skywalker'

Sturdy and reliable, this variety produces solid, bright white, domed heads and, as a bonus, has good resistance to wilt. The leaves have an erect habit and wrap around well to protect the curds. A touch of frost sweetens the flavor.

🪣	unsuitable for containers
🌱	spring
✳️	good resistance
❄️	hardy
🔒	fall

'Candid Charm'

Easy to grow and a consistent producer of early-maturing crops, this variety has achieved popularity with gardeners. The medium-large, attractively shaped, white heads are well protected by the stout leaves. Sow under cover in late winter.

🪣	unsuitable for containers
🌱	late winter to spring
✳️	poor resistance
❄️	not hardy
🔒	late summer

'Graffiti'

The deep purple heads of this award winner intensify in color if left exposed to light. Its sweet flavor makes it ideal for eating raw in salads, though it is also tasty when cooked. 'Graffiti' is considered to be superior to older purple-headed varieties.

 unsuitable for containers
 early to late spring
 some resistance
not hardy
summer to fall

'Goodman'

This vigorous summer variety produces heavy crops. The dense curds are well protected by the dark green, upright leaves. If sown outdoors in spring, it is ready to harvest in late summer or fall; sow under cover in winter for early summer crops.

 unsuitable for containers
early spring to early summer
 poor resistance
not hardy
 summer to fall

'Cheddar'

Beautiful yellow-orange heads, which contain a high level of the nutrient betacarotene, make this variety a stunning addition to the vegetable garden. The color deepens if the heads are left unwrapped and is retained during cooking.

 unsuitable for containers
spring
 poor resistance
not hardy
 summer to fall

'Snowball'

This old variety is a compact plant with medium-sized, tightly packed, snow-white heads. Frequently sown in late spring for a fall harvest, it can also be started indoors in late winter for a midsummer crop. It keeps well and is versatile in the kitchen.

unsuitable for containers
late winter to spring
poor resistance
not hardy
summer to fall

'Maystar'

After a late spring sowing, this hardy variety overwinters to mature in early summer the following year. An excellent flavor and texture make this a good all-purpose cauliflower for cooking or eating raw. The solid white curds freeze very well.

unsuitable for containers
spring
poor resistance
hardy
early summer

'Medallion'

This winter cauliflower produces a good crop early in the year following sowing. The large white curds form a round head with a full, rich flavor. Although hardy, it is less likely to overwinter well in very cold areas.

unsuitable for containers
early summer
poor resistance
hardy
spring

'Snow Crown'

One of the easiest varieties to grow, 'Snow Crown' has vigorous growth and produces substantial crops. The large white heads may develop a pink tinge in hot weather, but this does not impair the mild flavor. The variety keeps well in the ground for a week or two after maturing.

- 🪣 unsuitable for containers
- 🌱 spring
- 🐛 poor resistance
- ❄ not hardy
- 🔒 summer

'Cassius F1'

This vigorous hybrid cauliflower produces dense, self-blanching white heads 65 to 75 days after planting. Suitable for both spring and fall harvests, 'Cassius' plants are sturdy, resistant to fusarium and other diseases, and perform well in a wide range of conditions.

- 🪣 unsuitable for containers
- 🌱 mid-spring and midsummer
- 🐛 some resistance
- ❄ not hardy
- 🔒 early summer and fall

'Early White Hybrid'

Solid, pure-white self-blanching heads can reach a harvestable size just 52 days after transplanting. One of the earliest varieties of cauliflower, 'Early White' hybrid's fast-maturing habit and excellent flavor make it an adaptable choice for summer and fall harvests.

- 🪣 unsuitable for containers
- 🌱 mid-spring and late summer
- 🐛 some resistance
- ❄ not hardy
- 🔒 early summer and fall

BROCCOLI *Brassica oleraceam* Italica Group

The term "broccoli" is perhaps a little misleading, since it actually encompasses two distinct types of crop: calabrese, which produce the large, fluffy heads commonly referred to as "broccoli"; and sprouting broccoli, which produces an abundance of smaller florets on longer stalks. Sprouting broccoli has a long harvesting season and can be overwintered, making it a valuable winter crop when there is little else on offer.

	SPRING	SUMMER	FALL	WINTER
SOW/PLANT				
HARVEST				

SOWING

Give your broccoli a sheltered site in firm, fertile soil, with a pH of at least 6.8. Ensure that you choose a location where other brassicas have not been grown in the last three years. Dig in some well-rotted manure in the fall prior to planting.

Calabrese seed should be sown directly into the ground from mid-spring, successively through to early summer. Sow the seeds at a depth of .75 in (2 cm), and 12 in (30 cm) apart. Plants will grow fairly large so space rows at a distance of 18 in (45 cm).

Sow sprouting broccoli seeds at a depth of .75 in (2 cm) either in trays or modules under cover, or directly in the ground in early spring, covering them until

Harvest to encourage a second crop.

frosts have passed, or in mid-fall, if you want to overwinter them. Sprouting broccoli will grow larger than calabrese, so give them more space—24 in (60 cm) between plants and rows.

CROP CARE

Plants can become quite heavy once heads have developed, so earth up the stems as they

grow, and stake tall plants if necessary. Water and weed well while young. When established, avoid overwatering sprouting broccoli, to help it to overwinter.

HARVESTING

The central head of calabrese should be harvested before flower buds open. Then give the plant a mulch of compost to encourage it to produce a crop of side-shoots. Harvest spears of sprouting types before flower buds open, when they reach about 6 in (15 cm) in length. New spears will grow back and you may get a harvest for up to two months.

PESTS AND DISEASES

Broccoli is relatively problem-free, but rotating your crops will help to prevent persistant diseases such as clubroot from attacking. Cover plants with netting to deter pests such as birds and cabbage white butterflies.

Use netting as a barrier against pests.

'Belstar'

This F1 variety bears a mid-to-late season crop of attractive, well-domed, bluish-green heads. They have a good flavor and are excellent boiled, lightly steamed, or used in stir-fries. Heads will keep well once harvested; the plants will go on to produce plenty of extra side shoots.

- unsuitable for containers
- mid- to late spring
- some resistance
- not hardy
- midsummer to mid-fall

'Romanesco'

Resembling a cross between a very tall broccoli and a cauliflower, 'Romanesco' or 'Broccoflower', as it is sometimes called, was developed in Scotland and is grown for its outstanding flavor and texture, and its spiral of highly ornamental, domed, lime green curds.

- unsuitable for containers
- late spring
- poor resistance
- not hardy
- early winter

'Green Magic'

This variety is highly rated for its flavor and tightly packed, dark green heads, which are followed by a good crop of side shoots when the main head is harvested. Quicker to mature than many varieties, it makes a strong, bold display in the kitchen garden.

- unsuitable for containers
- mid- to late spring
- some resistance
- not hardy
- midsummer to mid-fall

'Fiesta'

This impressive variety produces numerous large, shapely, domed heads and bears a good number of secondary side shoots once the central portion has been removed. It is a good choice for hot summer sites because it withstands high temperatures.

- unsuitable for containers
- mid- to late spring
- some resistance
- not hardy
- midsummer to mid-fall

'Romanesco'

'De Cicco'

Early and extra-hardy, this Italian heirloom is a favorite of home gardeners, producing modest-sized central heads followed by a month or more of side shoots. Though less uniform than hybrids, 'De Cicco' can be more productive over the course of a season.

- 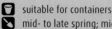 suitable for containers
- mid- to late spring; midsummer
- some resistance
- fairly hardy
- midsummer; fall

'Small Miracle Hybrid'

Uniquely compact, the 'Small Miracle' hybrid is a good container choice, producing small to medium size dark green heads that rise above the foliage of the 12-in (30-cm) plants. In a small garden they can be planted 8 in (20 cm) apart to optimize the space.

- suitable for containers
- mid- to late spring; midsummer
- good resistance
- fairly hardy
- midsummer; fall

'Waltham 29'

Developed in 1951 to withstand increasingly cold temperatures as it matures, this open-pollinated classic is good for fall planting and will not head properly if weather is too warm. Plants are stockier than most, and produce medium-sized heads and large side shoots.

- suitable for containers
- mid- to late spring; midsummer
- some resistance
- fairly hardy
- midsummer; fall

'Green Goliath'

This open-pollinated variety produces reliably large blue-green heads than tend to mature over time, rather than all at once, followed by three weeks of side shoots. Ready about 55 days after transplanting, it can be planted for spring or fall harvest.

- suitable for containers
- mid- to late spring; midsummer
- some resistance
- fairly hardy
- midsummer; fall

'Early Purple Sprouting'

This variety is an essential crop for the winter kitchen garden, providing the striking combination of tasty purple heads tucked into bluish-green leaves. Steam it to preserve its excellent taste and texture and add it to hot meals and salads.

- unsuitable for containers
- mid- to late spring
- poor resistance
- hardy
- late winter to early spring

'Arcadia F1'

This adaptable hybrid's tightly domed 5–8-in (13–20-cm) heads shed water well, which helps them resist bacterial rot during periods of wet weather. 'Arcadia' stands 2 ft (60 cm) tall, and produces flavorful dark green heads 65 to 70 days after transplanting.

- unsuitable for containers
- mid- to late spring; midsummer
- excellent resistance
- fairly hardy
- midsummer; fall

'Packman F1'

Known for its superior heat resistance, 'Packman' produces large, extra-early, flat-topped green heads. The relatively tall plants reach 27 in (69 cm) in height, and produce side shoots for a long period, provided they receive adequate water.

- unsuitable for containers
- mid- to late spring; midsummer
- some resistance
- fairly hardy
- midsummer; fall

'Claret'

This F1 hybrid is grown for its very tall plants that produce a heavy crop of dark purple spears, ready for picking from late winter. The plants are vigorous, even when grown in poor soils. The spears make a good addition to stews and pasta dishes.

- unsuitable for containers
- mid- to late spring
- some resistance
- hardy
- late winter to early spring

'Premium Crop'

When it was introduced in 1975, this hybrid broccoli won an AAS (All-America Selections) award for its consistently large, firm green heads that hold their quality well. 'Premium Crop' is ready to harvest 55 days after transplanting, and is resistant to downy mildew.

- suitable for containers
- mid- to late spring; midsummer
- good resistance
- fairly hardy
- midsummer; fall

'Santee'

This purple sprouting broccoli is ready for picking much earlier than other purple varieties, which tend to be picked over winter; it can crop in the same year as it is sown. It bears a good yield of tasty, tender spears, with an abundance of mini heads.

- unsuitable for containers
- mid- to late spring
- poor resistance
- not hardy
- midsummer to late fall

'Early White Sprouting'

One of the earliest broccolis of the year, 'Early White Sprouting' produces a heavy crop of sweet, tender, white spears. Harvest promptly and consistently and it will crop over a long period. It is an attractive plant and makes a strong visual contrast with overwintering purple varieties.

 unsuitable for containers
mid- to late spring
some resistance
hardy
late winter to early spring

'Red Spear'

Heavy-yielding and vigorous, this variety produces thick spears that will add striking purple color to the kitchen garden over winter. Harvest the tender spears in late winter and use them, and the subsequent crop of extra side shoots, in soups and salads.

 unsuitable for containers
mid- to late spring
some resistance
hardy
late winter to early spring

'Piracicaba'

Tender, mild-tasting 'Piracicaba' is unlike other varieties in appearance, producing small, loose, green heads with sweet stalks and large beads that are equally delicious raw and steamed. The leaves are tasty, too, and plants tolerate heat and cold.

 suitable for containers
mid- to late spring; midsummer
some resistance
fairly hardy
midsummer; fall

KALE *Brassica oleracea* Acephala Group

Kale is a hardy and adaptable plant, able to survive subzero winter temperatures and, in the case of some varieties, hot summers as well. Packed with high levels of vitamins and minerals, it is delicious eaten raw in salads when young and tender, or boiled or stir-fried when leaves are mature. Kale is also an ideal ornamental plant, since its leaves are striking in shape and color and look good throughout the winter.

	SPRING	SUMMER	FALL	WINTER
SOW/PLANT				
HARVEST				

SOWING

Kale plants can become relatively large, up to 3 ft (90 cm) high and 2 ft (60 cm) wide, so they need both space to spread and firm soil to support their eventual weight. Sow seeds in early spring to produce a crop in summer, and sow in late spring to early summer to produce a crop in the fall or winter.

Sow in pots or module trays at a depth of .75 in (2 cm). Plants will be ready to transplant when they are about seven weeks old; be careful not to damage the roots when planting out. Kale can be grown as a cut-and-come-again crop and planted densely, with seedlings spaced at a distance of 3–4 in (8–10 cm). If you plan to let crops grow to full

Harvest whole kale plants when mature.

size, they will need to be planted about 18–24 in (45–60 cm) apart.

CROP CARE

Keep seedlings well-weeded and give them plenty of water while young. However, when plants are established, resist overwatering, since this produces lusher growth that is less capable of overwintering. If the crop yellows in fall, remove affected

leaves and feed with high nitrogen fertilizer. Remove any flower buds that appear.

HARVESTING

Young, tender kale leaves can be harvested as required from cut-and-come-again crops and will resprout, producing new growth. Cut leaves when they are about 4 in (10 cm) in length and harvest until plants become bitter.

Fully grown kale can be left in the ground and harvested as required. Kale is one of the hardiest winter crops and can be left in the ground at temperatures as low as 5°F (-15°C).

PESTS AND DISEASES

Kale is less susceptible to the problems that plague other brassicas (see pp.246–7), but you may find that fine netting is needed to deter birds and butterflies. Rotate crops—plant where peas or beans have previously grown.

Netting will prevent attacks from birds.

'Redbor'

This variety, also called 'Redbor Hybrid' is a "must-have" for the kitchen garden. Its striking purple stems and frilly green leaves will last through winter. Use it as a cut-and-come-again crop, trimming off the tender young leaves to generate new, tasty growth.

- unsuitable for containers
- mid-spring to early summer
- some resistance
- hardy
- early fall to mid-spring

'Winterbor'

Also called 'Winterbor Hybrid', this is a top choice for exposed winter gardens. It withstands low temperatures to produce a thicket of short, bluish-green, curly leaves. Treat it as a cut-and-come-again kale into spring. Cook the leaves gently to preserve their flavor.

- unsuitable for containers
- mid-spring to early summer
- some resistance
- hardy
- early fall to mid-spring

'Vates Blue Curled'

This Scotch-type kale looks beautiful in the garden; its curled bluish-green leaves are vitamin-rich and good in soups, especially after a frost. Plants grow to 15 in (38 cm) or more, and can be harvested throughout the summer and, with protection, into winter.

- suitable for containers
- mid-spring and summer
- good resistance
- hardy
- spring to early winter

'Dwarf Green Curled'

This attractive variety produces dark green, tightly curled leaves; their good flavor is best retained through gentle cooking. It will grow to about 2 ft (60 cm) if left to develop, or it can be harvested as a cut-and-come-again type. It doesn't require staking and is a good choice for small plots.

- unsuitable for containers
- mid-spring to early summer
- some resistance
- hardy
- early fall to mid-spring

'Starbor'

Grow some plants especially for their tender baby leaves, harvesting them in summer for salads, while allowing others to mature over winter. Sow 'Starbor' in pots on a sunny windowsill, and harvest the flavorful, fresh growth in winter.

- suitable for containers
- mid-spring to early summer
- some resistance
- hardy
- early fall to mid-spring

'White Russian'

Excellent for cool-weather salads, 'White Russian' kale can withstand wet soil, and, with protection, temperatures well below freezing. Gray-green, dissected leaves are flat with whitish stems and veins. Tender when young, they are especially sweet after a frost.

- suitable for containers
- mid-spring and summer
- good resistance
- hardy
- spring to early winter

'Cavolo Nero'

Also known as 'Tuscan Kale', this traditional south Italian vegetable is widely available. It has a rich flavor, and should be cooked, steamed, or sautéed quickly to retain its dark green color. It can be used in all kinds of winter dishes, from soups and stews, to salads.

- unsuitable for containers
- mid-spring and early summer
- some resistance
- hardy
- early fall to mid-spring

'Fizz'

This unusual kale grows quickly, producing fleshy leaves on upright stems. Harvest the tender young growth for summer recipes, adding it raw to salads, and using in stir-fries. Grow near the front of the kitchen garden for easy picking.

- unsuitable for containers
- mid-spring and early summer
- some resistance
- hardy
- summer

'Siberian, Dwarf Siberian'

'Siberian' kale is not for garnish. The tender, bluish-green, frilled leaves are excellent in salads when young, and even better steamed once they mature. Plants are 15–30 in (38–75 cm) in height and are extremely cold-hardy.

- suitable for containers
- mid-spring and summer
- good resistance
- hardy
- spring to early winter

'Red Russian'

This frilly, highly decorative kale produces gray-green leaves with striking purple stems and veins. Some of the leaves can be harvested at the baby leaf stage for use in summer salads, leaving the rest to mature for winter recipes. Mature leaves can be braised, steamed, or blanched.

- unsuitable for containers
- mid-spring and early summer
- some resistance
- hardy
- early fall to mid-spring

'Ripbor'

This large kale will grow to about 2 ft (60 cm), and is packed with frilly, dark-green leaves, ready for cropping from fall; it lasts well in the ground over winter. Remove the first leaves from the crown and center, moving outward when cutting.

- unsuitable for containers
- mid-spring and early summer
- some resistance
- hardy
- early fall to winter

'Red Ursa'

This striking cross between 'Red Russian' and 'Siberian' kale has the broadleaf frills of 'Siberian' and the magenta veins of 'Red Russian'. Frilly foliage can be treated as a cut-and-come-again green from fall into winter. It can be stir-fried as it is heat tolerant.

- suitable for containers
- mid-spring and summer
- good resistance
- hardy
- spring into early winter

SPINACH *Spinacia oleracea*

Packed with vitamins and minerals, spinach is nutritious and has a delicious flavor; try the traditional thicker, wrinkled varieties for cooking, and thinner, smooth-leaved varieties for eating raw in salads. Happy to grow in cooler climates and shady positions, spinach is a very accommodating vegetable, however, be careful to keep it well-watered. Water more than once a day in hot, dry weather—since it will readily bolt.

	SPRING	SUMMER	FALL	WINTER
SOW/PLANT				
HARVEST				

SOWING

Spinach prefers a fertile soil, so apply well-rotted manure or compost in the fall before planting, or apply a compound fertilizer shortly before sowing. Spinach is a very versatile plant; it will happily grow in containers as a cut-and-come-again crop and it is ideal for intercropping, since it will tolerate partial shade.

Spinach can be sown year-round to provide a constant crop, so sow seed every few weeks throughout the year between midwinter and late summer. Sow at a depth of .75 in (2 cm) and space your rows 12 in (30 cm) apart. When seedlings have established, thin out, giving them 3–6 in (7–15 cm) of space, depending on how big

Sow in pots if your space is limited.

you want them to grow. Sow cut-and-come-again crops in wide drills; dig a 6–8 in (15–20 cm) wide trench the length of your row and sow two lines of seeds within it.

CROP CARE

Keep spinach well-weeded and, most importantly, keep it well-watered to help prevent bolting. If growth is slow, feed with a nitrogenous fertilizer.

HARVESTING

When plants reach approximately 2 in (5 cm) in height, harvest the outer leaves a few at a time for use in salads. When plants are about 10–12 weeks old, either cut a few leaves as and when you need them, or harvest the whole plant; either uproot completely, or cut the tops off leaving about 1 in (2.5 cm) above the ground. This stump may resprout and provide you with a second crop.

STORING

Spinach does not keep well after harvesting, so sow successively for a year-round crop instead.

PESTS AND DISEASES

Because spinach grows quickly, it is usually a relatively trouble-free crop, but you may need to use netting to deter birds. Slugs and snails may target crops, and diseases such as downy mildew may be a problem. This causes white mold on the underside of leaves, with yellowish-brown patches on the top. Remove and destroy the affected leaves to prevent the spread of infection, and spray the remaining crops with a fungicide. Giving plants plenty of space will help to reduce the risk. Resistant cultivars are available.

'Bordeaux'

This attractive variety produces dark-green leaves that contrast with its striking red stems and leaf veins. It is a good choice for a sweet baby spinach, and excellent for use in salads. If cooking, do so gently, since it has a tendency to reduce quickly and take on a soggy texture.

- suitable for containers
- early spring to early fall
- poor resistance
- fairly hardy
- mid-spring to mid-fall

'Melody Hybrid'

Hybrid vigor and resistance to downy mildew and mosaic virus earned this early-maturing variety an All-America Selections award in 1977. 'Melody' produces good yields in spring and fall, but it is not recommended for summer heat or overwintering.

- suitable for containers
- early spring to early fall
- good resistance
- fairly hardy
- mid-spring to mid-fall

'Olympia'

This smooth-leaved hybrid is exceptionally slow to bolt, and shows resistance to several types of downy mildew. 'Olympia' has an upright growing habit, and its thick, dark-green leaves have a mild flavor, and are easier to clean than savoyed types.

- suitable for containers
- early spring to early fall
- good resistance
- fairly hardy
- mid-spring to mid-fall

'Triathlon'

This mildew-resistant variety can
be sown from early spring onward
to provide batches of fresh, tasty
leaves. Plants grow quickly, and
their large, mid-green leaves can
be harvested young for use in
salads, or allowed to develop for
use in cooking.

- suitable for containers
- early spring to early fall
- good resistance
- fairly hardy
- mid-spring to mid-fall

'Samish F1'

One of the few available hybrids
tolerant of white rust (a problem
in the South), 'Samish' also resists
downy mildew. Although quick to
bolt in heat, it grows well in spring
and fall, and can be overwintered
for an early harvest of heavily
savoyed, triangular leaves.

- suitable for containers
- early spring to early fall
- good resistance
- fairly hardy
- mid-spring to mid-fall

'Renegade F1'

Compact and slow to bolt,
'Renegade' produces early yields
of tightly packed, dark-green
oval leaves. It is widely adaptable,
resistant to downy mildew and
cucumber mosaic virus, and has
proven to be a good choice for
winter high tunnel production.

- suitable for containers
- early spring to early fall
- excellent resistance
- fairly hardy
- mid-spring to mid-fall

'Lazio'

This variety is popular with supermarket spinach-suppliers because it checks all the right boxes: excellent mildew resistance, reliable, solid growth, a consistently high yield, and tasty, dark-green leaves. Its baby leaves are very good for tossing straight into salads or risottos.

- suitable for containers
- early spring to early fall
- excellent resistance
- fairly hardy
- mid-spring to mid-fall

'Giant Winter'

This variety is an excellent choice for its large, lance-shaped winter leaves, which have a strong flavor. It will need some protection in cold, exposed, windy areas. It is useful for cooking and, like other varieties, it can be frozen raw or cooked.

- suitable for containers
- early spring to early fall
- poor resistance
- fairly hardy
- mid-spring to mid-fall

'Viroflay'

Also known as 'Monstreux de Virofly', this heirloom is the parent to many modern hybrids. Its smooth leaves, up to 10 in (25 cm), are low in acid and very succulent. It prefers cool weather and overwinters with protection, but is quick to bolt in summer.

- suitable for containers
- early spring to early fall
- poor resistance
- fairly hardy
- mid-spring to mid-fall

'Tyee'

With exceptional bolting tolerance and disease resistance, this F1 hybrid produces semi-savoyed leaves into the summer. (A fall sowing will yield overwintered spring greens.) Its upright growth habit holds leaves above the soil, keeping them cleaner than most varieties.

- suitable for containers
- early spring to early fall
- excellent resistance
- fairly hardy
- mid-spring to mid-fall

'Space'

This fast-maturing, slow-bolting F1 hybrid has an extended harvest period that spans the seasons. Dark-green, smooth-to-slightly savoyed leaves are ready to harvest in 40 days. Good resistance to downy mildew keeps plants vigorous in cool, wet conditions.

- suitable for containers
- early spring to early fall
- good resistance
- fairly hardy
- mid-spring to mid-fall

'Bloomsdale Long Standing'

This classic, savoyed-leaf spinach has been popular for decades, and is one of the few open-pollinated varieties still on the market. The crumpled leaves are quick-growing and slow to bolt, though less so than some newer hybrids.

- suitable for containers
- early spring to early fall
- some resistance
- fairly hardy
- mid-spring to mid-fall

'Reddy'

This quick-growing F1 spinach was especially raised for its striking mix of red stems and veins and green leaves. Grow it in a prominent position for easy picking. Use it as a baby leaf and cook it gently to preserve the shape and color.

- suitable for containers
- early spring to early fall
- poor resistance
- fairly hardy
- mid-spring to mid-fall

SWISS CHARD *Beta vulgaris* subsp. *cicla* var. *flavescens*

Swiss chard and spinach beet are often referred to as "leaf beets," since both are related to the beet, but, conversely, they produce large, delicious leaves and insignificant, inedible roots. Swiss chard is an attractive plant often grown as an ornamental plant, since its leaves have veins and stems in a range of colors, from vivid red and yellow to purple. Swiss chard has a peppery flavor and is cooked and eaten like spinach.

	SPRING	SUMMER	FALL	WINTER
SOW/PLANT				
HARVEST				

SOWING

Swiss chard likes a fertile, moisture-retentive soil, so dig in some well-rotted manure or compost in the fall before sowing, or add a balanced fertilizer to the soil. If the pH of the soil is below 6.5, consider adding some lime to the soil, since Swiss chard likes alkaline conditions. Provide crops with a sunny, sheltered position.

Seed can be sown directly into the soil or grown in modules in a greenhouse or cold frame and then transplanted when established. Sow at a depth of 1 in (2.5 cm) and space rows 18 in (45 cm) apart. Once seedlings are established, thin out, depending on your requirements; if growing for

Leave cut stems in the ground to resprout.

salad crops, leave 4 in (10 cm) between plants; larger plants will need more space, so give them 12 in (30 cm) between plants.

CROP CARE

Keep chard well-watered and free from weeds. Remove any flowering buds to encourage the plant to direct its energy into its leaves. If you are leaving plants in the ground to overwinter,

a cloche offers some protection. Feed once with fertilizer.

HARVESTING

Harvest with a knife, leaving the stems in the ground to resprout; removing the plant's leaves will encourage further growth. Harvest young leaves for use in salads and older leaves for cooking, as and when you need them. Keep harvesting from the plant until it runs to seed.

PESTS AND DISEASES

Chard is usually trouble-free. Practice crop rotation and good garden hygiene for healthy yields.

GROW IN CONTAINERS

Swiss chard grows well for harvesting as a cut-and-come-again crop in a container, so why not sow in tubs on the patio, or intercrop with flowers in a windowbox. Harvest leaves regularly, before they outgrow their space.

Chard grows in even the smallest space.

'Lucullus'

While it is not one of the more decorative varieties, 'Lucullus' is popular for its flavor and for the profusion of its large, deeply puckered, light-green leaves and succulent white stems, which are broad and up to 20 in (50 cm) tall.

 suitable for containers
mid-spring to late summer
some resistance
fairly hardy
late spring to late fall

'Vulcan'

With fiery red stems and dark-green leaves, this is a highly ornamental variety with excellent flavor, both when young and raw in salads and when harvested mature and served as a steamed vegetable. The leaves are sweet-tasting and tender.

 suitable for containers
mid-spring to late summer
poor resistance
fairly hardy
late spring to late fall

'Bright Lights'

This handsome chard variety produces stems ranging in color from red to pink, purple, green, orange, and yellow, with large green or bronze foliage. Harvest as baby leaves 28 days after sowing, or when it reaches maturity in 50 to 60 days.

- suitable for containers
- mid-spring to late summer
- poor resistance
- fairly hardy
- late spring to late fall

'Rhubarb Chard'

This heirloom variety (also known as 'Ruby Red') produces heavily puckered, red-veined, dark green or purple leaves on red stems. It is both beautiful and delicious. The stems have a slight asparagus flavor and the flower stalks can be cooked like sprouting broccoli.

- suitable for containers
- mid-spring to late summer
- some resistance
- fairly hardy
- late spring to late fall

'Perpetual Spinach'

This variety has dull green stems with smooth, dark green leaves with small midribs, resembling spinach, but coarser. It is less likely to bolt than spinach and is hardier than other Swiss chards, making it easier to grow and suitable for a long harvest season.

- suitable for containers
- mid-spring to late summer
- poor resistance
- fairly hardy
- late spring to early winter

'Bright Yellow'

The broad, golden stalks and large, puckered, deep-green leaves of 'Bright Yellow' make it a candidate for the flower border as well as the vegetable patch. When the plant is young, the stalks can be eaten raw and are an attractive addition to a salad.

- suitable for containers
- mid-spring to late summer
- some resistance
- fairly hardy
- late spring to late fall

'Verde da Taglio'

Known as a cut-and-come-again-variety, this thin-stemmed green chard is popular among cooks for its sweet, spinachlike taste. It can be harvested throughout summer and into fall, and will respond by growing tender young leaves if cut back completely.

- suitable for containers
- mid-spring and late summer
- good resistance
- not hardy
- late spring to fall

'Silverado'

The bright, glossy green leaves are heavily savoyed with white stems and ribs, and can be harvested at baby size or larger. 'Silverado' is a compact, 18-in (45-cm) plant that resists bolting, allowing for a long harvest window in a variety of climates.

- suitable for containers
- mid-spring and late summer
- good resistance
- not hardy
- late spring to summer; fall

'Improved Rainbow Mix'

The reds, pinks, yellows, and oranges of this variety's thin stems intensify in color as it matures, providing a striking display against the dark green, puckered leaves. The colors are beautiful in salads and are retained during light cooking.

 suitable for containers
 mid-spring to late summer
 poor resistance
 fairly hardy
 late spring to late fall

'Bionda di Lyon'

Sow 'Bionda di Lyon' in spring and again in late summer. Large smooth, pale green leaves with thick white ribs can be harvested in 30 days for salads, or left in the garden for 50 days. Leaves are tender, and less fibrous than many chard varieties.

 suitable for containers
 mid-spring and late summer
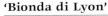 good resistance
not hardy
late spring to summer; fall

'Magenta Sunset'

Beautiful in the vegetable garden, the flower garden, or in a container, 'Magenta Sunset' produces crumpled green leaves with pink to magenta ribs, and grows to 2 ft (60 cm) in height. Baby leaves, picked at 30 days, make a tasty addition to salads.

 suitable for containers
 mid-spring and late summer
 good resistance
 not hardy
late spring to summer; fall

KOHLRABI *Brassica oleracea* Gongylodes Group

Kohlrabi's combination of striking ornamental leaves and a bulbous, alien-looking stem is both bizarre and beautiful. The swollen purple, green, or white stems have a mild, sweet flavor, and can be cooked or eaten raw in salads. This fast-growing vegetable can be grown in containers, but is ideal for use as a catch crop. It should be sown successively, since it does not keep very well once harvested.

	SPRING	SUMMER	FALL	WINTER
SOW/PLANT				
HARVEST				

SOWING

Kohlrabi will tolerate most soils, but it prefers a non-acidic pH, so consider adding lime to soil if the pH is much below 7. Sow under cover in early spring, or sow directly into the ground once the soil has warmed up. Kohlrabi needs a minimum temperature of 50°F (10°C) to prevent bolting.

Sow in modules at a depth of 1 in (2.5 cm), and plant the seedlings out before they reach 2 in (5 cm) tall, since this will also help to prevent bolting. When planting out, ensure that you leave at least 9 in (23 cm) between plants, and 12 in (30 cm) between rows. When sowing directly into the ground, thin out seedlings before they become too large or you risk damaging the roots.

Ensure that crops have space to develop.

Try sowing three seeds in each location, and then remove the weakest two once the seedlings have established. Plant faster-growing green and white varieties first and introduce slower purple varieties later.

CROP CARE

Ensure that you weed and water regularly—if kohlrabi dries out it becomes woody and unpalatable.

HARVESTING

Kohlrabi is best harvested when its stems have reached the size of tennis balls, although some varieties are still worth eating if left in the ground to grow larger. Cut them at the root and remove the oldest leaves; leaving young leaves will help to keep it fresh. If the weather is mild, kohlrabi can be left in the ground in winter, but lift if frosts are forecast.

STORING

Kohlrabi can be stored in boxes full of moist sand but it is best eaten fresh, so sow successively to ensure a continuous crop.

PESTS AND DISEASES

Kohlrabi is susceptible to attack from cabbage root fly, flea beetles, aphids, and slugs and snails (see pp.246–7). Since the leaves are not eaten, some damage might be tolerable. A bigger problem is clubroot; dig up and destroy affected plants and rotate crops.

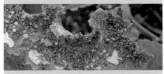

Some leaf damage can be tolerated.

'Superschmelz'

This is a giant variety, with bulbs up to 8–10 in (20–25 cm) across. The skins of 'Superschmelz' are pale green and the white flesh remains sweet and tender even into maturity. It grows quickly, maturing within 60 days, and is resistant to bolting and splitting.

- unsuitable for containers
- early spring to late summer
- poor resistance
- fairly hardy
- early summer to late fall

'Winner'

This hybrid produces round to slightly squashed bulbous stems that grow to about 18 oz (500 g) in less than two months. Best suited for late summer planting, pale-green 'Winner' bulbs hold well in the garden in cool fall weather.

- suitable for containers
- spring; late summer
- poor resistance
- fairly hardy
- early summer; autumn

'Kossak Hybrid'

This light-green, white-fleshed hybrid can be harvested in two months, or allowed to grow to the size of a bowling ball. Even at a giant size, 'Kossak' maintains its crunchy sweetness and does not become woody. It keeps for months in refrigerated storage.

- suitable for containers
- spring; late summer
- poor resistance
- fairly hardy
- summer; autumn

'Kolibri'

The flattened globe-shaped bulbs of this variety are 4–6 in (10–15 cm) across, purple-skinned, and white-fleshed. Since they retain their sweetness and juiciness when most other kohlrabi have become woody, this is a good choice for a late harvest.

 unsuitable for containers

 early spring to late summer

 some resistance

 fairly hardy

 early summer to late fall

'Grand Duke F1'

Hybrid 'Grand Duke', a 1979 All-America Selections winner, produces light-green bulbous stems in less than two months. Harvested at 4 in (10 cm), the flesh is sweet and finely textured. Young leaves can be cooked along with the "bulbs."

suitable for containers

spring; late summer

some resistance

fairly hardy

early summer; autumn

'Early Purple Vienna'

Harvest the purple-skinned, white-fleshed bulbous stem of 'Early Purple Vienna' at 55 to 60 days, when it reaches the size of a tennis ball. If left to grow larger, it will become woody. Leaves of this flavorful heirloom can be cooked like kale.

suitable for containers

spring; late summer

poor resistance

fairly hardy

 early summer; autumn

BOK CHOY *Brassica rapa* var. *chinensis*

Bok choy—or pak choi, as it is sometimes called—is a quick-growing member of the Oriental brassica family. Like Chinese cabbage, it is delicious in salads and is a useful late summer crop, but has larger, darker leaves and a more delicate taste. The leaves, stems, and flowering shoots of bok choy are all edible; harvest leaves when young for use in salads, or leave to mature for cooking lightly in stir-fries.

	SPRING	SUMMER	FALL	WINTER
SOW/PLANT				
HARVEST				

SOWING

Bok choy prefers a sheltered, sunny site with fertile, moisture-retentive soil. Dig in some well-rotted manure or compost in the fall before sowing the following year. Like spinach, bok choy benefits from a top-dressing of fertilizer shortly before sowing.

Sow seed directly into the ground in late spring or summer; avoid planting earlier than this, as bok choy will bolt if conditions are too cold. You can sow earlier in spring under cover in a heated greenhouse and transplant. Sow seed at a depth of .75 in (2 cm).

Plants will need about 12 in (30 cm) of spacing if they are to be harvested whole, but only 4 in (10 cm) if you plan to harvest just the leaves. Consider

Leave the cut stems to resprout.

intercropping among other, slower-growing crops such as sweet corn, since bok choy grows relatively quickly.

CROP CARE

Because of its shallow roots, bok choy needs to be watered regularly to ensure it doesn't dry out. Bok choy is relatively easy to grow, but does have a tendency to bolt. Keep plants well-weeded.

HARVESTING

Bok choy is ready to harvest in little more than a month. The leaves, stems, and flowering shoots are all edible. Either harvest the young leaves as a cut-and-come-again crop—the plant will resprout several times when it has matured, forming a proper "head." Stems and shoots can be harvested as needed when the plant is young.

STORING

Bok choy will wilt quickly after harvesting, so pick leaves as and when they are needed.

PESTS AND DISEASES

Bok choy is at risk from the same problems that affect other brassicas (see pp.246–7). Practice crop rotation and use brassica collars to protect against cabbage root fly. Make collars out of cardboard or carpet underlay.

Leaf diseases can spoil crops.

'Joi Choi'

This 12–15-in (30–38-cm) hybrid combines the benefits of being fast-growing and slow-bolting. It can be harvested leaf by leaf, or all at once. White-ribbed, dark-green leaves are ready to eat in about 50 days, and have a crunchy, juicy texture and a slightly mustardy flavor.

- suitable for containers
- mid-spring and late summer
- poor resistance
- fairly hardy
- late spring and fall

'Mei Qing Choi'

Just 8–10 in (20–25 cm) tall, this baby bok choy matures into a compact vase shape in about 40 days. Its leaves are rich green, with lighter green ribs and have a tender, sweet, and crunchy flavor. The heads can be gently braised whole, or chopped for stir-fries.

- suitable for containers
- mid-spring and late summer
- poor resistance
- fairly hardy
- late spring and fall

'White Stemmed Pac Choy'

This 12-in (30-cm) tall variety has thick white stems a bit like celery and large, rounded, glossy, dark-green leaves with a mild, sweet flavor. It grows fast, reaching maturity 50 days after sowing, is slow to bolt, and is cold-resistant.

- unsuitable for containers
- early spring to midsummer
- poor resistance
- hardy
- mid-spring to mid-fall

'Purple Pakchoi'

Reddish-purple leaves and purple-ribbed stems make this an attractive garden plant and productive salad vegetable: it produces a profusion of flavorful flowering stems. Harvest at 30 days for baby leaves, or at 45 to 70 days to eat all parts of the plant.

 unsuitable for containers
 early spring to midsummer
 poor resistance
fairly hardy
mid-spring to mid-fall

'Hon Tsai Tai'

A Cantonese variety, 'Hon Tsai Tai' produces purple stems with green leaves and yellow flowers. It is good in salads if cut young or can be left to mature for stir-frying: the flowering shoots are most tasty just before the flowers open.

 unsuitable for containers
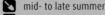 mid- to late summer
poor resistance
not hardy
early to late fall

'Black Summer'

This flavorful variety produces oval, dark green leaves on broad, flat, light green stems, which form a perfect broad vase shape. At 10–12 in (25–30 cm) tall, this very attractive variety is slightly smaller than the average. It is very slow to bolt.

 unsuitable for containers
 mid-spring to late summer
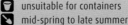 poor resistance
fairly hardy
 early summer to mid-fall

CHINESE CABBAGE *Brassica rapa* var. *pekinensis*

A member of the Oriental brassica family, Chinese cabbage has a delicate cabbage taste and succulent texture and is excellent for use in stir-fries or eaten raw in salads. As long as you give it plenty of water, Chinese cabbage is an easy vegetable to grow and makes a good cut-and-come-again crop. It is also relatively fast-growing, so consider growing it before or between slower-growing vegetables such as turnips or parsnips.

	SPRING	SUMMER	FALL	WINTER
SOW/PLANT				
HARVEST				

SOWING

Chinese cabbage needs very fertile soil in a sunny, sheltered position, so dig in plenty of well-rotted manure or compost in the fall before planting, or apply fertilizer.

Sow seed in late spring or early summer if sowing directly into the ground, since plants will try to bolt if sown outside earlier (bolt-resistant varieties are available). If you want to make an early start, sow under cover in module trays and transplant seedlings, when the risk of frost has passed.

Sow seed thinly at a depth of .75 in (2 cm) in rows 18 in (45 cm) apart. Once the seedlings are established, thin out to allow 12 in (30 cm) between plants.

Keep the fast-growing crops well weeded.

Chinese cabbage can be grown as a catch crop or intercropped with other plants since it is quick to grow and will be ready to harvest within eight to 10 weeks.

CROP CARE

Keep crops well-weeded and make sure that they have plenty of water—like bok choy, Chinese cabbage has very short roots and a tendency to dry out.

HARVESTING

When the "head" of the cabbage feels solid and well-developed, cut it off, leaving a 1 in (2.5 cm) stump left in the ground. Within the next few weeks this will resprout and provide a second crop. Young, late-sown plants can be harvested as cut-and-come-again crops when they are a couple of weeks old. Bolted leaves are also edible.

STORING

Cabbage heads can be stored in the refrigerator for several weeks, but are best eaten fresh, so harvest them just before use.

PESTS AND DISEASES

Chinese cabbage, as with all brassicas, is susceptible to clubroot and cabbage root fly (see pp.246–7). Place a brassica collar around seedlings to deter pests, and plant seeds where you have grown peas, beans, or fruiting vegetables the previous season.

Make a collar from a square of carpet.

'Wong Bok'

The large, barrel-shaped heads of 'Wong Bok' can reach 5.5 lb (2.5 kg) within 10 weeks of sowing, with light green leaves and faint white midribs. Fall crops will keep well for several weeks if wrapped in newspaper and stored in a cool place.

- unsuitable for containers
- mid-spring to late summer
- poor resistance
- fairly hardy
- midsummer to late fall

'Rubicon'

Firm heads that are 12 in (30 cm) tall can weigh as much as 6.5 lb (3 kg) and ripen in 52 days. Slow-bolting 'Rubicon' F1 hybrid is resistant to fungal diseases, and its firm heads store well for up to 6 weeks. Flavor is sweet, and excellent for Asian-style dishes.

- plant in containers
- mid-spring and late summer
- some resistance
- fairly hardy
- early summer and fall

'Minuet F1'

This early, disease-resistant Napa-type hybrid cabbage, harvestable in just seven weeks, produces small, slow-to-bolt heads that are delicious raw or cooked. Seed can be sown in late summer for a fall harvest of 9-in (23-cm), nearly-round heads.

- plant in containers
- mid-spring and late summer
- good resistance
- fairly hardy
- early summer and fall

'Wa Wa Tsi Hybrid'

This variety can be grown closely spaced, making it ideal for a small garden. It is excellent for baby leaves in salads or, when mature, a very tender, succulent, and sweet addition to stir-fries. The heads can reach a weight of 10–18 oz (285–510 g).

 unsuitable for containers
mid-spring to late summer
poor resistance
fairly hardy
early summer to mid-fall

'Kasumi'

This variety is a barrel-headed Napa type, with solid heads about 12 in (30 cm) tall, and attractive dark green leaves that have a mild, sweet flavor and tender texture. It is very slow bolting and is resistant to soft rot.

 unsuitable for containers
mid-spring to early summer
some resistance
fairly hardy
midsummer to late fall

'Kaboko F1'

This disease-resistant hybrid produces dense, cylindrical heads, 12–16 in (30–40 cm) tall, that mature in 55 to 60 days. The inner blanched leaves are crisp and sweet, and tasty cooked and raw. Slow to bolt, 'Kaboko' is a great choice for spring planting.

 suitable for containers
mid-spring, mid- to late summer
some resistance
fairly hardy
early summer and fall

Onion Family

- Onions
- Shallots
- Leeks
- Garlic
- Scallions and Bunching onions

ONIONS *Allium cepa*

For a low-maintenance crop, try growing onions. They are raised from seed or from sets, which are specially produced mini-bulbs. Aside from fertile soil and routine care, onions just need plenty of time to mature. If you want large bulbs, be prepared to wait. There are various onion cultivars available—most have brown or golden-yellow skins, but red-skinned onions are also popular and have a milder flavor.

	SPRING	SUMMER	FALL	WINTER
PLANT				
HARVEST				

SOWING

Onions need an open, well-drained site and non-acid soil. Dig in compost before sowing. To grow large onions, sow seed in midwinter in a heated greenhouse at 50–60°F (10–16°C) and harden off the seedlings in spring for planting out. For smaller bulbs, sow later in the winter or in early spring, under cover but without heat. When the weather warms up, you can sow seed directly into the soil, at about .75 in (2 cm) depth, in rows 12 in (30 cm) apart.

PLANTING

For a late summer or fall harvest, plant sets in spring. Push them into the soil, 2–4 in (5–10 cm) apart, depending on size, and cover, leaving the tips showing.

Dry onions thoroughly before storing.

CROP CARE

When planted-out seedlings are well established, thin them out according to the size of onion you want—closely planted onions are more likely to be smaller on harvest. Water both seedlings and sets moderately, since overwatering can delay swelling of the bulbs, and may make them more susceptible to disease. Weed the onion bed regularly.

HARVESTING
Onions are ready to harvest when their leaves die down and topple over. Carefully ease them out of the ground with a fork. If the weather is clear, leave them to dry on the ground. In wet weather, lifted onions rot quickly, so bring them indoors to dry off thoroughly on a rack or tray.

STORING
Once the skins have turned papery, store onions in a light, well-ventilated area. Braid the leaves into a rope and hang the onions up, or place them in single layers in slatted trays, or in a net.

PESTS AND DISEASES
Onions are susceptible to downy mildew in wet conditions. Other diseases include onion white rot, which affects the base, and onion neck rot, common in stored bulbs. Onion fly is a serious pest but less likely to affect onions grown from sets. Birds may target sets.

Remove and destroy infected foliage.

'Ailsa Craig'

This variety, named after a Scottish island, is over 100 years old but is still popular, especially for showing at exhibitions. It is also known as 'Ailsa Craig Exhibition'. The bulbs are large and globe-shaped with golden skin. They have a mild flavor |and keep well in storage.

- suitable for containers
- late winter to mid-spring
- poor resistance
- fairly hardy
- late summer to mid-fall

'Copra'

Market gardeners in the north swear that 'Copra' is the best hard storage onion. In the long days of summer, this hybrid produces firm, medium-sized bulbs, characterized by thin necks and yellow skins. The strong-flavored creamy flesh is best when cooked.

- suitable for containers
- early spring
- some resistance
- hardy
- late summer

'Red Wing'

This variety is a "long-day" producer of large, very firm 3–4-in (7.5–10-cm) purple-red bulbs with thick interior rings that become more colorful with storage. In latitudes above 43°, this reliable hybrid is considered the best red storage onion.

- suitable for containers
- early spring
- some resistance
- hardy biennial
- late summer

'Golden Bear'

This F1 hybrid variety produces high-shouldered bulbs with thin, golden-brown skin. It is a vigorous grower, resistant to downy mildew, gray mold, and white rot and has the advantage of cropping early, although it is not a good keeper.

 suitable for containers
 late winter to mid-spring
 good resistance
 fairly hardy
 late summer to mid-fall

'Cortland'

Bred for resistance to pink root and fusarium, this storage variety produces a uniform crop of 3–4-in (7.5–10 cm) firm bulbs with thick copper skins. Although it grows best in the long days of northern regions, 'Cortland' can also be grown in the South, too.

 suitable for containers
suitable for containers
early spring
good resistance
hardy biennial
late summer

'Red Candy Apple'

Sweet, beautiful 'Red Candy Apple' hybrid is a popular salad and sandwich onion. It is adaptable, developing bulbs in the short-day conditions of the South, and the long-day northern summers. The mild-flavored, red-ringed onions grow larger in lower latitudes.

 suitable for containers
 early spring
 poor resistance
hardy
late summer

'Purplette'

This unusual variety produces mini bulbs that can be harvested early for use in salads, or left until golf-ball-sized, at which time they are ideal for pickling or for cooking whole. The skin is a burgundy red, and the bulbs turn a pale-pink color when pickled or cooked.

🗂	suitable for containers
🌱	late winter to mid-spring
🐛	poor resistance
❄	fairly hardy
🔒	late spring to late summer

'Red Wethersfield'

This celebrated heirloom was named for the town of Wethersfield, Connecticut, where it was a valued crop in the 18th and 19th centuries. With its dark skin, pink-tinged flesh, and crisp, mild flavor, it is an attractive and flavorful slicer, and a good keeper.

🗂	suitable for containers
🌱	early spring
🐛	poor resistance
❄	hardy
🔒	late summer

'Yellow Granex'

Often sold as "Vidalia" onions (for Vidalia, Georgia), this hybrid variety develops super-sweet bulbs when day lengths are 10 to 12 hours, and cannot be grown in latitudes above 35°. The 3–4-in (7.5–10-cm) flattened globes store better than most sweet onions.

🗂	suitable for containers
🌱	mid-fall
🐛	no resistance
❄	hardy biennial
🔒	mid- to late spring

'Sturon'

This older variety is reliable and high yielding, and has a good flavor. The bulbs are medium in size and globe-shaped, with slightly high shoulders and good, even-toned, yellow-brown skins. It is slow to bolt in the ground and also keeps very well when in storage.

 suitable for containers
 late winter to mid-spring
 some resistance
 fairly hardy
 late summer to mid-fall

'Stuttgarter'

This strong-flavored, and long-day onion forms large, yellow-skinned bulbs that are excellent for cooking and store very well. This variety is commonly sold as sets, which should be planted as soon as the ground can be worked.

 suitable for containers
 early to mid-spring
 poor resistance
 hardy biennial
 late summer

'Borettana'

This Italian heirloom variety is traditionally planted at close spacing to produce small bulbs for pickling or cooking whole. It has pale, yellow-brown skin and crisp, white, sweet flesh. Grown at normal spacing, it produces medium-sized, flattened bulbs.

 suitable for containers
 late winter to mid-spring
 poor resistance
 fairly hardy
 late summer to mid-fall

'Red Brunswick'

This variety produces bulbs of medium to large size that have maroon-red skin and white flesh tinged with purple rings. 'Red Brunswick' is a reliable cropper, although with little resistance to disease, but it does store well, so is available through winter and into the spring.

> 🪴 suitable for containers
> 🔪 late winter to mid-spring
> 🦗 poor resistance
> ❄️ fairly hardy
> 🔒 late summer to mid-fall

'Red Baron'

This eye-catching variety has shiny, dark-red skin and pale purple-tinged flesh with purple rings. They have a strong flavor and are good for cooking or for eating raw. The bulbs are globe-shaped, of medium size, and store well.

> 🪴 suitable for containers
> 🔪 late winter to mid-spring
> 🦗 some resistance
> ❄️ fairly hardy
> 🔒 late summer to mid-fall

'Long Red Florence'

This Italian heirloom variety is also known as 'Rossa Lunga di Firenze', and produces elongated, torpedo-shaped bulbs with red skin and a mild, sweet flavor. They can be pulled young as scallions, or left to mature and become larger.

> 🪴 suitable for containers
> 🔪 late winter to mid-spring
> 🦗 poor resistance
> ❄️ fairly hardy
> 🔒 late spring to early fall

'Centurion'

This 'F1' hybrid variety has been developed from the popular 'Sturon'. 'Centurion' produces flattened, globe-shaped bulbs that have straw-colored skins of good thickness. It is a heavy cropper and produces crisp flesh. This variety is known to store well.

 suitable for containers
late winter to mid-spring
some resistance
fairly hardy
late summer to mid-fall

'Tropea Rossa Lunga'

Also called 'Tropeana Lunga', this variety from southern Italy produces long, torpedo-shaped bulbs with light, reddish-purple skin and pale-pink flesh. They have a mild flavor and high sugar content, so are ideal for eating raw, and are good roasted whole.

 suitable for containers
late winter to mid-spring
poor resistance
fairly hardy
late summer to mid-fall

'Texas Supersweet'

This sweet, mild onion was developed from the 'Grano' onion from Spain. In southern latitudes, 'Texas Supersweet' develops huge, 1-lb (450-g) bulbs when spring days are 10 to 12 hours long. When spring-planted in the north, it is not as large or as sweet.

suitable for containers
mid-fall
poor resistance
hardy
mid- to late spring

'Setton'

An F1 hybrid variety that was developed as an improvement to 'Sturon', 'Setton' produces attractive-looking bulbs of uniform shape, with smooth, russet-brown skin. It is a high-yielding variety that can be used fresh or stored through into spring.

🪴	suitable for containers
🗓	late winter to mid-spring
✳	some resistance
❄	fairly hardy
🔒	late summer to mid-fall

'Walla Walla Sweet'

Famous for its size and sweetness, this onion was originally introduced to Washington from the Mediterranean island of Corsica. The 4-in (10-cm), golden-skinned bulbs are best eaten raw, and do not store well.

🪴	suitable for containers
🗓	early spring
✳	poor resistance
❄	hardy
🔒	late summer

'Red Marble'

This small, flat, cipollini-type onion requires long summer days of the northern latitudes to develop. The dark-red bulbs grow to only 2 in (5 cm) wide, and with closer spacing can be harvested as smaller pearl onions. 'Red Marble' can be stored up to five months.

🪴	suitable for containers
🗓	early spring
✳	no resistance
❄	hardy
🔒	late summer

'Senshyu Semi-Globe Yellow'

An overwintering variety, this popular Japanese onion reliably produces heavy crops of round, straw-colored bulbs. It makes a good choice for sowing at close spacing in order to produce a crop of baby onions in early summer.

- suitable for containers
- early to late fall
- poor resistance
- hardy
- early to midsummer

'White Ebenezer'

This popular variety is commonly sold as easy-to-grow sets and is used as a green onion, a salad onion, and a storage onion. The flattened globes mature to 2.5–3 in (6–7.5 cm) and have papery wraps and crisp white flesh, with a medium-pungent taste.

- suitable for containers
- early spring
- poor resistance
- hardy
- late summer

'Candy'

This adaptable day-neutral sweet onion will develop large bulbs in both northern and southern latitudes. Started indoors and set out in early spring, 'Candy' produces mild, white-fleshed bulbs up to 6 in (15 cm) in diameter that store fairly well.

- suitable for containers
- early spring
- none
- hardy
- late summer

SHALLOTS *Allium cepa* Aggregatum Group

Small members of the onion family, shallots are less pungent than their larger relatives and are used for pickling and cooking. Shallots can be raised from seed, although the easier option is to grow them from small bulbs called sets. They need a long growing period but can be interplanted with faster-growing crops; after the companion crops are harvested, the shallots come into their own and will make use of the available space.

	SPRING	SUMMER	FALL	WINTER
SOW				
HARVEST				

SOWING

To raise shallots from seed, either start them off under cover in late winter, or outdoors, once the soil has warmed up in spring. Indoors, sow them in pots or trays, in good compost, and transplant them outside in mid-spring. Shallots need rich, well-drained soil. They will not thrive in very acidic soils, so check the pH levels of your plot and adjust the acidity with lime, if necessary. Once the seedlings are established, thin them out to approximately .75 in (2 cm) apart.

PLANTING

Plant sets outside in late winter or early spring. Rake the soil over, and then make a shallow drill, about 1 in (2.5 cm) deep.

Plant sets out in early spring.

Push each set into the drill, spacing them 6–8 in (15–20 cm) apart. Cover them gently with soil, leaving the points showing above ground level.

CROP CARE

Keep the bed free from weeds, taking care not to uproot the sets or seedlings as you work. Water sparingly, unless the weather is very warm and dry.

HARVESTING

Gently lift the clumps of shallots with a fork when the tops turn yellow in mid- to late summer. In dry, sunny conditions, it is safe to leave the bulbs to dry outside on the ground. Otherwise, bring them indoors and dry them on a slatted tray or wire rack.

STORING

Shallots are ready to store when their skins have turned papery. Place them in bags or in single layers on trays. The storage area should be light and frost-free, with good air circulation. Small shallots can be saved as sets for next year.

PESTS AND DISEASES

Like other members of the onion family, shallots are at risk from diseases such as downy mildew, especially in wet weather, and onion neck rot. Onion fly is a major pest, but it may be deterred by placing fleece over seedlings.

Onion neck rot softens lifted bulbs.

'Pikant'

Living up to its name, 'Pikant' is known for its strong, spicy flavor; this is a robust and prolific variety. It produces high yields of firm bulbs that have dark, reddish-brown skins. They are very resistant to bolting and also store well after they have been harvested.

 suitable for containers
 late winter to mid-spring
 some resistance
 fairly hardy
 mid- to late summer

'Echalote Grise'

Despite the French name, which means "gray shallot," this variety originated in Kazakhstan. It produces long bulbs that are easy to slice, 18 to 20 in a cluster, with gray-brown skin. The flavor is intense and concentrated.

 suitable for containers
 late winter to mid-spring
 poor resistance
 fairly hardy
 mid- to late summer

'Banana'

This is a very long shallot, with shiny, copper-brown skin and crisp, white flesh. It has a distinctive flavor, making it a popular choice with chefs, and it stores well after harvest. Overall, the size can be controlled by altering the planting distance.

 suitable for containers
 late winter to mid-spring
 poor resistance
 fairly hardy
 mid- to late summer

'Jermor'

This variety produces long, coppery-brown shallots in clusters that contain six to eight bulbs. The flesh is pink-tinged in color, and has a good flavor. The shallots have a good skin finish and are uniform in shape and size, making them suitable for exhibition.

suitable for containers
late winter to mid-spring
some resistance
fairly hardy
mid- to late summer

'Ambition'

Seed-grown shallots, a relatively new phenomenon, are becoming more and more popular due to their low cost and excellent storage capabilities. Hybrid 'Ambition' yields firm, 2-in (5-cm) rust-colored bulbs with delicately flavored white flesh.

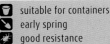
suitable for containers
early spring
good resistance
hardy biennial
late summer

'French Gray'

Many chefs consider the 'French Gray' shallot as the one true shallot. Grown only from sets, planted early in spring or in fall along with the garlic, it is not a long-keeping shallot. Mature bulbs are an elongated pear shape with thick, gray outer skins.

suitable for containers
early spring or mid-fall
poor resistance
cold hardy
late summer or eary summer

'Red Sun'

This attractive variety has firm, red-brown skin and solid, crisp, red-tinged flesh with a punchy taste. 'Red Sun' produces high yields, and it is a versitile onion variety. It is well-suited for a range of uses: for salads, cooking, and pickling, and has long storage potential.

- suitable for containers
- late winter to mid-spring
- poor resistance
- fairly hardy
- mid- to late summer

'Prisma'

Planting seed-grown shallots reduces the risk of diseases that can occur when sets are used. Hybrid 'Prisma' produces dependable yields of round, flattened, rose-colored bulbs with purple-tinged interiors that store exceptionally well.

- suitable for containers
- early spring
- good resistance
- hardy
- late summer

'Golden Gourmet'

This reliable variety consistently produces high yields of large, good-quality, yellow-skinned bulbs. The flavor is mild, making them suitable for use in salads as well as for cooking. They have good resistance to bolting and store well after harvest.

- suitable for containers
- late winter to mid-spring
- some resistance
- fairly hardy
- mid- to late summer

'Longor'

The 'Longor' variety produces a good yield of long bulbs that are pinky-brown in color. They are uniform in size, with a good shape, making them a solid choice for exhibition purposes. The pink-tinged flesh has a robust flavor and the bulbs store well.

 suitable for containers
late winter to mid-spring
some resistance
fairly hardy
mid- to late summer

'Picasso'

The mild-flavored 'Picasso' variety has red-brown skin and pink flesh, which is good for use in salads, for cooking, or for pickling. It crops early, producing uniform bulbs that show very good resistance to bolting.

suitable for containers
late winter to mid-spring
poor resistance
fairly hardy
mid- to late summer

'Matador'

This 'F1' hybrid variety produces a substantial yield of uniform bulbs. The flesh is crisp and white and the thick, reddish-brown skins give it excellent potential for long storage through into spring and early summer.

suitable for containers
late winter to mid-spring
some resistance
fairly hardy
mid- to late summer

LEEKS *Allium porrum*

Hardy, resilient leeks can be planted to provide a succession of crops from late summer all the way through the winter months. Early varieties are generally taller, with longer portions of blanched stem, while later crops tend to be shorter, with darker stems and a tougher texture. Delicious used in stews, casseroles, soups, or served up with white sauce, leeks are a versatile, valuable source of fresh winter food.

	SPRING	SUMMER	FALL	WINTER
SOW				
HARVEST				

SOWING

Although they will probably cope in any soil you care to plant them in, leeks prefer a deep, fertile soil with a slightly acidic pH. Dig in plenty of well-rotted manure or compost before planting.

Seed can be sown from as early as late winter in trays or modules under cover. Sow at a depth of 1 in (2.5 cm). Otherwise, sow successionally into an outdoor seed bed through spring; seedlings should be ready to plant out in eight weeks, when they are about as thick as a pencil.

Harden seedlings off before you transplant them. Trim their roots down to about 1 in (2.5 cm) and leaves to 6 in (15 cm). With a dibber, create holes about 6 in (15 cm) deep, and 6 in (15 cm)

Trim seedling roots before transplanting.

apart. Place the seedlings into the holes and water around them, allowing the water to drag the soil into the surrounding hole.

CROP CARE

Feed plants with a nitrogen fertilizer in summer, but do not overwater them. To give leeks their customary white stems, you will need to earth up soil around them as they grow.

HARVESTING

Within four to five months, your leeks will be ready to harvest, although they can be left in the ground for longer, if necessary.

STORING

Out of the ground, leeks do not store very well. If you need to use the space for planting other crops, they can be dug up and then "heeled in" elsewhere.

Dig a shallow trench, deep enough to submerge the leeks' roots fully. Place the leeks in the hole, leaning them against the side. Cover the roots over with soil. Lift as required.

PESTS AND DISEASES

Leeks are prone to the same problems as other members of the onion family, most notably onion fly, leek moth, and downy mildew. They may also suffer from leek rust—remove and destroy infected leaves. Sow seed in modules to discourage fusarium wilt.

Leek moth grubs burrow into stems.

'Hannibal'

'Hannibal' is an early variety of leek that develops quickly, making it a good choice for cultivating as baby leeks in the late summer. If left to mature, it does show good resistance to bulbing and produces long, white shafts with healthy mid-green foliage.

	suitable for containers
	early to mid-spring
	some resistance
	hardy
	early fall to early winter

'King Richard'

This well-established, early favorite is a good choice for a quick crop of baby leeks, but will also go on to produce mature plants with very long shafts and pale-green leaves. It is popular for showing and slow to bolt, with a sweet, tender flavor.

	suitable for containers
	early to mid-spring
	some resistance
	hardy
	early fall to early winter

'Lancelot'

This early variety is a good choice for producing an early crop of baby leeks and it can also be left until early winter to produce a full-sized crop. It is an easy-going variety and is also well-suited to being grown in containers.

	suitable for containers
	early to mid-spring
	poor resistance
	hardy
	early fall to early winter

'Bandit'

This late variety produces dark blue-green foliage and has some resistance to rust disease. The leaves make an attractive contrast with the thick, white stem, which has a good flavor. 'Bandit' stands well once it is mature and it exhibits little tendency to bolt.

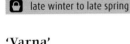

🪣 suitable for containers
🌱 early to mid-spring
🕷 some resistance
❄ hardy
🔒 late winter to late spring

'Varna'

This quick-maturing leek was developed for dense planting, and yields clumps of slender plants with scallionlike qualities. Though not winter-hardy, 'Varna' can be harvested from summer into fall, as gourmet baby leeks or slender mature stalks.

🪣 suitable for containers
🌱 early to mid-spring
🕷 some resistance
❄ fairly hardy
🔒 summer to fall

'Blue Solaise'

A French heirloom leek also known as 'Bleu de Solaise', this maincrop variety has attractive deep purplish-blue foliage and thick, white, medium-length stems. It is a very hardy variety that stands well once mature and will crop until late spring.

🪣 suitable for containers
🌱 early to mid-spring
🕷 poor resistance
❄ hardy
🔒 late fall to late spring

'Apollo'

Vigorous, high-yielding, and with uniform shafts, this maincrop 'F1' hybrid variety has pale leaves that exhibit a good resistance to leek rust. The leaves of the hardy 'Apollo' are held semi-erect, which makes this variety a good choice for close planting.

	suitable for containers
	early to mid-spring
	good resistance
	hardy
	late fall to mid-spring

'Atlanta'

This late variety produces healthy, blue-green foliage that stands more erect than most, making it easier to fit a greater number of plants into the vegetable bed or container. The blanched white stem is of average length.

	suitable for containers
	early to mid-spring
	some resistance
	hardy
	late winter to late spring

'Musselburgh'

This old, maincrop variety takes its name from a town in Scotland and it is still popular, thanks to its hardiness and reliability. 'Musselburgh' produces short but sturdy stems with a good flavor. The blue-green leaves have some resistance to leek rust.

 suitable for containers
early to mid-spring
some resistance
hardy
late fall to mid-spring

'Lincoln'

Sow 'Lincoln' leek seeds directly in the ground and harvest as pencil-thin babies at 50 days, or allow them another month to develop into long, thick, white shanks. This early-maturing "summer leek" has a mild flavor that is delicate enough to eat raw.

 suitable for containers
mid- to late spring
poor resistance
hardy
midsummer to fall

'Jolant'

An early variety, 'Jolant' is one of the fastest-growing leeks, producing a dense shaft with a mild flavor. This is a good choice for producing an abundance of baby leeks. Grow them in containers, since they can be planted at high density.

 suitable for containers
 early to mid-spring
 some resistance
hardy
early fall to early winter

'Toledo'

A maincrop variety, 'Toledo' tends to be a little late in getting into its stride, but once it does it is a good cropper, producing smooth and uniform, medium-to-long shafts that are topped by dark-green flags, from early winter on. It is also suitable for containers.

- 🪣 suitable for containers
- 🌱 early to mid-spring
- ✳️ some resistance
- ❄️ hardy
- 🔒 early winter to mid-spring

'Lyon 2—Prizetaker'

More than 100 years old, this early variety retains its popularity as a show leek. It quickly develops long, thick, white stems that possess good flavor. Once mature, it will stand well and has a good tolerance of low temperatures.

- 🪣 suitable for containers
- 🌱 early to mid-spring
- ✳️ poor resistance
- ❄️ hardy
- 🔒 early fall to early winter

'Tadorna'

This large leek, planted in spring for fall into winter harvesting, will overwinter in moderate climates. 'Tadorna' produces medium-length white shafts that have a delicious mild flavor. The dark blue-green foliage is resistant to leaf diseases.

- 🪣 suitable for containers
- 🌱 early to mid-spring
- ✳️ good resistance
- ❄️ fairly hardy
- 🔒 mid-fall to winter

'Carlton'

The first 'F1' hybrid leek, this early variety grows quickly, producing uniform plants with long, straight shafts. The leaves are tightly packed so little soil gets trapped and they are quick and easy to clean. However, it tends to bolt if left too long before harvest.

 suitable for containers
 early to mid-spring
 some resistance
 hardy
 early fall to early winter

'Upton'

This hybrid "summer leek" achieves a thickness of 3–4 in (7.5–10 cm) about 90 days after transplants are set out. Tall and vigorous, 'Upton' plants have dark, blue-green foliage and uniformly good quality in a variety of growing conditions.

 suitable for containers
early to mid-spring
poor resistance
hardy
late summer to fall

'Pancho'

An early variety, 'Pancho' produces a good yield of medium to long, solid shafts, which have only a slight tendency to bulb. It has a crisp texture and good flavor. The foliage is mid-green and shows good resistance to the fungal disease leek rust.

 suitable for containers
 early to mid-spring
good resistance
hardy
early fall to early winter

GARLIC *Allium sativum*

Its distinct aroma and strong flavor make garlic a vital component of many of our everyday dishes, and it is also known for its medicinal properties and health benefits. Despite needing a relatively long growing period, it is very easy to grow, even in cooler climates, making it a popular choice with gardeners. Garlic can either be planted straight into the ground, or indoors in module trays to be planted out once it has sprouted.

	SPRING	SUMMER	FALL	WINTER
PLANT				
HARVEST				

PLANTING

Garlic grows best in a sunny, open site with fertile, well-drained, and mildly alkaline soil. Plant in fall or early winter, since garlic needs cold weather at the start of its growth. Spring planted garlic will still succeed, but it does tend to produce smaller bulbs, since there is less time for it to mature.

To plant, split open a bulb and divide it into individual cloves. Push these about 4 in (10 cm) deep into the soil with their points facing up, either directly into the ground or in modules. Space the plants 8 in (20 cm) apart.

Create deep holes for bulbs with a dibber.

CROP CARE

Plant it in the right conditions and garlic is relatively easy to grow. Keep it well-weeded, and water it so that the soil is kept fairly moist; be careful not to overwater. If the weather is cold, consider giving plants some protection with a cloche.

Watch for signs of bolting, since this will decrease the final size of the bulb. To prevent this from happening, cut the stem down to about half its height a couple of weeks prior to harvesting.

HARVESTING

Garlic is ready to be harvested when its leaves turn yellow and start to die down. This usually happens in early summer. Alternatively, harvest while the leaves are still green and use the cloves fresh; they have a milder flavor and must be used quickly this way, since they do not keep for long.

STORING

Hang the garlic up to dry in braids or individually. Take care not to bruise the bulbs and they will store for up to 10 months in a well-ventilated place.

PESTS AND DISEASES

Buying good quality, disease resistant bulbs will help to keep most diseases at bay, as will rotating crops. One common problem is leek rust—orange blisters filled with powdery spores appear on leaves—remove promptly and it may not prove fatal.

A garlic leaf infected with leek rust.

'Elephant'

Although this variety is not a true garlic, and is more closely related to leeks, it looks like a giant garlic bulb and is grown in the same way. The bulbs are huge—up to 6 in (15 cm) across—and have a mild flavor. They are particularly good for roasting whole.

	suitable for containers
	fall
	poor resistance
	hardy
	early to midsummer

'Premium Northern White'

This late-season porcelain hardneck variety can withstand winter temperatures of well below 0°F (-18°C). Averaging six large cloves per bulb, it is an excellent all-purpose garlic that stores well. The flavor is strong and spicy.

	suitable for containers
	mid- to late fall
	some resistance
	hardy
	midsummer

'Silver Rose'

This silverskin softneck garlic produces large, white bulbs ideal for braiding. Late-maturing 'Silver Rose' bulbs are among the longest-keeping of garlic varieties, and contain a dozen or more rose-colored cloves each. This is a good warm-climate choice.

	suitable for containers
	mid- to late fall
	some resistance
	hardy
	midsummer

'Pioneer'

This softneck, artichoke-type variety is known for its large, white bulbs wrapped in papery skins. The bulbs can contain up to 20 cloves, and are ready to harvest earlier than most other garlic varieties. They are good keepers, and are ideal for braiding.

- suitable for containers
- mid- to late fall
- some resistance
- hardy
- early to midsummer

'Bogatyr'

This hardneck garlic originated in Moscow, and grows well in areas with cold winters. Bulbs average four to seven plump cloves, and are among the longest-storing of the marbled purple stripe varieties. Cloves have a spicy flavor and are particularly good for roasting.

- suitable for containers
- mid- to late fall
- some resistance
- hardy
- midsummer

'Music'

Hot when raw, but sweet and pungent when roasted, 'Music' is a popular porcelain hardneck variety. It is known for vigor, cold tolerance, and heavy harvests of bulbs, each of which contains four to seven large cloves. Bulbs store well for nine months or more.

- suitable for containers
- mid- to late fall
- some resistance
- hardy
- midsummer

'Inchelium Red'

An artichoke-type, softneck variety, 'Inchelium Red' produces 3-in (7.5-cm) bulbs that are layered with up to 20 large and small cloves. It is popular for its exceptionally large size, rich, mild garlicky taste, and because it keeps well.

- suitable for containers
- mid- to late fall
- some resistance
- hardy
- midsummer

'Mediterranean'

This softneck cultivar is originally from southern France. It produces large, white bulbs and is a good choice for producing "wet" garlic, which can be eaten while it is still fresh and juicy, or used for aioli. It can also be dried off and stored until late fall.

🪣	suitable for containers
🍂	fall
🕷	poor resistance
❄	hardy
🔒	early to midsummer

'Early Italian Purple'

This artichoke-type, softneck garlic is adaptable to both northern and southern growing conditions. The large, white-skinned bulbs, packed with numerous small cloves, mature a week or more earlier than others, and store up to 10 months with proper curing.

🪣	unsuitable for containers
🍂	mid- to late fall
🕷	some resistance
❄	cold hardy
🔒	early to midsummer

'Siberian'

'Siberian' thrives in cold winter climates, as expected, and produces huge hardneck bulbs of four to eight cloves with pinkish-brown skins. A purple-striped variety, it has a medium to strong taste that mellows with storage, and with roasting.

🪣	unsuitable for containers
🍂	mid- to late fall
🕷	some resistance
❄	cold hardy
🔒	midsummer

'Early Wight'

This hardneck cultivar produces a very early crop that can be ready to lift by the late spring. It develops good, fat cloves that have the advantage of being easy to peel. It should, however, be used very soon after it is harvested, since it does not keep well in storage.

- suitable for containers
- fall
- some resistance
- hardy
- late spring to early summer

'St. Helen's Red'

An attractive choice for braiding, this large, softneck garlic produces bulbs covered with silvery skin tinged with purple. Bulbs contain about seven cloves, which are hot when eaten raw, but take on a subtle flavor when roasted. 'St. Helen's' is an excellent keeper.

- unsuitable for containers
- mid- to late fall
- some resistance
- cold hardy
- midsummer

'Georgian Fire'

'Georgian Fire' is a large and beautiful porcelain-type hardneck that produces about six cloves per bulb. It grows best in cold-winter areas, and can be marginally successful in warm-winter areas. The flavor of the raw cloves is robust and pleasantly hot.

- unsuitable for containers
- mid- to late fall
- some resistance
- cold hardy
- midsummer

SCALLIONS AND BUNCHING ONIONS *Allium cepa*

Mostly enjoyed as a salad vegetable when their stems are still slender, scallions will also develop into sizeable bulbs if left in the ground to grow on. Bunching onions can be harvested at scallion size, or allowed to mature to the size of leeks. Both are very easy to raise and need minimal care.

	SPRING	SUMMER	FALL	WINTER
SOW				
HARVEST				

SOWING

Grown from seed, scallions and bunching onions need a sunny, fertile, well-drained site and will not do well on very acid soils. Test the pH levels of your soil and add lime if necessary. Dig in plenty of well-rotted manure or compost before sowing.

Sow the seed directly into the ground from early spring. If you want to harvest scallions throughout the summer, sow successive batches at two-weekly intervals until the fall. You can also sow hardy varieties in the fall for overwintering crops that will be ready to harvest the following spring.

Prepare shallow drills .5–.75 in (1–2 cm) deep and 12 in (30 cm) apart, and space the seeds about

Pull scallions as required.

.5 in (1 cm) apart. Carefully rake back the soil to cover the drills. Plants will not need thinning.

CROP CARE

Weed the bed regularly and water if the weather is very dry, since this can cause the onions to become bulbous. If you live in an area where there is a high risk of frosts, protect overwintering crops with cloches.

HARVESTING

The longer you leave scallions in the ground, the bigger the bulbs will grow. If you want them at their youngest and most delicate, you can start harvesting as soon as the onions reach approximately 6 in (15 cm) high. Harvest bunching onions as required, either when young and slender, or leave to mature and thicken.

STORING

Although scallions do not store well, they will keep fresh in the refrigerator for a few days. For best results, pick them for immediate use.

PESTS AND DISEASES

Scallions and bunching onions are vulnerable to the same problems that afflict larger varieties of onion (see pp.316–7). Downy mildew and onion white rot are the most common diseases; remove infected plants and destroy, as there is no effective cure. To reduce the risk and spread of disease, practice good garden hygiene and keep plants well ventilated.

You may also need to cover your seedlings with fleece to protect them from onion fly. Scallions and bunching onions grown from sets are less at risk.

'Crimson Forest'

This very striking scallion variety produces conventional green foliage, but has a deep red shaft. The coloration can penetrate for several layers, making this a very attractive variety to use in salads, especially since the flavor is mild.

 suitable for containers
 early spring to midsummer
 poor resistance
 fairly hardy
 late spring to fall

'Deep Purple'

These vigorous scallions have bright, medium-green leaves and attractive deep red-purple bases. The bulbous, torpedo-shaped base colors up whatever the age of the plant or the temperature. Overall, this is a good-looking variety with a pleasant flavor.

 suitable for containers
 early spring to midsummer
 poor resistance
fairly hardy
late spring to fall

'Lilia'

This Italian scallion has a strong, pungent flavor. It has a very attractive appearance with dark green leaves and shiny, deep purple-red stems. It does tend to be bulbous and, if planted at wider spacing or thinned, it can be left to form full-sized onions.

 suitable for containers
early spring to midsummer
poor resistance
fairly hardy
late spring to fall

'Performer'

This is an upright scallion variety with dark-green leaves. The stems have a mild flavor and do not become bulbous with age. If provided with cloche protection, this variety will continue to crop through into the winter months.

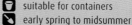 suitable for containers
 early spring to midsummer
 poor resistance
 fairly hardy
late spring to early winter

'Mini Purplette'

This dual-purpose onion can be direct-sown and harvested either as attractive scallions with purple ends or as delicately flavored pearl onions. Started indoors, 'Mini Purplette' forms purple-skinned bulbs that mature about two months after they are transplanted.

 suitable for containers
early- to mid-spring
poor resistance
fairly hardy
early- to midsummer

'Ishikura Improved'

The growth habit of this bunching onion is similar to a leek, with "hilling up" producing long white stems. Seeds can be direct-sown at two to three week intervals for a continuous harvest of mild-tasting green onions lasting from summer through late fall.

suitable for containers
early spring and summer
poor resistance
fairly hardy
summer to fall

'Eiffel'

A very upright grower, with improved disease resistance, the 'Eiffel' scallion variety produces mid-green leaves and long, white shafts that stay narrow through the summer, showing a high resistance to developing bulbs at the base.

suitable for containers
late summer to mid-fall
some resistance
hardy
early to late spring

'Ramrod'

This very upright-growing scallion produces stiff, medium-green leaves and a good length of white shaft. It has a mild flavor and is a good choice for overwintering as it can produce an early contribution to the salad bowl.

 suitable for containers
late summer to mid-fall
some resistance
hardy
early to late spring

'Guardsman'

This very vigorous F1 bunching variety produces medium-to-dark green leaves. The lower part is well-blanched, with some tendency to form bulbs. It stands well, remaining in good condition for longer than older varieties, and can be harvested over several weeks from one sowing.

- suitable for containers
- early spring to midsummer
- poor resistance
- fairly hardy
- late spring to fall

'Parade'

This non-bulbing, bunching onion produces uniform stands of upright, dark green stalks that are ready to harvest about two months after sowing. Successive sowings will yield a continuous "parade" of nutritious and mild-tasting green onions for salads and cooked dishes.

- suitable for containers
- early spring to summer
- poor resistance
- fairly hardy
- early summer to fall

'Red Beard'

Clusters of tender stalks take on a red color in cold temperatures, which distinguishes this bunching onion from most others. The plants grow up to 2 ft (60 cm) tall and form thicker bunches the longer they're left in the ground.

- suitable for containers
- spring
- some resistance
- hardy
- midsummer to fall

'Evergreen'

These clusters of slender scallions are excellent in stir-fries, soups, and salads and can be harvested over a long period, beginning as early as 60 days from seed. The plants are resistant to pink smut and can overwinter for a spring crop in many regions.

- suitable for containers
- early spring and summer
- good resistance
- hardy
- spring; summer into fall

'White Lisbon'

The best-known scallion of all, this variety is quick and easy to grow. It has dark green leaves, a mild flavor, and a tendency to become bulbous at the base as it matures. It is a good choice for growing in containers.

 suitable for containers
 late summer to mid-fall
 some resistance
 hardy
early to late spring

'White Spear'

A vigorous, bunching variety with dark, blue-green leaves and long, straight, slender stems. The crop is uniform in appearance and is quick-growing, making it a good choice for sowing early or late in the season.

suitable for containers
early spring to midsummer
some resistance
fairly hardy
late spring to fall

'Beltsville Bunching'

This tall, bunching variety produces a good length of blanched white stem. It has a crisp texture and mild flavor, and tolerates hot, dry weather conditions well. This is a good choice for late summer and fall cropping.

suitable for containers
early spring to midsummer
some resistance
fairly hardy
late spring to fall

'Emerald Isle'

This variety produces a very uniform crop, which could make it a good choice for gardeners interested in showing their produce at exhibition. This bunching onion develops medium size, strong stems, with straight tops and an average balance between green and white.

- suitable for containers
- early spring to late summer
- some resistance
- fairly hardy
- late spring to fall

'Shimonita'

A hardy bunching onion that can stand through the winter, this variety has very thick foliage. The blanched shaft is sweet at the base and pungent near the leaves. If thinned out to wider than normal spacing, the plants can grow on to become as thick as leeks.

- suitable for containers
- early spring to late summer
- poor resistance
- hardy
- mid-spring to late fall

'Toyko Long White'

This Japanese bunching onion produces long white stalks and green leaves that can be used fresh or cooked in soups, salads, or as a topping for potatoes. The non-bulbing onions are resistant to root rot and smut, and can be harvested over a long period.

- suitable for containers
- early spring and summer
- good resistance
- fairly hardy
- summer and fall

'Photon'

This bunching onion produces neat plants, so would make a good choice for growing in containers. It is also attractive to look at, with uniform growth, dark green leaves, and a long portion of blanched white stem.

- suitable for containers
- early spring to midsummer
- some resistance
- fairly hardy
- late spring to fall

'Summer Isle'

This relatively late-cropping variety of bunching onion is vigorous and uniform. It produces strong, bright green tops with plenty of blanched white shaft below. It has a sweet flavor, with low pungency, so makes a good choice for eating raw.

- suitable for containers
- early spring to midsummer
- some resistance
- fairly hardy
- late spring to fall

'Red Baron'

Intensely red from the base to the lower leaves, 'Red Baron' makes a beautiful contribution to salads. Seeds can be densely sown and harvested at a tender 12-15 in (30-38 cm), just as the bulbs begin to swell. Summer plantings will yield fall scallions.

- suitable for containers
- early- to mid-spring
- poor resistance
- fairly hardy
- early to midsummer

'Ishiko'

Also sold as 'Heshiko', this is a strong-growing variety that produces high yields suitable for using fresh in salads or cooking in stir-fries. The leaves of this bunching onion are mid- to dark green and contrast attractively with the white part of the stem.

- suitable for containers
- early spring to midsummer
- some resistance
- fairly hardy
- late spring to fall

'Feast'

This F1 hybrid variety has medium to dark green upright leaves. The bases are a good pure white, and are long and slender. This bunching onion copes well with hot weather, stands well, and is slow to bolt. 'Feast' is resistant to downy mildew.

- suitable for containers
- early spring to midsummer
- some resistance
- fairly hardy
- late spring to fall

Stem
Vegetables

- Asparagus
- Rhubarb
- Celery
- Celeriac
- Florence fennel

ASPARAGUS *Asparagus officinalis*

Asparagus is a valuable crop, yielding succulent produce that is costly to buy, at a time of year when little else is available. It has a reputation for being difficult to grow, but modern high-yielding, high-quality cultivars are available and make success much easier; all-male varieties now dominate, since they produce a greater number of thicker spears. Two years must elapse before the first crop, but the wait is well worth it.

	SPRING	SUMMER	FALL	WINTER
SOW/PLANT				
HARVEST				

SOWING AND PLANTING

Any fertile, well-drained garden soil in full sun will support asparagus. Dig in plenty of well-rotted manure or compost shortly before planting, and consider adding lime to the soil if it is acidic; asparagus does best with a pH between 6.3–7.5.

If you are raising asparagus from seed, sow it indoors in late winter. Sow singly in module trays and keep warm using a heated propagator. The seedlings can be planted out in late spring.

However, most gardeners buy dormant asparagus crowns and plant them directly into the ground in early spring. Dig trenches 8 in (20 cm) deep and incorporate fertilizer into the base. Set the plants in the soil

Spread the roots on the trench base.

in the bottom of the trench. Although close planting is possible, allowing 16 in (40 cm) between crowns and 4 ft (1.2 m) between trenches will give a longer lasting plantation.

CROP CARE

Asparagus plants should be well watered and fed with a balanced fertilizer every spring. Once established, no further

watering is needed, but fertilizer should be applied each year in midsummer after stalks have been harvested. In the fall, the ferny foliage will become strawlike and should be cut down.

HARVESTING

After two years, asparagus will be ready to harvest. In the third year, a light crop is taken in mid-spring, and subsequently full cropping can begin. Use a knife to slice stems free, taking care not to harm emerging spears nearby. Cut the stems 1 in (2.5 cm) below the soil surface when they reach about 5–7 in (13–18 cm) tall.

PESTS AND DISEASES

Asparagus beetle is the only serious pest. Treat infected plants with an appropriate insecticide or by picking off the beetles and larvae. Root diseases sometimes occur; fresh crowns must be planted on a new site. Slugs may also damage emerging spears.

Asparagus beetles strip plant foliage.

'Jersey Knight'

This high-quality, robust, all-male hybrid is reliable and produces good yields of thick but tender spears. The green stems are succulent and numerous, with attractive purple tips. Best-suited to warmer regions, it has good resistance to root diseases.

 unsuitable for containers
early spring
good resistance
hardy
mid-spring to midsummer

'Grolim'

This all-male hybrid produces many stems of exceptional thickness and succulence, with fewer thin stems than other varieties. Cropping peaks early in the season; stems are produced even when closely spaced, making it good for small gardens.

 unsuitable for containers
early spring
poor resistance
hardy
mid-spring to early summer

'Ariane'

This vigorous and reliable all-male hybrid bears purple tips on deep-green stems. The shoots are thick and succulent. It crops early in the picking season when asparagus is most appreciated, and the overall yields are heavy throughout the season.

 unsuitable for containers
early spring
poor resistance
hardy
mid-spring to midsummer

'Connover's Colossal'

Although old-fashioned and consisting of both male and female plants, this variety can give fair yields, especially if you seek out the better strains. Seed is much cheaper than for hybrid types, so this variety is useful where resources are limited.

- unsuitable for containers
- early spring
- poor resistance
- hardy
- mid-sping to midsummer

'Jersey Supreme Hybrid'

This all-male hybrid has proved reliable, giving very good yields of high-quality spears, even in cold regions. Cropping starts early, but yields are high throughout the season. It has good tolerance of cold and of root and foliage diseases.

- unsuitable for containers
- early spring
- good resistance
- hardy
- mid-spring to mid-summer

'Martha Washington'

This old-fashioned, non-hybrid variety has both male and female plants. Its yields and quality are fair, and it has more poor-quality spears than hybrid plants. But, despite this, there are reasons to grow it: seed is cheap and it has a reputation for longevity.

- unsuitable for containers
- early spring
- some resistance
- hardy
- mid-spring to midsummer

'Backlim'

This long-established, all-male hybrid has stood the test of time, giving good yields year after year in a wide range of conditions. Its stems are thick, succulent, and numerous. Most of the stems are ready to harvest later in the season, but yields are high overall.

🗑	unsuitable for containers
🗲	early spring
🕷	some resistance
❄	hardy
🔒	mid-spring to early summer

'Jersey Giant'

This high-quality, all-male hybrid has proved reliable, giving good yields, even in cooler regions. The green stems are thick, succulent, and numerous with attractive purple tips. Cropping begins early and continues over a long period with high yields overall.

🗑	unsuitable for containers
🗲	early spring
🕷	some resistance
❄	hardy
🔒	mid-spring to midsummer

'Purple Pacific'

This non-hybrid variety produces purple stems of good flavor. Color is lost with prolonged cooking, but can be retained by careful steaming or microwave cooking. The tender stems are especially suited to eating raw and are often especially sweet.

🗑	unsuitable for containers
🗲	early spring
🕷	poor resistance
❄	hardy
🔒	mid-spring to midsummer

'Gijnlim'

This long-established, all-male hybrid has proved reliable and will crop well over many years. The mid-green stems are thick, succulent, and numerous, and have pronounced purple tips. Production peaks early in the season, with high yields overall.

 unsuitable for containers

 early spring

 some resistance

hardy

mid-spring to early summer

'Lucullus'

This all-male hybrid has proved reliable over many years in a wide range of gardens. It bears high yields of good-quality spears, with yields peaking later in the season. Arguably, however, it is not in the same class as more modern asparagus cultivars.

 unsuitable for containers

early spring

 some resistance

 hardy

mid-sping to midsummer

'Purple Passion'

This non-hybrid variety has purple stems of good flavor. Color is lost during cooking, but can be retained by careful steaming or microwaving. The tender stems lack string, and are especially suited to eating raw—they can be especially sweet.

 unsuitable for containers

 early spring

 some resistance

 hardy

mid-spring to midsummer

RHUBARB *Rheum x hybridum* syn. *R. cultorum*

Rhubarb is an anomaly; it is a vegetable that is eaten as a fruit, and one that produces plenty of tasty stalks at a time of year when little else is available, especially if "forced." Although it can get by with little care and attention, it repays generous treatment with greater yields of better produce. Unlike most vegetable crops, it is perennial, and can give several years of productive growth before it needs to be replaced.

	SPRING	SUMMER	FALL	WINTER
PLANT				
HARVEST				

PLANTING

Rhubarb prefers an open site and should be planted in soil that has been improved with plenty of manure or other bulky organic matter—it needs soil that will drain well, but not become waterlogged. Additional balanced fertilizer is helpful and should be applied annually in late winter.

It is possible to raise your own rhubarb from seed, but buying a plant, or separating a piece of long root, complete with at least one bud taken from the outside of the parent clump in winter or early spring, is better. Plant out immediately; make sure that the bud is at the same depth as when it was dug out. Allow 36 in (90 cm) space between plants.

Pull stems gently to protect the clump.

CROP CARE

Newly planted rhubarb should be watered during dry spells for the first year. Mulch it with a 3 in (7 cm) layer of organic matter.

FORCING

Forcing your rhubarb results in earlier, sweeter, and more tender stems. Pile organic matter around the forcing container to ensure that no

light can reach the plant. Forced rhubarb should be left for a year or two to recover.

HARVESTING

Do not harvest any rhubarb stems in the first year and only remove a light crop in the second. Full harvests can be taken thereafter for many years. When stems reach a sufficient size, harvest them by grasping the base and pulling the sticks away from the clump, taking care not to snap them. Light crops can be harvested until early summer; heavy crops until late summer.

PESTS AND DISEASES

Rhubarb suffers from few pests but fungal diseases such as honey fungus and crown rot can damage the crowns, particularly if the soil is poorly drained. Both can cause the plant to rot and die, but may not be fatal if you act promptly to remove any diseased parts of the plant. Destroy rather than compost infected material, to reduce the risk of infection spreading.

Viruses are common and any rhubarb that fails to thrive should be replace. Buy healthy new plants mail order or from garden centers.

'Grandad's Favorite'

One of the few rhubarb varieties bred in recent times, this midseason variety has an excellent flavor. It is highly productive, bearing large yields of bright-red stems, and is especially well-suited to producing later crops rather than being forced.

- unsuitable for containers
- winter to early spring
- some resistance
- hardy
- spring to early summer

'Early Champagne'

This long-established and widely grown variety is sold as plants, rather than seed. It produces pink stalks with redder bases. The early stems have good flavor and texture and can be readily forced; they are well-suited to any good garden soil.

- unsuitable for containers
- winter to early spring
- some resistance
- hardy
- spring to early summer

'MacDonald'

This very vigorous rhubarb strain produces large, tender red stalks and crinkled leaves, and has shown resistance to wilt and root rot. Due to its dependable growth and high productivity, it is one of the most common varieties on the market.

- unsuitable for containers
- early spring
- good resistance
- hardy
- spring to summer

'Stein's Champagne'

This long-established rhubarb is suited to all good garden soils. It has the typical 'Champagne' rhubarb attributes of good, deep red color and sweet tender flavor. It is an early variety, so is suitable for both forced and unforced cultivation.

- unsuitable for containers
- winter to early spring
- some resistance
- hardy
- spring to early summer

'Early Champagne'

'Glaskins Perpetual'

This vigorous rhubarb variety has stood the test of time; it is widely grown and sold. It produces long red stems of fair texture and flavor, which are borne over a long cropping period from spring into summer. It is available as plants, but seldom as seed.

- unsuitable for containers
- winter to early spring
- some resistance
- hardy
- spring to early summer

'Chipman's Canada Red'

Brilliant red stems keep their color with cooking, and are sweet and delicious in pies and sauces. This cold-hardy perennial prefers a sunny site with moist, but well-drained soil. In warmer climates it appreciates some shade in the heat of the day.

- unsuitable for containers
- early spring
- some resistance
- hardy
- spring to early summer

'Victoria'

This long-established and widely grown rhubarb is sold as both plants and seed. It produces high yields of late growing stalks with fair texture and flavor. The stems have a greenish tint and are produced for a long period from spring into summer.

- unsuitable for containers
- winter to early spring
- some resistance
- hardy
- spring to early summer

'Crimson Red'

This vigorous, strong-growing rhubarb produces thick, succulent, deep red stems of very good flavor, texture, and appearance. It is well-suited to all climatic zones with cold winters, including areas with very harsh winter weather.

- unsuitable for containers
- winter to early spring
- some resistance
- hardy
- spring to early summer

'Reed's Early Superb'

This strong-growing, vigorous, and long-established rhubarb will thrive in any garden soil and position. It is moderately early and suitable for forcing, but also very attractive when grown outside, producing long red stems of good texture and flavor.

- unsuitable for containers
- winter to early spring
- some resistance
- hardy
- spring to early summer

'Valentine'

Reliable and robust, this very vigorous North American variety will grow well in any good garden soil in all climatic zones with sufficiently cold winters. Stalks are dark red, thick, and succulent, with good flavor. It seldom produces seed stalks.

- unsuitable for containers
- winter to early spring
- some resistance
- hardy
- spring to early summer

'Paragon'

This 19th-century heirloom variety produces mild-flavored, bright red stems and vigorous foliage. Originally from Britain, it is now available only in North America. It is not recommended for forcing, but is hardy and likely to thrive in cold climates.

- unsuitable for containers
- winter to early spring
- some resistance
- hardy
- spring to early summer

'Fulton's Strawberry Surprise'

This long-established, strong-growing cultivar is best-suited for outdoor production and will grow in any good garden soil. If it is left unforced, its bright red stems are especially attractive, and are tender and well-flavored.

- unsuitable for containers
- winter to early spring
- some resistance
- hardy
- spring to early summer

CELERY *Apium graveolens* var. *dulce*

Celery comes in four kinds: self-blanching celery is most common and
should be closely planted in blocks, where the plants shade each other
enough to blanch their stems. Trench celery is grown in trenches and
earthed up as it grows, to give blanched, tender stems that are free
from bitterness. Green celery is bred to be succulent without blanching,
while some celery is grown as a leafy herb, in the same way as parsley.

	SPRING	SUMMER	FALL	WINTER
SOW				
HARVEST				

SOWING

Celery plants flower prematurely
if planted out too early. To prevent
this, planting should be done in
early summer from sowings made
indoors in mid-spring, as the seed
takes a long time to germinate.

Sow seed thinly, barely
covering it with soil, in shallow
pots or module trays. Seedlings
should be grown under cover
until they develop a few leaves
and their roots fill their pots.
Keep them in a moderately
warm environment, such as a
greenhouse, with plenty of light.

Celery does best in soil that
has been enriched with plenty
of organic matter and has been
supplemented with a balanced
fertilizer before planting.
Space trench seedlings 12–18 in

Dig up the plants from midsummer.

(30–45 cm) apart in a prepared
trench; self-blanching and green
types in blocks, spaced 10 in
(25 cm) apart. Allow leaf celery
5 in (13 cm) between plants.

CROP CARE

Water seedlings after planting
and keep them free of weeds.
Water frequently, since tender
stems will not form if the plants
dry out. Add extra fertilizer if

growth slows. Trench celery may require tying together as it forms, to keep the plants free from mud.

HARVESTING

Harvest and trim when the heads are big enough. Water before harvesting for longer storage.

STORING

Trench celery can be left in the ground in mild regions if heads are protected with soil and boards, to exclude rain and frost. Other celery must be harvested when it matures. Kept in the refrigerator, it will store in usable condition for several weeks.

PESTS AND DISEASES

Foliage may be "mined" by celery fly, which cause brown patches on leaves and slow the overall growth. Picking affected leaves before the problem spreads is usually sufficient control.

Celery leaf spot causes small brown rings to appear on leaves—destroy infected plants immediately, since fungicides are seldom available for later control. Plants may also be at risk from foot and root rots, violet root rot, and sclerotina. These diseases have no treatments, so remove and destroy any infected plants.

'Celebrity'

This non-hybrid, self-blanching celery produces pale, slender sticks of celery. It is well-ribbed and succulent, and has exceptional flavor and texture. It resists bolting, making it suitable for summer crops and for indoor growing for winter crops.

🪣	unsuitable for containers
🌱	spring
🕷	some resistance
❄	hardy
🔒	summer

'Tendercrisp'

When conditions are suitable, this tall, green, non-hybrid celery produces large, leafy heads with long stems of good texture and flavor. Although 'Tendercrisp' can be blanched by earthing up or using opaque collars, it is often used unblanched instead.

🪣	unsuitable for containers
🌱	spring
🕷	some resistance
❄	hardy
🔒	summer

'Victoria'

This green hybrid celery produces tall stems with dense, heavy heads. It is vigorous and tolerates a wide range of conditions, maturing early to produce succulent, fleshy stems. It resists bolting and will store in good condition for long periods.

🪣	unsuitable for containers
🌱	spring
🕷	some resistance
❄	hardy
🔒	summer to fall

'Golden Self Blanching'

This traditional, non-hybrid, self-blanching variety produces medium-quality stalks of good texture and flavor. They are thick and wide, but not as long as more modern varieties, and are more variable. It requires no exclusion of light to blanch its stems.

 unsuitable for containers
 spring
 poor resistance
hardy
summer to fall

'Giant Pascal'

This traditional trench celery produces long, crisp stems that can grow up to 2 ft (60 cm) high and 2 in (5 cm) thick. For optimum crispness and mild flavor, grow in rich soil conditions with plenty of water; exclude light to blanch stems.

 unsuitable for containers
spring
 poor resistance
hardy
summer

'Afina'

Although the stems can be eaten, this celery is more commonly grown for its foliage, which can be used fresh or dried; its celery flavor is pronounced. 'Afina' is much less demanding in cultivation conditions than ordinary celery.

 unsuitable for containers
spring
 some resistance
hardy
summer to winter

'Tango'

This non-hybrid, self-blanching celery produces long, bright, succulent stems of very good flavor. It resists bolting and remains in good condition for long periods, even in hot weather. It is relatively slow-growing, however, and is not best-suited to early crops.

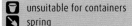 unsuitable for containers
spring
some resistance
hardy
summer to fall

'Octavius'

This hybrid green celery produces medium-green stems that are especially suited to fall cropping. The plant is tall and vigorous and the heads are large and dense; the total yield is very high. 'Octavius' has good flavor and texture.

unsuitable for containers
spring
some resistance
hardy
summer to fall

'Gigante Dorato'

Also known as 'Giant Gilded', this Italian variety is valued for its mild, crisp flavor and the slightly golden color of its stems. Unless the stalks are shielded from the sun for three weeks before harvesting, the stalks will be green.

unsuitable for containers
late spring
no resistance
fairly hardy
late summer

'Green Utah'

This long-established, tall, green-stemmed variety bears crisp, succulent, well-flavored stems in tight hearts that keep well in cool storage. Although more variable and less reliable than modern varieties, it is still valuable. No blanching is required.

- unsuitable for containers
- spring
- poor resistance
- hardy
- summer to fall

'Conquistador'

This widely adapted celery produces crisp, dark green heads with a good tolerance to bolting. Plants perform well under heat and drought stress and in soils of average fertility, but are only slightly resistant to fusarium yellows.

- unsuitable for containers
- late spring
- some resistance
- fairly hardy
- late summer

'Redventure'

This hybrid celery has bold red stems that are much less coarse than traditional red celery. Although not as succulent as self-blanching and green types, it has a robust flavor and texture. It is especially suitable for cooking.

- unsuitable for containers
- spring
- some resistance
- hardy
- summer

CELERIAC *Apium graveolens* var. *rapaceum*

Celeriac is, botanically speaking, very similar to celery but with a swollen lower stem that can be eaten cooked, or grated and eaten raw. The texture of celeriac is similar to that of turnips and its flavor is mild and celerylike. Unlike celery, however, it is lifted in late fall and will store well in frost-free sheds and cellars. It is popular in cooler regions, where celery is easily damaged.

	SPRING	SUMMER	FALL	WINTER
SOW				
HARVEST				

SOWING

Celeriac is tolerant of most locations and should be treated in the same way as celery: enrich the soil with plenty of compost or organic matter, adding general fertilizer shortly before planting. Add lime, too, if the soil is acidic.

Sow seed thinly in shallow pots and barely cover with a layer of soil. Move seedlings into small, individual pots when they have developed three leaves, and place them in moderate warmth in a bright greenhouse or similar environment until the roots have grown to fill the pot. Plants will usually benefit from supplementary fertilizer.

Like celery, celeriac bolts if planted out too early, reducing the crop. To avoid this, plant out

Allow seedlings plenty of space to grow.

greenhouse-grown, mid-spring sowings in early summer.

CROP CARE

Water plants frequently, especially in dry periods, since they must not be allowed to dry out; celeriac is a little more tolerant of dry soil than celery. Apply additional general fertilizer if growth is slow. Any side-shoots or fallen foliage

should be removed, to allow the roots to become smooth and large.

HARVESTING

Roots can be lifted when they are the size of tennis balls, but will go on swelling until early winter.

STORING

Celeriac can be left in the ground over winter in mild regions; pull a layer of soil up over the roots to protect them. In cold areas, dig up the roots, remove the foliage, and store in boxes of sand or soil to prevent the roots from drying out. Roots will remain sound until early spring.

PESTS AND DISEASES

Celeriac is vulnerable to several pests and diseases. The maggots of celery leaf fly mine holes in foliage, creating brown, dry patches and causing the stem to become stringy. Remove and destroy infected leaves and treat with fungicide. Carrot fly is also strongly attracted to celeriac—cover crops with fine, insect-proof mesh or horticultural fleece to prevent them from reaching and mining the roots (see pp.174–5).

Celery leaf spot disease creates brown patches on leaves. Remove and destroy any infected plant material.

'Brilliant'

This excellent celeriac variety produces bold white roots. It responds well to generous feeding and to soils that have been enriched with organic matter, producing a fine texture and flavor. It has good resistance to bolting, and stores well.

	unsuitable for containers
	spring
	poor resistance
	hardy
	summer

'Diamant'

This high-quality celeriac has medium size, slightly flattened white roots. It responds to generous feeding producing bulbs with a fine texture and flavor. It has good resistance to bolting, and stores well.

	unsuitable for containers
	spring
	some resistance
	hardy
	summer

'Giant Prague'

This traditional celeriac has smaller than average white roots. It requires generous feeding and a soil that is enriched with ample organic matter to produce a fine texture and flavor. 'Giant Prague' has fair storage potential.

	unsuitable for containers
	spring
	poor resistance
	hardy
	summer

'Prinz'

This very high-quality variety has excellent early vigor, abundant healthy foliage, and high resistance to bolting. The medium size, slightly flattened roots have good storage potential and an outstanding texture and flavor. It responds well to generous feeding and watering.

 unsuitable for containers

 spring

 some resistance

❄ hardy

🔒 summer

'Monarch'

This high-quality variety has refined, well-finished, bold, white roots and upright deep green foliage. Although remarkable for quality, it is also heavy-yielding and has good storage potential. It has good resistance to bolting.

 unsuitable for containers

 spring

 some resistance

 hardy

🔒 summer

'Mars'

High-quality celeriac has large white roots and upright, deep green, healthy foliage. If well-watered and fed, texture and flavor will be excellent, and roots will last for many months in storage. Good resistance to premature flower production.

 unsuitable for containers

spring

 some resistance

 hardy

🔒 summer

FLORENCE FENNEL

Foeniculum vulgare var. *azoricum*

If you can provide Florence fennel with the conditions it needs it makes a wonderful garden plant—the crisp, swollen stems have a mild aniseed flavor and are good cooked or shredded raw, while the attractive feathery foliage can also be used as a herb. It grows best, and is less likely to bolt, where the weather is cool and nights are mild and short.

	SPRING		SUMMER		FALL		WINTER	
SOW								
HARVEST								

SOWING

Before sowing or planting out, prepare the site by digging in well-rotted manure or compost and adding a balanced fertilizer. Florence fennel prefers well-drained, sandy soil, which may need liming if its pH is too acidic.

It is best to sow seed directly into the ground in early summer, although seedlings can be sown from as early as spring under cover or in a greenhouse, or outside if you choose a bolt-resistant variety and protect it with a cloche or cold frame.

If you are sowing under cover, place three seeds into each small pot or module, and thin out as soon as they are strong enough to be handled. Plant them out as soon as the roots can bind the soil.

Harvest once the bulbs are fully formed.

Plants will need to be spaced about 12 in (30 cm) apart, so if sowing directly into the ground, sow several seeds where each plant is to grow and then thin out the weakest as seedlings develop.

CROP CARE

If plants are subjected to too much heat or too little water they are prone to bolting, so it is essential to give them plenty of

water during dry spells. Their foliage casts little shade to smother weeds, so careful weeding is needed. Earth up around the bulbs as they mature, to whiten them and provide frost protection.

HARVESTING AND STORING

The foliage can be used as a herb, in moderation, at any time. Bulbs will be big enough to harvest from early to late fall; lift them and discard unwanted foliage. Bulbs will stand in good condition for some weeks if earthed up outdoors or kept in the salad crisper of the refrigerator.

PESTS AND DISEASES

Generally, fennel has no significant pests or diseases and bolting is the most likely problem. Discourage this by sowing in summer when days are long and nights are mild, and by ensuring that the soil does not dry out. Bolt-resistant varieties are available.

One fungus that sometimes affects fennel is rhizoctonia, which stunts plant growth and causes colorful sores on both the bulb and the stem. This disease has no cure, so dig up and destroy any infected plants and practice crop rotation in future years.

'Perfection'

This selected, non-hybrid cultivar has larger bulbs and better resistance to bolting than older types. It is potentially suitable for sowing from spring until fall, but it may need protection in cooler regions that are prone to cold springs and short summers.

- suitable for containers
- spring to summer
- some resistance
- hardy
- late summer to early winter

'Orion F1'

This high-yielding F1 hybrid variety produces large, uniform, pure white bulbs with excellent flavor and crispness. It is excellent used in cooking, or for eating raw in salads. The plants are resistant to bolting, so can be sown early in the season.

- suitable for containers
- spring to summer
- some resistance
- hardy
- late summer to early winter

'Di Firenze'

This Italian variety produces large, crisp, white bulbs, and attractive, mid-green, feathery foliage. The fennel has a tasty, aniseed flavor, and is good used in cooking. It does not have good resistance to bolting, so does best in warm regions.

- suitable for containers
- spring to summer
- some resistance
- hardy
- late summer to early winter

'Zefa Fino'

This long-established Swiss, non-hybrid variety matures fast, producing quick-swelling, large, white bulbs. The bulbs are a uniform, rounded shape, and of excellent quality. It is especially well-suited to summer sowing in areas with cooler conditions, and has some resistance to bolting.

- suitable for containers
- spring to summer
- some resistance
- hardy
- late summer to early winter

'Victorio'

Also known as 'Victoria', this hybrid fennel has strong vigor, producing robust foliage and a heavy crop of large, dense, quick-maturing fennel. The bulbs are of good quality and have a green tinge. It is well-suited to cooler regions for summer sowing.

- suitable for containers
- spring to summer
- some resistance
- hardy
- late summer to early winter

'Finale'

This non-hybrid fennel produces strong, feathery foliage and large, heavy, rounded bulbs with good white color. It has good bolt resistance so can be sown early, and is reliable from mid- to late summer, even in cooler regions.

- suitable for containers
- spring to summer
- some resistance
- hardy
- late summer to early winter

Peas and Beans

- Peas
- Runner beans
- Green beans
- Fava beans
- Beans for drying

PEAS *Pisum sativum*

Harvested and eaten fresh, peas are a real sweet treat. Most peas will need to be shelled, but some, such as snow peas and sugar peas (also known as mangetouts) are edible-podded and can be eaten whole. Both are delicious eaten raw or cooked, and many varieties are grown for their edible pea shoots, which can be added to salads. Easy to grow, peas will also brighten up the garden with an attractive display of flowers.

	SPRING	SUMMER	FALL	WINTER
SOW/PLANT				
HARVEST				

SOWING

Dig in well-rotted manure or compost in the fall before sowing. Pea roots are nitrogen-fixing; they convert nitrogen from the air and store it in nodules on their roots. For this reason, they don't need any extra nitrogenous fertilizer. Peas prefer a sunny, moist site that will not get too hot or become waterlogged. A slightly alkaline pH is ideal.

Sow seed any time from late winter onward—seedlings can be started indoors and and then transplanted when the soil warms up, or sown directly in the ground, although seedlings will need protection from frost with a cloche or cold frame. In some regions, seed can be

Plant out strong seedlings in springtime.

sown successively through spring until midsummer. Sow at a depth of 1.5–2 in (4–5 cm); leave at least a 2 in (5 cm) space between plants. Sow in single or double rows.

CROP CARE

Most peas will require at least a little support, so construct a framework for them using canes or netting—this will keep them upright and make the best use

of the space available. Peas are attractive to birds, so use netting to keep them at bay. Keep well-watered, ensuring that peas get plenty of water when in flower and when pods are swelling.

HARVESTING

Peas should be ready to harvest in early summer, within two to three months of sowing. Once the first pods are ready, pinch out the top growing shoots of each plant to encourage more pods to develop. Shoots can also be harvested and eaten. Peas can be stored for a short while, but taste sweetest when fresh.

PESTS AND DISEASES

Slugs and snails are troublesome on young plants and birds on older plants. Protect with netting. To prevent a soil buildup of diseases such as pea leaf and pod spot or downy mildew, ensure that you practice crop rotation.

Downy mildew (left) shrivels leaves. Pea moths (right) devour young peas.

'Sugar Snap'

This variety bears a large crop of delicious pods on vigorous growth, so needs good support. Pick pods early when crisp and succulent, so that they can be added to salads and stir-fries. The young shoots and new leaves at the tip ends are also very tasty.

🪣	unsuitable for containers
🌱	mid- to late spring
🐛	poor resistance
❄️	not hardy
🔒	late summer to early fall

'Sugar Ann'

This very popular sugar snap variety produces a large crop of pale green, delicious, sweet pods. Its strong vines and medium height means that plants don't need supporting. The peas can be eaten raw or can be used in stir-fries or risottos.

🪣	unsuitable for containers
🌱	mid- to late spring
🐛	some resistance
❄️	not hardy
🔒	late summer to early fall

'Oregon Sugar Pod'

This first-rate variety is well-known and widely sold. It is popular for its heavy crops of medium-length, broad, flat, very tasty pods, which keep appearing over a long period. Although they can become larger, pick at 3 in (7.5 cm), before they get stringy.

🪣	unsuitable for containers
🌱	mid- to late spring
🐛	some resistance
❄️	not hardy
🔒	late summer to early fall

'Ambassador'

This is a maincrop pea that is grown for its medium-sized pods with sweet, tender peas. The shoots and side shoots can also be used in salads. Keep picking from the bottom of the plant, working up, and use promptly for the maximum flavor.

 unsuitable for containers
early to mid-spring
poor resistance
not hardy
midsummer to late summer

'Cascadia'

This virus-resistant snap pea produces an abundance of edible-podded peas on 32-in (81-cm) vines. The juicy, stringless, 3-in (7.5-cm) pods are ready to harvest 60 days from sowing. Vines can be trellised or staked between plants.

 unsuitable for containers
early spring
excellent resistance
fairly hardy
late spring to early summer

'Mammoth Melting'

Trellis this 4–6-ft (1.2–1.8-m) heirloom for high yields of 5-in (13-cm) flat, edible pods that remain tender even when large, and are delicious fresh or stir-fried. Plants are resistant to fusarium wilt and bear white blossoms as pretty as cut flowers.

 unsuitable for containers
early spring
some resistance
fairly hardy
late spring to early summer

'Waverex'

This first-rate variety produces tiny, sweet-tasting peas that appear on 2-ft (60-cm) tall plants. Cook them quickly and gently to preserve their texture and flavor, and use them in risottos, salads, and stews. They also make a delicious pea soup, with stock, garlic, and butter.

- unsuitable for containers
- mid- to late spring
- poor resistance
- not hardy
- late summer to early fall

'Maestro'

'Maestro' bears 4.5-in (11-cm) pods filled with up to 10 tender peas over an extended period, beginning 60 days after sowing. The compact, 2-ft (60-cm) vines are resistant to pea enation mosaic virus and powdery mildew, ensuring a healthy harvest.

- suitable for containers
- early spring
- excellent resistance
- fairly hardy
- late spring to early summer

'Dakota'

This early-maturing dwarf pea produces slender pods borne doubly at the nodes, each with six or more easy-to-shell peas. The mildew-resistant 2-ft (60-cm) vines produce in a concentrated period; it is a good choice for gardeners wanting to preserve their harvest.

- unsuitable for containers
- early spring
- good resistance
- fairly hardy
- late spring to early summer

'Douce Provence'

This French first early variety grows to around 30 in (75 cm) high, producing a large crop of particularly sweet-tasting, tender peas. Being hardy, it can be sown outside in late fall for an early summer crop, or the following spring when the soil has warmed up.

	unsuitable for containers
	mid-fall or late spring
	poor resistance
	hardy
	early summer to early fall

'Canoe'

A second early, this variety is grown because it bears more peas per pod than most: a maximum of 12. It also produces a heavy crop of pods, each slightly curved and pointed like a canoe. When grown in blocks the plants are almost self-supporting.

	unsuitable for containers
	early to mid-spring
	poor resistance
	not hardy
	early to late summer

'Green Arrow'

These vigorous, mildew- and wilt-resistant plants can grow up to 2–2.5-ft (60–76-cm) and bear heavy yields of slim pods, each containing up to 11 petite peas. 'Green Arrow' is a late-maturing shelling pea; to maximize yields it needs an early start.

	unsuitable for containers
	early spring
	good resistance
	fairly hardy
	late spring to early summer

RUNNER BEANS *Phaseolus coccineus*

Attractive and easy to grow, runner beans are used by gardeners in the US mainly for ornamental purposes. In Europe, however, they are a delicious garden staple. Most varieties will grow very tall and add structure and interest to your garden. They will also produce an abundance of beautiful red, white, or bi-colored flowers. Dwarf varieties are also available, and beans can be found in a range of colors.

	SPRING	SUMMER	FALL	WINTER
SOW/PLANT				
HARVEST				

SOWING

Site your runner beans carefully: most will grow fairly tall and can become top-heavy, so give them plenty of support and a sheltered location to protect them from strong winds. They thrive in deep, fertile soil, so dig in some well-rotted manure or compost in the fall before planting the following spring. Also, be sure not to plant them where peas or beans have grown in the last two years.

Sow seed in mid-spring for a midsummer crop, or sow in midsummer for an fall crop. If the weather is cold, warm up the soil with a cold frame or cloche. Construct the supports for your beans; use bamboo canes to create teepees or double rows of supports, and sow seed

Train bean seedlings up bamboo supports.

at a depth of 2 in (5 cm) at the base of each cane. Seed can be sown under cover before planting out, but bear in mind that roots will grow deep, so use long paper "tube pots" that can be planted straight into the ground.

CROP CARE

Train the young seedlings around the canes, tying them in with string if necessary. Once plants

reach the top of the supports, pinch out the growing tips. In order to produce pods, it is crucial that beans not be allowed to dry out once pollinated, so mulch around the bases of the plants, and water frequently.

HARVESTING

If beans are left too long they will become tough and stringy, so harvest when they are still young and tender; this may be up to two or three times a week. This will also encourage the plants to produce more pods. Beans do not store long, but seeds can be stored for future crops.

PESTS AND DISEASES

Discourage the diseases that affect runner beans, such as halo blight and foot and root rot, by practicing careful crop rotation—plant where root crops have grown the previous year. Halo blight causes dark spots ringed with yellow "haloes" on leaves. Remove and destroy any infected plants.

Black bean aphids are strongly attracted to the growing tips, so pinch these out when plants have reached full height. Bad infestations may need treating with an insecticide. Mice may eat seed sown in the soil.

'Painted Lady'

An old variety, 'Painted Lady' produces a beautiful display of both red and white flowers, and makes a striking feature in ornamental beds and borders. The flowers are followed by large, medium length pods that have a fine flavor and tender texture.

 unsuitable for containers
late spring to early summer
poor resistance
not hardy
midsummer to mid-fall

'Titan'

This variety is very reliable, giving strong, vigorous growth, a good show of flowers, and a crop of long, tasty pods. Keep the plants well-watered during dry periods, and pick runner beans regularly to encourage more pods to develop.

 unsuitable for containers
late spring to early summer
some resistance
not hardy
midsummer to mid-fall

'Wisley Magic'

Although its bright red flowers are very attractive to birds, 'Wisley Magic' still produces a huge, flavorful crop of 15-in (38-cm) long, straight, smooth pods from the end of summer through into fall. It has won awards for its heavy yields.

 unsuitable for containers
late spring to early summer
some resistance
not hardy
midsummer to mid-fall

'Polestar'

This attractive red-flowering variety produces a good show of attractive summer flowers, which are eye-catching in beds and borders. It then produces a good yield of 10-in (25-cm) long, flavorful pods. It is vigorous, and will easily reach the top of a 5.5 ft (1.7 m) high support.

 unsuitable for containers
 late spring to early summer
 poor resistance
 not hardy
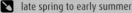 midsummer to mid-fall

'Flare'

This red-flowering variety is well-regarded for its high yields of straight, narrow, and virtually stringless pods that can reach up to 12 in (30 cm) in length. It is an attractive plant, which makes it a good addition to the ornamental garden.

 unsuitable for containers
late spring to early summer
some resistance
not hardy
 midsummer to mid-fall

'Achievement'

This improved, very popular variety bears an abundance of red flowers that are followed by tasty beans in long, straight pods. It produces excellent results for the kitchen and show bench. Pick regularly, before the pods mature, for continuous flowering.

 unsuitable for containers
 late spring to early summer
some resistance
not hardy
 midsummer to mid-fall

'White Lady'

This excellent runner bean produces vigorous growth and a multitude of white summer flowers that are largely ignored by birds; it will need a sturdy support. The heavy crop develops over a long period, well into fall, and the long pods are smooth, fleshy, and stringless.

- unsuitable for containers
- late spring to early summer
- some resistance
- not hardy
- midsummer to mid-fall

'White Apollo'

This vigorous, prolific variety produces long, straight, stringless pods, up to 14 in (36 cm) in length, which emerge over a long cropping season. The beans are flavorful and excellent for cooking. Its pretty white flowers are largely ignored by birds.

- unsuitable for containers
- late spring to early summer
- some resistance
- not hardy
- midsummer to mid-fall

'Aintree'

This red-flowering variety produces long, very slender, smooth, flavorful pods, which are stringless if picked young. It is a good choice in regions with high summer temperatures, and looks striking when grown beside a white-flowering variety.

- unsuitable for containers
- late spring to early summer
- some resistance
- not hardy
- midsummer to mid-fall

'Red Rum'

This very reliable variety is highly rated because the plants generate showy red flowers and a large crop of stringless, flavorful pods, even in adverse weather. The pods are straight, fleshy, and should be harvested when they grow to about 9 in (23 cm).

- 🪣 unsuitable for containers
- 🌱 late spring to early summer
- 🕷 some resistance
- ❄ not hardy
- 🔒 midsummer to mid-fall

'Desiree'

This outstanding bean has many attributes: its vigorous growth generates about 40 flavorful, 12-in (30-cm) long, broad, stringless pods per plant. Its white flowers are largely untouched by birds, and it is also very productive, even through long, dry summers.

- 🪣 unsuitable for containers
- 🌱 late spring to early summer
- 🕷 poor resistance
- ❄ not hardy
- 🔒 midsummer to mid-fall

'Scarlet Runner'

Scarlet runner bean vines quickly climb 12–15 ft (3.7–4.6 m) and are grown mainly for their beautiful flaming red flowers, which attract hummingbirds. The flowers are edible, and the green pods, when picked at a tender 3–4 in (7.5–10 cm), are delicious.

- 🪣 unsuitable for containers
- 🌱 late spring
- 🕷 poor resistance
- ❄ not hardy
- 🔒 mid- to late summer

'Enorma'

This heavy-cropping variety produces runner beans that can reach up to 18 in (46 cm) in length. They are highly flavorful and will remain crisp and tender even when mature. The plants have good vigor and need a strong support system to thrive.

- unsuitable for containers
- late spring to early summer
- some resistance
- not hardy
- midsummer to mid-fall

'Celebration'

This early-cropping variety is highly prized for its abundance of delicate, ornamental, pale salmon-pink colored flowers. These are followed by high yields of straight, smooth, fleshy pods, containing numerous flavorful beans.

- unsuitable for containers
- late spring to early summer
- some resistance
- not hardy
- midsummer to mid-fall

'Lady Di'

This variety will regularly produce good crops of showy, red flowers followed by 12-in (30-cm) long, dark green, stringless pods, which are borne over a prolonged season. The beans have a good flavor and are excellent for exhibitions.

- unsuitable for containers
- late spring to early summer
- some resistance
- not hardy
- midsummer to mid-fall

'St. George'

This early-cropping variety bears numerous bi-colored red and white flowers, followed by a large crop of juicy, crisp pods. It has won awards for its heavy yields. It makes a flamboyant feature in beds or borders when grown up strong supports.

 unsuitable for containers
late spring to early summer
poor resistance
not hardy
midsummer to mid-fall

'Scarlet Empire'

This improved version of 'Scarlet Emperor' has higher levels of disease resistance, and is grown for its high yields of narrow, stringless pods, which grow to about 12 in (30 cm) long with good flavor. Plants are vigorous and will do well from early sowings.

 unsuitable for containers
late spring to early summer
poor resistance
not hardy
midsummer to mid-fall

'Summer Medley'

This variety puts on a colorful show with a lively mix of red, white, and pink flowers. The mid-green runner beans are borne over a long cropping season, and have a good flavor and texture. The plants are often grown as ornamentals.

 unsuitable for containers
late spring to early summer
poor resistance
not hardy
midsummer to mid-fall

GREEN BEANS *Phaseolus vulgaris*

Call them what you like: snap, string, French, wax, borlotti, cranberry, Kenya, or flageolet, Green beans are delicious eaten when pods are young and fresh, eaten podded like peas, or grown to produce a crop of dry beans. Custom choose your favorite—green beans generally have a bush or climbing habit, and are available in a wide variety of colors, from yellow, gold, and purple to multicolored or traditional green.

	SPRING	SUMMER	FALL	WINTER
SOW/PLANT				
HARVEST				

SOWING

Green beans like a sheltered, warm site; frost will kill them, and climbing varieties will need protection from the wind. Dig in well-rotted manure or compost in the fall before sowing. Green beans need a moisture-retentive, fertile soil, but do not usually need nitrogenous fertilizer, since their roots fix and store nitrogen in the soil.

Sow beans any time from early spring onward, depending on the weather in your region. If starting indoors, plant seed in extra-deep multipacks or individual pots, at a depth of 2 in (5 cm). Harden off; plant out when seedlings have reached 3 in (8 cm), and the soil has warmed up. Alternatively, wait until the last frosts have passed,

Sow three seeds to a pot in early spring.

and sow seed directly into the ground at a depth of 2 in (5 cm). Construct bamboo cane supports for climbing varieties, and sow or plant at the bottom of each cane.

CROP CARE

Mulch well around seedlings and water regularly; ensure that plants do not dry out once their flowers appear. Bush varieties will become quite top-heavy, so

support them with twigs or short canes, and earth them up to give stability. Guide climbers up their supports and pinch out growing tips when they reach the top.

HARVESTING

Harvest once pods are large enough for use and eat while they are still young and tender. The more pods you pick, the more are produced, so check plants every few days for new growth. If beans are grown for drying, leave them on the plant until they dry out and the seed pods rattle. Green beans can also be frozen for later use.

PESTS AND DISEASES

Protect seedlings against slugs and snails, and be wary of bean beetles and black bean aphids, which will target leaves and young pods. Discourage diseases such as halo blight and fusarium rot by practicing crop rotation.

Bean seed maggots attack germinating seeds—protect by sowing under cover.

'Golddukat'

The long, slightly curved, pale-yellow pods of this attractive early variety are borne in very high yields, over a long harvesting season. The pods are stringless and tender, with a good flavor. The plants look striking when grown next to a dark-green variety.

 suitable for containers
 late spring to midsummer
some resistance
not hardy
 early summer to mid-fall

'Blue Lake 274'

Developed in 1961, this firm, tender bean is a favorite of gardeners. Bushy, disease-resistant plants produce heavy yields of 6-in (15-cm) pods that are ready to pick two months after sowing. The quality beans are great for freezing and canning.

suitable for containers
late spring to midsummer
good resistance
not hardy
midsummer to fall

'Tavera'

These extra-slender, dark-green filet beans should be picked at 4–5 in (10–13 cm), when they are exceptionally tender and perfect for green bean salads. 'Tavera' plants are compact and high yielding, and resistant to anthracnose and mosaic virus.

suitable for containers
late spring to midsummer
good resistance
not hardy
midsummer to fall

'Jade'

Resistant to multiple viruses and tolerant of some strains of rust, 'Jade' has a vigorous upright habit and produces large yields of straight, slender, dark-green pods. The harvest often extends later in the season than it does for other bean varieties.

 suitable for containers
late spring to midsummer
excellent resistance
not hardy
midsummer to fall

'Carson'

Highly resistant to bean mosaic virus, and tolerant of bacterial brown spot, 'Carson' delivers impressive yields of fancy, slim, yellow wax beans over a long period. The gourmet-quality pods are best when harvested young, usually around 5.5 in (14 cm) in length.

 suitable for containers
late spring to midsummer
good resistance
not hardy
midsummer to fall

'Provider'

This adaptable, early bush bean germinates well in cool soil, and its resistance to multiple diseases helps it to perform well in adverse conditions. Its very high yields of tender 5.5-in- (14-cm-) long pods are ready to harvest in just 50 days.

suitable for containers
late spring to midsummer
excellent resistance
not hardy
midsummer to fall

'Dragon Tongue'

This dual-purpose bush bean produces beautiful yellow pods streaked with purple, which can be picked when small and tender or left to mature until the beans dry to a mottled light brown inside the pods. The crisp, juicy, young pods are popular with chefs.

 suitable for containers
 late spring to midsummer
poor resistance
not hardy
 midsummer to fall

'Safari'

The 18-in (46-cm) high, upright growth of this variety makes for easy picking. "Safari" is also suited to growing in containers. The fairly short, stringless pods have a good flavor and texture, although yields can be slightly variable. For the best results, cook quickly to preserve the flavor of the beans.

- suitable for containers
- late spring to midsummer
- some resistance
- not hardy
- midsummer to mid-fall

'Maxibel'

Gourmet-quality, dark green, filet beans average a straight, slender 6–8 in (15–20 cm) and have excellent flavor. The 2-ft (60-cm) plants are resistant to anthracnose and mosaic virus, and the clusters of pencil-thin beans are easy to hand pick.

- suitable for containers
- late spring to midsummer
- good resistance
- not hardy
- midsummer to fall

'Royal Burgundy'

Erect, very attractive 'Royal Burgundy' plants are resistant to white mold and mosaic virus, and perform well in cool weather. They produce gorgeous, glossy purple 5–6-in (13–15-cm) pods that turn dark green when cooked.

- suitable for containers
- late spring to midsummer
- good resistance
- not hardy
- midsummer to fall

'Speedy'

As the name implies, everything about this variety is a little quicker than the average, with early growth and quick emergence of the sweet-tasting, small pods, sometimes in as little as just seven weeks. Either pick for flavorful young beans for fresh eating or dry them for later use.

 suitable for containers
 late spring to midsummer
 poor resistance
 not hardy
 early/midsummer to mid-fall

'Derby'

These medium-dark green beans are at their best when harvested at 5–6 in (13–15 cm), but stay tender even when slightly longer. Strong growth, resistance to bean mosaic virus, early maturation, and prolific yields make 'Derby' an excellent home garden choice.

suitable for containers
late spring to midsummer
good resistance
not hardy
midsummer to fall

'Roc d'Or'

This classic tender, crisp, golden yellow bean is excellent for fresh eating and preserving. 'Roc d'Or' produces long, 6–9-in (15–23-cm) pods with a delicious buttery flavor. As with all bush beans, successive sowings will provide a continuous harvest.

 suitable for containers
 late spring to midsummer
 some resistance
 not hardy
midsummer to fall

'Goldfield'

This climbing French variety puts on an attractive show with its dangling array of yellow pods, and is worth growing in the flower border as it makes a strong focal point. The tasty pods are flat, stringless, and flavorful, and are borne over a long cropping period.

🪣	unsuitable for containers
🌱	late spring to midsummer
🕷	poor resistance
❄	not hardy
🔒	midsummer to mid-fall

'Kentucky Wonder'

This heirloom pole bean, grown by gardeners for over 100 years, produces generous yields of long, round, slightly curved pods beginning about 67 days after sowing. The vigorous vines are resistant to rust and successful in many growing conditions.

🪣	unsuitable for containers
🌱	late spring to early summer
🕷	some resistance
❄	not hardy
🔒	late summer to fall

'Helda'

Growing to 8 ft (2.4 m), 'Helda' begins producing stringless, flat-sided, 9-in (23-cm) pods just two months after sowing, and continues all summer if they are harvested regularly. The vine shows good resistance to Common Mosaic Virus.

🪣	unsuitable for containers
🌱	late spring to early summer
🕷	some resistance
❄	not hardy
🔒	midsummer to fall

'Romano'

This reliable variety produces wide stringless bean pods with what many consider the classic Italian flavor. A favorite for generations, 'Romano' produces a continuous harvest when young pods are picked regularly. Shelled mature brown beans have a delicate flavor.

- unsuitable for containers
- late spring to early summer
- some resistance
- not hardy
- late summer to fall

'Trionfo Violetto'

As ornamental as it is tasty, this Italian heirloom sports lavender flowers and purple-streaked foliage along with its slender purple pods. The gourmet-quality beans are at their tender best when harvested at 6 in (15 cm) in length, and pencil-thin.

- unsuitable for containers
- late spring to early summer
- poor resistance
- not hardy
- late summer to fall

'Kentucky Blue'

Bred for multiple disease resistances, 'Kentucky Blue' is a gardeners' favorite because of its reliable and abundant yields of straight, dark-green pods. Bean pods can be harvested at 9 in (23 cm); they are most flavorful at 6–7 in (15–18 cm).

- unsuitable for containers
- late spring to early summer
- good resistance
- not hardy
- midsummer to fall

'Fortex'

'Fortex' filet beans can be harvested at 6 in (15 cm), but are tender and sweet even at 11 in (28 cm). This productive, disease-resistant climbing bean yields stringless pods about 70 days after sowing, and continues to produce for a long period.

- unsuitable for containers
- late spring to early summer
- good resistance
- not hardy
- late summer to fall

FAVA BEANS *Vicia faba*

Eat homegrown favas, also know as broad beans, as soon as possible after harvesting, since this is when they are at their sweetest and most delicious, beating any store-bought version hands down. Or, try picking while pods are very young and tender and cooking them whole or eating in salads. Dwarf varieties can be grown in containers on a patio or in small gardens and their beautifully scented flowers will attract bees.

	SPRING	SUMMER	FALL	WINTER
SOW/PLANT				
HARVEST				

SOWING

Dig in plenty of well-rotted manure or compost in the fall before sowing—fava beans will probably not need any extra fertilizer, since nodules on their roots fix and store nitrogen in the soil. They prefer well-drained, fertile soil, and taller varieties will appreciate some shelter. Plant where root crops have previously grown.

Seed can be sown directly in the ground and protected from frost, if necessary, or it can be sown in pots and transplanted later. Sow at a depth of 2 in (5 cm), leaving 6 in (15 cm) between plants and 24 in (60 cm) between rows. In warm-winter areas, favas can be fall-sown; otherwise, spring seeding will produce a summer harvest.

Create deep planting holes with a dibber.

CROP CARE

Construct supports for taller varieties using bamboo canes. Dwarf varieties may need some support or earthing up as they develop and become top-heavy. Use sticks or canes to prevent dwarf varieties from trailing on the ground, where they will be at greater risk from pests. Mulch well around plants and ensure that they are kept well-watered.

As soon as tiny seed pods begin to appear, pinch out the plants' growing tips—this encourages the plant to channel its energy into developing pods, and will also help to discourage attack from black bean aphid.

HARVESTING

Young pods can be cooked and eaten whole, but the fava beans themselves are ready to harvest in about three to four months, once they can be felt through their pods. Harvest from the bottom of the plant first. Do not leave them on the plant too long or they will become tough.

PESTS AND DISEASES

Use netting if attacks from birds and mice are particularly bad, and spray with a pyrethroid insecticide before the plant flowers to deter black bean aphids. Broadbean weevils may also be a problem and will damage pods.

Black bean aphids distort leaves.

'The Sutton'

This is a bush fava bean (also called broad bean) that can be repeat-sown outdoors in spring, and under cloches during fall and winter, to give a sustained harvest. It is a good choice for smaller gardens and exposed sites. Pick frequently; this variety is good for freezing.

- suitable for containers
- spring or fall
- some resistance
- hardy
- late spring to fall

'Express'

This is one of the quickest varieties to mature and a good choice for a second sowing in spring. It produces a heavy crop of greenish-white beans that are ready in time for summer. They can be frozen, and will still be tender when defrosted.

- unsuitable for containers
- mid- to late fall
- some resistance
- hardy
- late spring

'Extra Precoce Bianco'

This fava bean variety yields cylindrical pods containing six to seven rounded white beans. 'Extra Precoce Bianco' is an earlier producer than most varieties, and a good choice for areas that do not experience long stretches of cool spring temperatures.

- unsuitable for containers
- early spring
- poor resistance
- fairly hardy
- early summer

'Bunyard's Exhibition'

This traditional variety gives a reliable crop of large, tasty beans, producing up to nine per pod. It is a tall plant, growing to 4.5 ft (1.4 m), and needs support as it grows. Pinch out the tips to restrict their height on smaller plots or in exposed regions.

 unsuitable for containers
 spring or fall
some resistance
hardy
late spring to fall

'Jubilee Hysor'

This early variety gives an excellent crop of pods filled with six to eight tasty, light-green beans. It is quick to mature from a spring sowing, or if raised earlier under a cloche, which gives ample time for further sowings and late summer crops.

 unsuitable for containers
late winter to late spring
some resistance
fairly hardy
early to late summer

'Windsor'

Plant in very early spring, or in fall in Southern regions, for a summer harvest of flat, light-green beans about the size of large limas, as these beans require cool temperatures. The upright, non-branching plants stand 4 ft (1.2 m) tall.

 unsuitable for containers
 early spring
 poor resistance
 fairly hardy
early summer

BEANS FOR DRYING *various*

Growing beans for drying means that you can enjoy these nutritious vegetables long after the summer crops of fresh beans are over. There is no special technique; you simply leave your beans to dry on the plant until the end of their growing season. Once harvested, they take up little storage space and will keep for several months. Easily grown varieties suitable for drying include lima, cranberry, and kidney beans.

	SPRING	SUMMER	FALL	WINTER
SOW/PLANT				
HARVEST				

SOWING

Beans need full sun and warmth, so delay spring sowing outside until the minimum temperature is around 54°F (12°C). Otherwise, start the seeds off indoors and plant out seedlings only when there is no danger of late frosts. Work plenty of well-rotted compost into the soil before sowing or planting out.

Drying beans come in both bush and climbing varieties. If you are growing bush beans, sow the seeds approximately 2 in (5 cm) apart in staggered rows.

For climbers, make a row of canes or poles, or a teepee, for the plants to scramble up; sow a couple of seeds at the base of each cane, allowing about 12 in (30 cm) space between each plant.

Construct netting for drying beans outside.

CROP CARE

Unless conditions are very dry, there is no need to water your beans until the first flowers appear. Then water generously and regularly, never allowing the soil to dry out completely.

Bush beans may need short supporting canes as they grow. Climbing beans usually twine around their supports without needing to be tied in.

HARVESTING

Beans for drying will be ready to harvest once the bean pods have withered and the plants are starting to shed their leaves. If the pods are completely dry, you can shell the beans as soon as you pick them. In a particularly wet season, leave the pods to dry in a well-aired, rodent-free place before removing the beans.

STORING

Place the shelled beans in an airtight container and use as required. If stored in a cool, dry place, they should keep for several months.

PESTS AND DISEASES

Slugs and snails are among the enemies of emerging bean seedlings because they eat the tender tips. To deter them, set up beer traps around your plot to attract them away from the developing plants, or use diatomaceious earth (DE), grit, or a line of copper tape as a barrier. Pick them off by hand as you spot them. Birds may target pods, so construct netting to deter them. In summer, bean beetles and black bean aphids may skeletonize or wither leaves; spray with an appropriate control or wash off and hand-pick the pests.

'Lingua di Fuoco'

The borlotti, Italian "tongue of fire" takes on a spectacular red-splashed appearance as the pale green pods ripen, although it disappears on cooking. The young pods can be eaten as flageolets or the seeds can be left to fully mature for use as haricot beans.

 suitable for containers
late spring to early summer
good resistance
not hardy
midsummer to early fall

Cannellini Beans

This is a popular Italian bean that has a kidney shape with slightly squared-off ends and a creamy-white color. When cooked, they have a fluffy texture and a nutty, mild flavor. Harvest when the pods turn pale yellow.

 suitable for containers
late spring to midsummer
good resistance
not hardy
early fall

Kidney Beans

As the name suggests, these beans have a distinct kidney shape. The most popularly used variety is a dark-red color with a soft, creamy flesh. They need to be cooked well before eating to destroy the toxins that are in their skins.

 suitable for containers
late spring
good resistance
not hardy
midsummer

'Blue Lake'

This traditional, dual-purpose variety is a climbing bean, bearing long, round, stringless, green pods that are tender and have a characteristic French-bean flavor when eaten young. When left until the end of the season, the white seeds can be dried and used as haricots.

🗑	suitable for containers
🌙	late spring to early summer
🕷	good resistance
❄	not hardy
🔒	midsummer to early fall

'Supremo'

This is a dual-purpose French variety that bears kidney-shaped borlotti beans. Although it is only a dwarf bush, it produces heavy yields of good-quality pods and beans, both of which are a cream color, and flecked with red.

🗑	suitable for containers
🌙	late spring to early summer
🕷	good resistance
❄	not hardy
🔒	midsummer to early fall

Lima Beans

Part of the kidney bean family, these are available as large or baby types (and include "butter beans"). All have a buttery texture and delicate flavor. Harvest in the late summer or the fall for fresh eating or for drying.

🗑	suitable for containers
🌙	late spring
🕷	good resistance
❄	not hardy
🔒	late summer to early fall

'Goldfield'

This attractive variety bears flat, stringless, yellow pods, up to 11 in (28 cm) in length, which dangle from the bushy plants. Harvesting can last for many weeks if the beans are picked regularly. The pods can be eaten in salads or the beans dried as haricots.

- suitable for containers
- late spring to midsummer
- poor resistance
- not hardy
- midsummer to mid-fall

'Rattlesnake'

Dark green 'Rattlesnake' bean pods have purple streaks when fresh, but the color fades with cooking. The pods are best picked young, when they are practically stringless, but can also be left to mature, and shelled for use as dried beans. Their flavor is excellent, both green and dry.

- unsuitable for containers
- late spring to early summer
- poor resistance
- not hardy
- late summer to fall

Lablab Beans

A dual-purpose plant, this ornamental climber also produces edible pods. Known as the hyacinth bean, in warm temperatures it bears fragrant, bi-colored pink flowers that precede brown seed pods. Boil harvested beans before eating.

- suitable for containers
- early summer
- good resistance
- not hardy
- late summer to early fall

'Yin Yang'

This dwarf plant produces high yields of dual-purpose kidney beans. The green pods can be eaten when young and tender or left to mature for drying. The mild beans have a black and white pattern reminiscent of the Chinese Yin Yang symbol.

- suitable for containers
- late spring to midsummer
- good resistance
- not hardy
- midsummer to mid-fall

Soybeans

Hailed as the new "super food," soybeans are a highly nutritious bean that can be eaten hot or cold. The short pods contain two or three beans each and are ready for harvesting when the leaves have fallen and the pods are dried up. They are a suitable container crop.

 suitable for containers
late spring to midsummer
good resistance
not hardy
late summer to early fall

'Solista'

This Italian, climbing, green bean bears heavy yields of pods all the way up the plant. The kidney-shaped, maroon-speckled, white beans have a creamy texture and a sweet flavor; they can be eaten fresh or left to mature for drying.

suitable for containers
late spring to early summer
good resistance
not hardy
mid- to late summer

Southern Peas

A popular cooking ingredient, Southern peas are also known as cowpeas or field peas, because they can be fed to livestock or used as green manure. There are several varieties available, but the best-known one is the black-eyed pea.

 suitable for containers
late spring
good resistance
not hardy
mid-summer

Salad Vegetables

- Lettuce
- Salad greens
- Chicory/Radicchio
- Endives

LETTUCE *Lactuca sativa*

Freshly picked, homegrown lettuce tastes so much better than supermarket salad greens. There are two main types of lettuce, "loose-leaf" and "hearted", distinguished by whether or not they form heads. With the correct care and conditions, it is possible to have a continuous crop of lettuce all year round. Getting seeds to germinate can be tricky, but once they have started, lettuces are among the easiest crops to grow.

	SPRING	SUMMER	FALL	WINTER
SOW				
HARVEST				

SOWING

Lettuces will grow well in most types of moisture-retentive soil, and as long as you provide them with enough water and soil depth, they are suited to growing in containers, too. Site them next to taller crops to provide shade in high summer, since full sun may cause them to bolt.

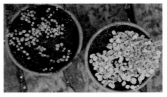

Shallow-rooted lettuce will thrive in pots.

The best time to plant lettuces is soon after the soil has warmed up in the spring, but if you want a harvest earlier in the summer, sow the seed under cover then transplant outside. For winter harvests, a heated greenhouse is essential in most regions of the United States.

Make shallow furrows and sow at a depth of .5 in (1 cm). Small and medium lettuces will need

around 6–10 in (15–25 cm), and larger, headed lettuces about 14 in (35 cm), since they will need more space to expand.

Sow seed in the afternoon, once the heat of the day has passed, since the cooler temperature increases the chance of seeds germinating. If necessary, thin out the seedlings as they grow, leaving only the strongest ones to develop to full size.

PLANTING

Seedlings that have been started indoors, whether in multi-packs or individual planting pots, will be ready to plant out when they have grown four or five mature leaves. Keep them moist and lift them out carefully, trying not to disturb the roots too much, since this can damage later growth.

Plant into a moist bed of soil and provide seedlings with temporary shade to help prevent wilting. If the weather turns cold, or you are worried about pests and diseases, protect vulnerable seedlings with a cloche or cold frame.

CROP CARE

Once lettuces have been planted out, keep them free from weeds and well-watered at all times.

Harvest as cut-and-come-again crops.

This is especially important in the one or two weeks before harvesting, because too much heat or a lack of water can cause the lettuces to bolt. It can also cause them to become bitter.

Most lettuces will not need any extra fertilization, but if growth seems slow, feed them with a nitrogenous fertilizer.

TIP PREVENTING A GLUT

Lettuce can be grown in every season with managed planting, especially if you can provide winter protection. Plant carefully to avoid gluts, because lettuce doesn't keep well once picked. To ensure a steady harvest, sow seeds frequently and in small batches—a handful of seeds every few weeks. Intercrop lettuces to harvest as early season "catch crops" to maximize space.

Seed sown in batches will provide you with a continual supply of lettuce.

HARVESTING

Lettuces with hearts take longer to mature than the loose-leaf varieties, but all lettuces are fairly quick to grow and can be harvested at the baby stage in as little as five weeks. When harvesting, make sure to cut the heading lettuces as soon as they are mature; otherwise, you run the risk that they will rot in wet conditions or bolt in hot or dry conditions.

You can harvest loose-leaf lettuces to use whole, or use them as cut-and-come-again crops. Remove the outer leaves as you need them and leave the inner ones to continue growing. Or, if cutting the entire lettuce, use scissors and cut away the leaves, leaving around 1 in (2.5 cm) of the plant in the ground.

Lettuce stumps regrow and may provide you with a second crop of leaves—continue to care for them as usual and in a couple of weeks the new leaves will resprout.

STORING

Lettuce can be kept for a little while in a sealed plastic bag in the refrigerator, but it is best eaten as fresh as possible. Try to harvest only as much as you need at any given time, to prevent spoilage and waste.

PESTS AND DISEASES

Lettuces are susceptible to these pests and diseases in particular, so guard against them wherever possible.

- Slugs and snails love tender young leaves and may munch their way into the hearts of larger lettuces. Use pellets, or create a barrier to crops using a cloche.
- Cutworms, leatherjackets, and wireworms attack the roots of lettuces, causing them to wilt.
- Lettuce root aphids can be a big problem. They feed on lettuce roots, causing the plant to wilt. Remove Lombary poplars, the pest's other host. Or grow resistant varieties.
- Botrytis—or gray mold—might strike lettuces if weather is wet. Fluffy gray mold will appear on the leaves and can destroy the entire plant.

Slugs (left) can devastate an entire row of vulnerable lettuce seedlings. Use a line of grit or sand (right) to keep slugs or snails away from seedlings.

'Little Gem'

One of the best-known cos varieties, this dwarf, compact lettuce produces crisp, medium-sized hearts, which have an outstanding sweet flavor. This fast-growing mid-green lettuce is perfect for smaller gardens and can be grown well under cloches.

- suitable for containers
- early spring to midsummer
- good resistance
- fairly hardy
- late spring to late fall

'Sylvesta'

One of the few organic lettuce varieties that shows resistance to aphids, it has big butterheads with thick but tender green outer leaves and tightly packed, blanched hearts. Resistance to downy mildew and mosaic virus adds to its productiveness.

- suitable for containers
- spring; late summer
- excellent resistance
- fairly hardy
- late spring to summer; fall

'Roxy'

This standard European butterhead variety produces large beautiful heads that are slow to bolt and resist tip burn. Glossy red, slightly rumpled outer leaves conceal a bright-green, tender heart. It has a soft texture and a mild and tasty flavor.

- suitable for containers
- spring; late summer
- good resistance
- fairly hardy
- late spring to summer; fall

'Freckles'

This unusual heirloom romaine lettuce variety bears bright-green leaves splattered with crimson "freckles." It is a hardy variety that can be successively sown from early spring to fall, producing crisp, upright heads with a buttery texture and sweet flavor.

 suitable for containers
 early spring to early fall
 good resistance
 fairly hardy
 late spring to early winter

'Optima'

One of the darkest green butterhead lettuces sold, 'Optima' offers superior nutrient levels and resistance to multiple diseases. Big-framed and thick-leaved, it matures in about 55 days, and demonstrates excellent tolerance to summer heat.

 suitable for containers
 spring; late summer
excellent resistance
fairly hardy
late spring to summer; fall

'Esmeralda'

This slow-bolting, green butterhead produces large, firm heads that are resistant to tip burn, downy mildew, and mosaic virus. As is typical for a butterhead lettuce, 'Esmeralda' has a sweet flavor and a smooth, tender texture.

 suitable for containers
 spring; late summer
 excellent resistance
 fairly hardy
late spring to summer; fall

'Jericho'

This summer romaine, bred for Israel's desert climate, has a reputation for excellent heat tolerance, as well as sweet succulent flavor long past the time when most lettuces have turned bitter. The heads are tall and robust, and have good tip-burn resistance.

- suitable for containers
- spring; late summer
- good resistance
- fairly hardy
- late spring to summer; fall

'Rouge d'Hiver'

A popular winter variety, as its name suggests, 'Rouge d'Hiver' is also good for fall and spring crops. A French romaine lettuce, the red-tinted leaves turn deeper red in cold weather and can be harvested as baby leaves or as compact heads when mature.

- suitable for containers
- mid-fall to early spring
- good resistance
- hardy
- late spring to midwinter

'Outredgeous'

The reddest of the red romaines, 'Outredgeous' makes a colorful addition to baby salad mixes, and forms a loose head as it matures. Leaves are thick and slightly ruffled, full of antioxidants, and maintain their redness even when grown in low light conditions.

- suitable for containers
- spring; late summer
- good resistance
- fairly hardy
- late spring to summer; fall

'Flashy Troutback'

This beautiful, heirloom, romaine-type lettuce, also sold as 'Forellenschluss', is prized for its unique red-speckled leaves and superior sweet, crunchy flavor. It holds up in summer heat, and can be harvested as baby greens or as tender, mature leaves.

- suitable for containers
- spring; late summer
- some resistance
- fairly hardy
- late spring to summer; fall

'Rouge d'Hiver'

'Winter Density'

This hardy, semi-cos lettuce is sown in the fall to overwinter for a spring harvest. Upright, densely packed heads have, crisp leaves with a sweet flavor that rivals the excellent taste of 'Little Gem'. It is slow to bolt and tolerates the heat well.

🪣	suitable for containers
🌱	late summer to early fall
🐛	good resistance
❄	hardy
🔒	early spring

'Michelle French Batavian'

Bolt-resistant 'Michelle' is mostly green, with crisp leaves that become tinged with red in the cool of spring and fall. Baby leaves can be picked for salads. The dense, crispy heads mature in 55 days and hold up well in summer heat.

🪣	suitable for containers
🌱	spring; late summer
🐛	good resistance
❄	fairly hardy
🔒	late spring to summer; fall

'Summertime'

Bred to form a crisp, solid head that matures in summer heat without bolting, 'Summertime' is an easy-growing, iceberg-type lettuce. The medium-sized heads are resistant to rib discoloration and tip burn, and have a mild, sweet flavor.

🪣	suitable for containers
🌱	spring; late summer
🐛	good resistance
❄	fairly hardy
🔒	early to midsummer; fall

'Yugoslavian Red'

This name of this butterhead variety says it all. A Yugoslavian discovery, it produces large, loose heads of puckered green leaves that are tinged with red, and which when cut in half reveal a solid bright-greeny yellow center. It has an excellent mild, buttery flavor.

 suitable for containers
 early spring to late summer
 good resistance
 not hardy
 late spring to early fall

'Cardinale'

This heat-tolerant summer crisp, or Batavian-type lettuce, forms open rosettes of bronze-red leaves that fold themselves in as the heads mature in 55 to 60 days. The outer leaves are crisp and sweet, and can be harvested as loose leaves before the heads develop.

suitable for containers
spring; late summer
some resistance
fairly hardy
late spring to summer; fall

'Loma'

This loose-leaf Batavian lettuce forms apple-green heads if left to mature, but the frilly, crunchy leaves can also be harvested at 3–6 in (7.5–15 cm). Heat-tolerant, bolt-resistant, and very flavorful, 'Loma' is a reliable producer in all but the hottest weather.

suitable for containers
spring; late summer
good resistance
fairly hardy
late spring to summer; fall

'Marvel of Four Seasons'

Also known as 'Merveille de Quatre Saisons', this large, round, butterhead variety is a traditional favorite. It is a very hardy, semi-hearting lettuce that can be grown almost all year round to produce dark green leaves with an attractive brownish-red tinge.

🪣 suitable for containers
🌱 early spring to late summer
🕷 good resistance
❄ hardy
🔒 mid-spring to early winter

'Mottistone'

This reliable, new Batavian variety produces upright, wavy, green leaves with red speckling, set around a blanched center. The pretty leaves are excellent for decoration or eating, and have a crisp texture. It is slow to bolt and resistant to mildew.

🪣 suitable for containers
🌱 late spring to midsummer
🕷 good resistance
❄ not hardy
🔒 early to late summer

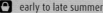

'Nevada'

Like most summer crisps, 'Nevada' can be harvested as flavorful young leaves, or left to form large, open, crunchy heads of vibrant green. Resistance to mildew, mosaic virus, and tip burn make this slow-bolting variety a good performer in difficult conditions.

- suitable for containers
- spring; late summer
- excellent resistance
- fairly hardy
- late spring to summer; fall

'Magenta'

A resistance to downy mildew, mosaic virus, bottom rot, and tip burn sets this Batavian-type lettuce apart from similar varieties. Performance and taste are excellent, with red-tinged leaves forming a slow-bolting head with a crispy green heart in 48 days.

- suitable for containers
- spring; late summer
- excellent resistance
- fairly hardy
- late spring to summer; fall

'Flashy Butter Oak'

This blend of 'Emerald Oak' and 'Flashy Troutback' produces compact heads of red-speckled, puckered leaves that have a crisp, tender crunch. Leaves can be harvested young for use in salad mixes. The heads mature in 54 days.

- suitable for containers
- spring; late summer
- some resistance
- fairly hardy
- late spring to summer; fall

'Oscarde'

This compact oakleaf lettuce is a good choice for fall planting or winter greenhouse production. Full rosettes of attractive, lobed leaves are red on the outside, turning bright green at the tender hearts. 'Oscarde' is resistant to a full range of downy mildews.

- suitable for containers
- spring; late summer
- good resistance
- fairly hardy
- late spring to summer; fall

'Lollo Rossa'

A very popular, beautiful Italian lettuce with frilled, pale-green leaves that have a crimson edge, this variety has a crisp texture and excellent flavor. The plants are compact and non-hearting and are very easy to grow and can be placed anywhere in the garden.

 suitable for containers
early spring to late summer
good resistance
not hardy
late spring to early fall

'Red Deer Tongue'

This widely adaptable heirloom lettuce is a favorite of many gardeners because of its ruggedness and its mild, nutty flavor. 'Red Deer Tongue' forms tender rosettes of triangular red-edged leaves that stand up well to both heat and cold.

 suitable for containers
 spring; late summer
some resistance
fairly hardy
 late spring to summer; fall

'Sunset'

'Sunset' lettuce plants deserve a spot where they can be admired for their good looks as they grow into gorgeous 12-in (30-cm) wide, glowing red heads. Mature heads are slow to bolt, and yield tasty, nice-textured salad greens.

 suitable for containers
 spring; late summer
good resistance
 fairly hardy
 late spring to summer; fall

'Waldmann's Dark Green'

This uniform variety produces frilled, wavy leaves on large, loose heads. Preferred by market growers for its productivity, 'Waldmann's Dark Green' is a good nutritional choice as well, due to the higher than average levels of vitamin A in its dark colored leaves.

- suitable for containers
- spring; late summer
- good resistance
- fairly hardy
- late spring to summer; fall

'Merlot'

One of the darkest red lettuces, bordering almost on purple, 'Merlot' is beautiful in the garden and on the plate, and is high in antioxidants. The upright, frilly-margined leaves can be harvested as babies or left longer so that they form 10-in (25-cm) open heads.

- suitable for containers
- spring; late summer
- good resistance
- fairly hardy
- late spring to summer; fall

'Red Sails'

This 1985 All-America Selections award-winner is a popular variety because of its attractiveness and its long harvest period. The soft, buttery, burgundy-tinged green leaves resist bolting and bitterness. 'Red Sails' is also a beautiful container choice.

- suitable for containers
- spring; late summer
- good resistance
- fairly hardy
- late spring to summer; fall

'Emerald Oakleaf'

Labeled an oakleaf, 'Emerald Oak' has "deer tongue" and butterhead in its lineage, as evidenced by its dense buttery heart. Tidy and compact, the tasty, crunchy, ruffled green heads grow best in cool weather, and mature to a size perfect for salad for two.

- suitable for containers
- spring; late summer
- some resistance
- fairly hardy
- late spring to summer; fall

SALAD GREENS *various*

Salad doesn't have to mean small and expensive supermarket portions—there is a huge range of distinctively flavored leaves that you can grow at home. Sow seed in batches throughout the year and enjoy an almost perpetual harvest of crops. Red orache and texsel greens may sound exotic but they are just as easy to grow as the more familiar cress or arugula. Or try Oriental cut-and-come-again leaves such as mibuna.

	SPRING	SUMMER	FALL	WINTER
SOW				
HARVEST				

SOWING

Leafy salad plants all share a preference for fertile soil that is moisture-retentive but not prone to waterlogging. Some varieties, such as corn salad, thrive in full sun; others, including arugula and purslane, are happier if grown in partial shade. Salad greens sown in late spring will be ready to harvest in summer. For fall and early winter crops and for most Oriental leaves, start sowing in late summer and early fall.

If you are sowing directly into the ground, wait until the soil has warmed up in spring. For successional crops, sow the seeds a few at a time in short rows. Repeat every two to three weeks, or as soon as the previously sown batch of seeds begin to shoot.

Seedlings will need thinning as they grow.

PLANTING OUT

Salad greens can also be sown in successive batches under cover, either for planting outside later or as an indoor winter crop.

Seedlings should be ready to transplant about four weeks after sowing. To minimize disturbance of fragile roots, sow them in modules, one or two seeds per cell, or in coir pots. Thin to about 4 in (10 cm) as seedlings develop.

CROP CARE

Hoe regularly between the planted rows to control weeds and promote good air circulation. This also reduces the risk of pests and diseases (see opposite).

Keep your plants well watered and do not let the soil dry out— salad crops have a very shallow root system, so require frequent watering. Lack of moisture will spoil the flavor and texture of salad greens and encourages the plant to bolt. In hot weather, water either in the early morning or evening to avoid scorching the delicate leaves.

Many salad crops appreciate top-dressing with a nitrogen-rich fertilizer, which can be applied around the base of the plants. Apply fertilizer when growth

Harvest your greens using scissors.

appears to be slowing down; check the requirements of individual crops before using.

Plants sown outside in early spring may need protection if there is a exceptionally cold spell. Keep an eye on the weather and be prepared to cover your crops with fleece or cloches if the temperature drops.

TIP GROWING IN CONTAINERS

In a small garden, salad greens can be container-grown successfully on the patio or beside the kitchen door.

- Water plants regularly and take care not to let containers either dry out or become waterlogged.
- Make sure you choose the best position for your containers. Once filled, large pots are heavy to move.
- Raise containers on blocks or feet to improve drainage.

With their shallow roots, most salad greens will happily grow in a container.

HARVESTING

Pick young leaves as soon as they are large enough to use. Leaves should be ready within a couple of months. Salad plants reach maturity quickly, after which they become coarse and bitter, with tough stems.

If you are growing your crops for cut-and-come-again salads, keep harvesting the leaves a few at a time, working your way through the successive sowings. Picking encourages the plants to produce more leaves. Just one small batch could supply you with harvests over several weeks.

You can also cut a whole plant while it is still young. The stump left behind will rapidly grow another crop of leaves. Once a plant has bolted, its leaves will no longer be useful, so pull it up.

STORING

Once harvested, salad greens are best used almost immediately, as they soon lose freshness. The leaves do not freeze well, because they become mushy when thawed. However, repeated cropping means that storing salad greens will not be necessary. If you happen to pick more leaves than you need, they will keep for a short while if wetted and kept in a plastic bag in the refrigerator.

PESTS AND DISEASES

Pest damage and infections can destroy tender salad crops. Stay vigilant for signs of trouble.

- Slugs and snails can rapidly demolish a row of seedlings. Deter them with barriers and traps, use nematodes as a biological control, or hunt for them at night and pick them off by hand.
- Arugula in particular is susceptible to attack by flea beetles, which chew holes in leaves. Cover plants with fleece or fine mesh to help deter these and other pests such as cabbage root fly and caterpillars, which target Oriental brassicas.
- Downy mildew is a disease that causes a fluffy white mold to develop on leaves. It is common in plants grown under cover. Pull off the leaves and improve air circulation.

Snails can rapidly demolish leafy salad crops so use defenses to keep them at bay. Ensure that you wash leaves thoroughly before use.

Land Cress

Also known by the name of "American Cress", these spicy leaves are often used as a substitute for watercress. This variety is easy to grow and can be harvested as a cut-and-come-again crop. It can be picked throughout winter if it is protected from frost.

- suitable for containers
- early spring to late summer
- some resistance
- hardy
- year round

Watercress

Despite its name, this crop doesn't need to be grown in water; sow into pots placed in deep saucers, or in polyethylene-lined trenches, keeping the soil permanently wet. Harvest the young shoots regularly to encourage regrowth.

- suitable for containers
- late spring and summer
- some resistance
- hardy
- summer

Sorrel

This salad leaf is used in French cuisine, particularly in soups and sauces. The bright-green leaves are produced in abundance and have a sharp, refreshing taste that becomes bitter with age. Although it is a perennial it can be grown as an annual.

- suitable for containers
- mid- to late spring
- some resistance
- hardy
- early to late summer

Purslane

This sprawling plant produces juicy, succulent stalks and rosettes that are bright green in color; the oval-shaped leaves taste a little like snow peas. Its leaves are quick to mature and can be harvested as a cut-and-come-again crop for use in salads or stir-fries.

- suitable for containers
- late spring to midsummer
- some resistance
- fairly hardy
- early to late summer

Mibuna

A vigorous Japanese plant with long, narrow leaves possessing a peppery flavor, 'Mibuna' can regrow after cutting up to five times in a season; successional sowing will give a long-lasting crop. The leaves are good in salads or lightly cooked.

- unsuitable for containers
- mid-spring to early fall
- poor resistance
- hardy
- late spring to late fall

Wild Arugula

This salad crop is closely related to garden arugula but has a much stronger, peppery taste. It is a perennial, often grown as an annual. The leaves should be cropped when young and tender, although the flowers of more mature plants can also be eaten.

- suitable for containers
- early spring to late summer
- some resistance
- hardy
- late spring to early winter

Arugula

The deep-green, oval-shaped, and often serrated leaves have a distinctive peppery flavor and are ideal as a salad on their own or mixed with other leaves. Pick regularly as a cut-and-come-again crop, since it has a tendency to bolt when temperatures become hot.

- suitable for containers
- early spring to late summer
- some resistance
- fairly hardy
- late spring to early winter

Par-cel

Par-cel is an easy-to-grow variety of celery that was developed for its pretty, curled leaves rather than for its stalks. The finely cut, dark-green leaves are glossy and have a strong celery taste. They are often used as a garnish, but are also very good in soups, stocks, and stews.

- suitable for containers
- early spring to midsummer
- some resistance
- hardy
- early summer to late fall

Perilla

Perilla is grown for its crinkled red or green leaves, which are widely used in Japanese cuisine, and have a distinctive cinnamon scent and taste. It is an attractive plant that doubles as an ornamental, making it a good choice for smaller gardens.

- suitable for containers
- late spring and summer
- some resistance
- not hardy
- summer and fall

Greek Cress

These quick-growing microgreens are best eaten as young seedlings. The curled, bright-green leaves add a spicy, peppery flavor to salads, sandwiches, and stir-fries. They can be grown year-round indoors, and also outdoors, if protected from frost.

- suitable for containers
- year round
- some resistance
- fairly hardy
- year round

Par-cel

Red Orache

This easy-to-grow plant is as attractive and ornamental as it is productive. The dark-red leaves are good in salads when they are young, or can be cooked as spinach once they have matured. Red Orache has a tendency to bolt so is best grown from successional sowings.

- suitable for containers
- early spring to late summer
- some resistance
- not hardy
- early summer to mid-fall

Chop Suey Greens

This new variety of Japanese chrysanthemum lacks the bitterness of other types and is very easy to grow. The fine, deeply cut, bright-green leaves have a sweet, peppery, and slightly fragrant flavor and are ideal for salads or stir-fries.

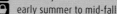

- suitable for containers
- mid-spring to late summer
- some resistance
- not hardy
- midsummer to late fall

Texsel Greens

Also known as "Ethiopian Greens," this quick-growing salad leaf has a mild, mustard-like flavor. Mature leaves can be cooked as a vegetable, or they can be picked young and used for salads or stir-fries. Grow it under cover and have a year-round crop.

 suitable for containers
early spring to late summer
some resistance
hardy
late spring to early winter

Celtuce

This dual-purpose crop get its name from its celerylike stems, which can be harvested by cutting off mature plants; and its lettucelike leaves, which can be cut young and used in salads. Crop leaves as needed and cut the stem at 8 in (20 cm) long.

 unsuitable for containers
early spring and summer
some resistance
not hardy
early- to late-summer

Corn Salad

Also known as "Lamb's Lettuce," this popular salad variety grows slowly to produce rosettes of small, green leaves that can be picked during the winter months. It can be sown successively year round, and the hardy leaves can withstand frost.

suitable for containers
early spring to mid-fall
some resistance
hardy
year round

Tatsoi

A type of bok choy, this rosette-shaped salad leaf is hardy and prolific. The dark green, spoon-shaped leaves grow on short, sturdy, greenish-white stems and can be used at any stage of growth. They are mild-flavored and good for salads or winter dishes.

 unsuitable for containers
early spring to mid-fall
poor resistance
hardy
late spring to midwinter

New Zealand spinach

Unrelated to traditional spinach, this plant can be cropped in the same way, and has small, green, fuzzy leaves. It has a spreading habit and grows well in hot, dry conditions, but keep it well-watered to encourage plenty of growth. Harvest it regularly.

 unsuitable for containers
mid-spring to early summer
some resistance
not hardy
midsummer to fall

Mustard Greens

This group of vegetables offers good nutritional values and tangy flavors that intensify to hot as the plants mature. According to variety, the leaves may be large and savoyed or pretty fronds, several possessing attractive colors from purple to red or golden.

 suitable for containers
 late spring to early fall
 poor resistance
fairly hardy
late summer to late fall

Mizuna

Related to Mibuna but with a milder taste and slower to bolt, Mizuna has slender white stalks and dark green, serrated leaves that can be harvested young for salads or later for cooking. It regrows prolifically after cutting and is easy to grow.

 unsuitable for containers
mid-spring to early fall
poor resistance
hardy
late spring to late fall

Buckler Leaf Sorrel

This type of sorrel has small, soft, slightly succulent leaves, with a sharp, lemony flavor. Although perennial, it can be sown each year as an annual, and can be used raw in salads, or cooked in soups and fish dishes. It self-seeds freely, if allowed.

 suitable for containers
 early spring and summer
 some resistance
 hardy
 summer to fall

Chinese Broccoli

Chinese Broccoli

Also known as Chinese kale, this is similar to European purple sprouting broccoli in both appearance and flavor, but it is more refined and tender. The leaves, stems, and flowers are all edible, and the leaves can be used raw in salads when they are young.

- suitable for containers
- late spring to early fall
- poor resistance
- fairly hardy
- midsummer to late fall

Komatsuna

This is a fast-growing Japanese vegetable that can be harvested at about 30 days after sowing for baby leaves, or when it reaches the size of kale, at around 70 days. The flavor of the leaves, flowers, and stems is mild and fresh, and excellent in salads and stir-fries.

- suitable for containers
- early spring to early fall
- poor resistance
- hardy
- mid-spring to late fall

Oriental Saladini

This seed mix provides a range of Oriental leaf vegetables such as Bok Choy, Mibuna, Mizuna, Mustard, and Komatsuma, which will provide salad leaves over a long period. Sow them successively and treat them as cut-and-come-again plants.

- suitable for containers
- mid-spring to late summer
- poor resistance
- fairly hardy
- late spring to mid-fall

Choy Sum

This vegetable is grown for its broad, crisp leaf stalks, which can be green, white, or purple, and are harvested just before flowering. The stalks can be eaten raw in salads or stir-fried. It is a quick-growing crop that does best in milder regions.

- suitable for containers
- early summer to early fall
- some resistance
- not hardy
- summer to fall

CHICORY *Cichorium intybus*

A highly ornamental plant, there are three distinct, attractive types of chicory: Witloof or Belgian, which has elongated heads of tight, white leaves, and is usually forced and blanched; radicchio or red chicory, which has tight heads of crisp, red leaves, similar in appearance to a small lettuce; and sugarloaf, which has looser, green leaves. All types have a decidedly bitter taste, but can be eaten raw in salad, or cooked.

	SPRING	SUMMER	FALL	WINTER
SOW				
HARVEST				

SOWING

Chicory is a very tolerant crop, and will grow well even in poor soils and partial shade. It is best not to sow seed too early or plants might bolt, so begin in late spring and sow through to midsummer.

Sow seed directly into the ground at a depth of .5 in (1 cm). Once seedlings develop, thin Witloof chicory to leave about 9 in (23 cm) space between plants, and about 12 in (30 cm) between radicchio or sugarloaf types, as these will develop larger heads.

CROP CARE

Ensure that chicory crops are kept weeded and well-watered to discourage them from bolting. Protect with cold frames or cloches if frosts are forecast.

A large box is ideal for forcing.

HARVESTING

Chicory is usually ready to harvest in a month, once heads are firm. Raddichio or sugarloaf types will store once lifted, or they can be left in the ground for longer if not immediately needed. Dig up Witloof types and force (see above). Once chicons (Belgian endives) have been cut, recover the stumps—you may get a second crop.

FORCING AND BLANCHING

Forcing Witloof chicory will produce a crop of blanched leaf shoots that are less bitter in taste than the green leaves. Dig up mature plants in late fall to early winter. Cut the leaves off the plant to within 1 in (2.5 cm) above the root collar, and trim the bottom of the root so that it measures 8 in (20 cm) in length. Plant these trimmed roots in boxes of moist potting compost, so that their tops are just showing above the soil surface. Then cover with 9 in (23 cm) of compost. Move the box to a warm dark place for three to four weeks.

PESTS AND DISEASES

Chicory may be at risk from slugs and snails, which will happily munch their way through leaves. To deter them, create a protective barrier using a cloche or cold frame; set up beer traps to draw them away from crops; and lay a ring of coarse material such as sand or diatomaceious earth (DE) around the planting area. Alternatively, use slug pellets, as these are the most effective control. Keep a close eye out for aphids, too. If infestations are severe, spray with insecticide.

'Red Rib'

Also known as 'Italian Dandelion', this variety bears serrated, long-stemmed leaves that resemble dandelions. The dark-green leaves have distinctive, bright-red stems and mid-veins. Eaten raw or cooked, the leaves have a pleasant, bitter flavor with a little sweetness.

suitable for containers
late spring to late summer
good resistance
fairly hardy
midsummer to fall

'Palla Rossa Verona'

This Italian variety produces round, compact, firm heads with heart-shaped, deep-red leaves with white ribs. The excellent quality of the leaves and their sharp flavor makes them popular with chefs. It is a good variety for forcing.

suitable for containers
midsummer to early fall
good resistance
hardy
fall to early winter

Belgian Endive

Known also as Witloof chicory, this winter delicacy is grown in two stages. At the end of summer, roots are lifted, replanted, and placed in absolute darkness to produce blanched heads with a crunchy texture and mild flavor. 'Totem' is a popular US variety.

suitable for containers
mid- to late spring
good resistance
fairly hardy
winter

'Indigo'

Also called 'Indigo F1', this reliable variety produces dense, round heads, green outer leaves, and red hearts, with white midribs and a good flavor. The heads are ready for harvesting early in the season and are resistant to bolting, tip burn, and bottom rot.

 suitable for containers
 early to mid-spring
 good resistance
hardy
midsummer to late fall

'Fiero'

This hybrid chicory produces reliable, attractive heads of elongated, purple leaves with white ribs 66 days after transplanting. The leaves have a dense texture and a mild bitterness that adds an interesting taste to salads or sautéed dishes.

 suitable for containers
mid-spring; late summer
good resistance
fairly hardy
summer; fall

'Leonardo'

This vigorous variety produces large, round, dense heads of red leaves. The hearts are well-developed, with a red color that deepens as the weather becomes colder. The flavor of the leaves is enhanced by cooler temperatures and frost.

 suitable for containers
 mid- to late summer
 good resistance
 hardy
fall to midwinter

'Palla Rossa'

This round, red, ball-type originates from Chioggia in Italy. The green leaves of the medium-to-large, firm, and well-filled heads have white midribs, and turn red as the temperatures drop. The crisp leaves have a sweet flavor with a touch of bitterness.

 suitable for containers
 mid- to late summer
 good resistance
hardy
midwinter

'Pan di Zucchero'

Also known as 'Sugar Loaf', this popular variety produces upright, tight heads with dark-green outer leaves. The crunchy hearts are ideal for shredding into salads. It is good for forcing or for growing as a cut-and-come-again crop.

 suitable for containers
mid- to late summer
good resistance
hardy
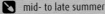 late fall to midwinter

'Treviso Precoce Mesola'

This Italian chicory produces firm, long heads with red leaves and white midribs. The leaves have a distinctive flavor and texture and are ideal for use in fall or winter, raw or cooked. The baby leaves are excellent in spring salads.

 suitable for containers
mid-spring to late summer
good resistance
hardy
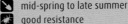 fall to midwinter

'Rossa di Treviso'

This classic Italian variety, also known as 'Treviso', bears slender, tall, upright radicchios, which have white midribs and need cold temperatures for the leaves to take on their distinctive red color. Good raw or grilled, the leaves have a pleasant bitter taste; remove outer leaves before eating.

 suitable for containers
 mid- to late summer
 good resistance
hardy
mid-fall to midwinter

'Orchidea Rossa'

This early-maturing variety produces attractive, rosette-shaped heads. The small to medium-sized heads are round, and the leaves red with white midribs. The crisp leaves can be cooked to remove their bitterness, or used raw in salads.

 suitable for containers
late spring to late summer
 good resistance
hardy
fall to midwinter

'Castelfranco'

Also referred to as 'Castelfranco Variegated', in summer, this variety produces creamy-green leaves with a red mottling that deepens as winter approaches. The round, closed heads are good for forcing. It is a late-maturing variety with a crunchy texture.

 suitable for containers
mid- to late summer
 good resistance
hardy
 midwinter

ENDIVE *Cichorium endivia*

Endive is closely related to chicory and forms sprawling rosettes of bitter-tasting, lettucelike leaves. There are two main types of endive—those with flat, broad leaves that are known as "escarole" or "Batavian," and those with frilly, finely serrated leaves known as "Frisée" or chicory endive. The feathery leaves are blanched to reduce the bitterness of their taste, and can be used in salads like lettuce.

	SPRING	SUMMER	FALL	WINTER
SOW/PLANT				
HARVEST				

SOWING

Endives like a fertile, well-drained soil and a pH of around 5.5–7.5. They are generally quite tolerant plants and are not too fussy about location—they will grow happily in full sun and will tolerate partial shade, too.

Exposure to cold weather may encourage plants to bolt, so don't plant them out too early. Instead, sow under cover in spring and then plant seedlings out once the soil has warmed up in early or midsummer. Alternatively, sow seed directly into the ground in early summer. Sow seed at a depth of .5 in (1 cm), and later thin seedlings out, depending on type: allow compact varieties about 9 in (23 cm) between plants, and give spreading varieties about

Clay pots can be used to blanch leaves.

15 in (38 cm). Space rows of plants 10–15 in (25–38 cm) apart.

CROP CARE

Keep plants weeded and well-watered at all stages of their growth. Protect crops with cloches or cold frames if the weather turns cold—this will discourage them from bolting and will also extend the length of the harvesting season.

HARVESTING

Harvest endives as required—either cut the whole head off and wait for new leaves to resprout, or harvest individual leaves as a cut-and-come-again crop.

BLANCHING

Preventing light from reaching the leaves will blanch them and reduce their bitter flavor. Cover frisée types with a plate or gather up and tie together the leaves of Batavian types shortly before crops are ready to harvest. Block the light for about 10 days. After this time, the leaves will have whitened and be ready to eat.

PESTS AND DISEASES

Be vigilant against slugs, since they will probably be the biggest threat to your crop. Use slug pellets, or if you prefer, protect plants with cloches or set up beer traps. Also consider laying grit, diatomaceious earth (DE), or copper tape as a barrier. Aphids and caterpillars may also target your crops: pick off any caterpillars that you find, and spray infested plants with an appropriate insecticide. Lettuce root aphid, which feed on plant roots, and tip burn, which shrivels the rims of leaves, might pose a problem.

'Natacha'

This is an attractive and vigorous escarole that produces big, heavy heads of bright-green, strong-flavored leaves around a central, creamy heart. It is the best-performing variety, and disease-resistant, with excellent resistance to bolting, tip burn, and bottom rot.

- suitable for containers
- early spring to midsummer
- excellent resistance
- hardy
- late spring to early fall

'Tres Fine Maraichere'

This classic mesclun mix ingredient requires cool temperatures to grow well. Finely cut inner leaves are mild and delicious, and add interesting texture to salads. 'Tres Fine Maraichere' is sensitive to tip burn, particularly if grown in soils that lack calcium.

- suitable for containers
- spring and late summer
- poor resistance
- hardy
- early summer and fall

'Kentucky'

This variety is a very productive, robust, easy-to-grow, intermediate frisée type. Seeds produce large heads of very fine, deep-green leaves around a yellow heart that has a distinctive, sharp taste. This type is ideal for blanching.

- suitable for containers
- late spring to midsummer
- good resistance
- hardy
- midsummer to late fall

'Batavian Full Heart'

Also known as escarole, this variety has large, thick, dark-green leaves around a creamy-colored center. The outer leaves have a sharp flavor, while the heart is milder in taste. It can be harvested into the winter since it is very hardy.

- suitable for containers
- early spring to late summer
- good resistance
- hardy
- late spring to early winter

'Frenzy'

This compact, uniform variety is a Tres Fine type. The dense heads produce finely curled, deeply cut leaves around a center that self-blanches to a creamy yellow color. The leaves can be picked when young or left to mature. This is popular choice among chefs.

 suitable for containers
 early spring to midsummer
 good resistance
hardy
midsummer to fall

'Frisée Glory'

This frisée endive has uniform, deeply, yet finely cut, lacy leaves that have a distinctive, slightly bitter flavor. The tender young leaves are a traditional ingredient of Mesclun, the classic French salad. Harvest as whole heads or as baby leaves.

 suitable for containers
early spring to midsummer
good resistance
hardy
late spring to late fall

'Rhodos'

This frisée-type endive has a naturally self-blanching heart with mild-flavored, tender, white leaves that are a salad delicacy. Maturing in 42 days, 'Rhodos' is sensitive to tip burn and bottom rot, and should be harvested before signs of either appear.

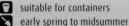 suitable for containers
spring and late summer
 poor resistance
 hardy
early summer and fall

Fruiting Vegetables

- Globe artichokes
- Tomatoes
- Sweet and Chili peppers
- Eggplant
- Corn

GLOBE ARTICHOKES *Cynara scolymus*

The succulent petal bases and centers of tender, immature globe artichoke flowers are delicious boiled, while young shoots can be blanched for use in salads. When grown from seed, globe artichokes can be variable in quality, so, if possible, purchase named offsets that have been propagated. It is also possible to select from the best of your seed-raised plants to produce a good quality offset.

	SPRING	SUMMER	FALL	WINTER
SOW				
HARVEST				

SOWING

Give globe artichokes a sheltered but sunny position. They do best in well-drained, fertile, moisture-retentive soil, so dig in plenty of well-rotted manure or compost before planting and apply some balanced fertilizer.

In spring, sow seed in pots indoors, or in outdoor seedbeds, at a depth of 2 in (5 cm). The young seedlings should be transplanted to their final positions in early summer.

Offsets taken in spring from the sides of mature plants are a better way of raising new plants if good quality mother plants are available. Offsets are also sold by specialty nurseries. Ensure that plants have enough space, allowing 30 in (75 cm) between

Apply a compost mulch every spring.

plants and 36 in (90 cm) between rows. Push offsets deep enough into the soil that they can stand upright, then water in well.

CROP CARE

Keep plants free of weeds and apply plenty of water in dry spells. Apply fertilizer and an organic mulch every spring. In the fall, plants die back and the dead material should be removed.

In cold regions, protect the crown of the plant with a layer of straw or other insulating material. Plants should be replaced every three years, since clumps become less productive with age.

HARVESTING

Abundant flowerbuds are borne from late spring to early summer, and if the stem is cut back, may fruit again in early fall. Cut the heads from about golf-ball size; they can become unappetizingly woolly if larger than a tennis ball. They should be cut with a slight amount of edible stalk; long stalks tend to be woody.

PESTS AND DISEASES

Globe artichokes are largely problem-free, but blackfly and root aphids may target plants. As blackfly affect stalks, wash off by hand or treat with an appropriate insecticide. Little can be done about root aphids, but water and feed plants to help overcome the effect.

Ladybugs will help control aphids.

'Purple Globe'

The rather unruly, thistlelike plants of this highly ornamental variety produce variable artichokes in early summer. The smallish globes tend to lack firmness and are on the spiny side, but they do have a good flavor and are best gathered when small.

- unsuitable for containers
- spring to summer
- some resistance
- hardy
- early summer to fall

'Green Globe Improved'

This hybrid artichoke variety is more reliable than its parent plant, and more vigorous, producing larger, firmer artichokes on more even plants. The globes are suitable for harvesting when they are both large and small in size.

- unsuitable for containers
- spring to summer
- some resistance
- hardy
- early summer to fall

'Violetto di Chioggia'

This handsome, seed-raised variety originates in Italy. The spiked and variable artichokes are carried on thistlelike foliage. Fairly hardy and productive, the plants are not very uniform, but this is outweighed by the fact that cropping is good.

- unsuitable for containers
- spring to summer
- some resistance
- hardy
- early summer to fall

'Gros Vert de Laon'

This hardy, high-quality variety will survive winters in northern maritime climatic regions. The artichokes are round, green, and can be gathered when small or large. The best forms are propagated by offsets and are of superior quality to seed-raised cultivars.

 unsuitable for containers
 spring to summer
 some resistance
❄ hardy
🔒 early summer to fall

'Romanesco'

This productive variety produces rounded, purple-tinted artichokes that are relatively tight and firm, which is unusual for a seed-raised variety. Tall, vigorous, and variable, the plants are very ornamental, even without their colored flower buds.

🪴 unsuitable for containers
🍴 spring to summer
🕷 some resistance
❄ hardy
🔒 early summer to fall

'Imperial Star'

This selection of 'Green Globe' benefits from being less variable. It is raised from seed. Since it matures quickly and can produce artichokes in its first year, it can be grown in regions with winters that are more severe than artichokes normally tolerate.

🪴 unsuitable for containers
🍴 spring to summer
🕷 some resistance
❄ hardy
 early summer to fall

TOMATOES *Lycopersicon esculentum*

With flavorful, attractive fruits that range from tiny, currantlike types to huge, fleshy, beefsteak varieties, in colors as diverse as, pink, red, yellow, maroon, and even purple, it is no wonder that the easy-to-grow tomato is loved by gardeners. A wide range of varieties are available as seed, but young plants are also widely sold. These are valuable for gardeners without the warm conditions needed to raise seedlings.

	SPRING	SUMMER	FALL	WINTER
SOW/PLANT				
HARVEST				

SOWING

Sow seed in early spring, ensuring a temperature of between 64–77°F (18–25°C). Good, sturdy growth depends on ample warmth and light; crowded plants become elongated and hard to handle later. As soon as they are large enough, seedlings should be set out into individual containers and grown on either in a greenhouse or outdoors. Containers, filled with fertile potting media, will support good crops.

For outdoor tomatoes, plant out only once the danger of frost has passed, after hardening off. A warm, sunny, sheltered site is essential outdoors. Mix a 2 in (5 cm) layer of rotted organic manure or compost and balanced fertilizer into the soil.

Support vine tomatoes with stakes.

CROP CARE

Water plants during dry periods. Tomatoes are self-fertile but may need shaking to effect pollination.

Bush tomatoes need no special treatment—each shoot ends with flowers and therefore will not grow very long. With many such shoots, bush tomatoes require minimal staking. Vine tomato flowers grow out from the stem.

The stem also has growing points that give rise to many trailing side-shoots. These should be cut out, and the main stem tied to a stake. When the plant reaches the top of the stake, remove its growing tip. A few varieties have aspects of both bush and vine and require minimal trimming; merely tie them to a stake. Plants will need regular feeding with tomato fertilizer.

HARVESTING
Gather fruits once they have attained their full color and have begun to soften. They will not keep long in storage.

PESTS AND DISEASES

In greenhouses, caterpillars, whitefly, and red spider mite may be a problem. Tomatoes also share several problems with potatoes, such as potato cyst eel worm and potato blight. Outdoor crops are prone to blight in cool damp weather; its effects can be devastating.

Tomato blight causes fruits to rot.

'Chocolate Cherry'

Recently introduced, this heavy-cropping vine variety bears small, very dark purple fruits with excellent flavor. Perfect for use in salads, these tomatoes are especially rich in beneficial antioxidants. Plants will need support with sticks or string.

 suitable for containers
 late spring to early summer
 some resistance
 not hardy
 summer to early fall

'Sweet Million'

A hybrid cherry tomato that can be grown in greenhouses or outdoors, and has a vine habit so should be trained up sticks or string. The trusses are very long and carry large numbers of small, bright red, very sweet, round, cherry fruits.

 suitable for containers
 late spring to early summer
 some resistance
 not hardy
 summer to early fall

'Sun Cherry'

This high-yielding, cherry, vine variety bears numerous bright red fruits, borne on large trusses, which ripen to a sweet flavor. Plants need to be supported by sticks or string, and are suitable for either greenhouse cultivation or outdoor cultivation.

 suitable for containers
 late spring to early summer
 some resistance
not hardy
summer to early fall

'Chadwick'

A juicy cherry variety, this tomato is named after its originator and is sometimes called 'Camp Joy'. Its fruits are on the large side for cherry types, and are borne on plants with a vine habit, in greenhouses or outdoors.

 suitable for containers
late spring to early summer
some resistance
not hardy
summer to early fall

'Gardener's Delight'

This long-established cherry tomato has a vine habit and should be supported with sticks or string. Famed for its flavor, this variety bears medium yields of larger than usual fruits, on long trusses. The fruits mature early, even in cooler regions.

 suitable for containers
 late spring to early summer
 some resistance
not hardy
 summer to early fall

'Matt's Wild Cherry'

A tomato originally of Mexican origin, this variety produces cherry-sized, round, red fruits possessing a good flavor. Plants have good cropping potential and need to be supported with sticks or string. They require a warm, sunny site in which to thrive.

 suitable for containers
 late spring to early summer
 some resistance
 not hardy
 summer to early fall

'Gold Nugget'

This heavy-cropping bush variety of tomato bears round, cherry-sized, yellow fruits, whose succulent, firm flesh is ideal for slicing or stuffing. 'Gold Nugget' is suitable for regions that have a cooler, maritime climate.

 suitable for containers
 late spring to early summer
 some resistance
 not hardy
 summer to early fall

'Garden Peach'

Originally from Peru, this unusual variety bears heavy crops. The mottled-yellow fruits ripen to pink, with peachlike skin and succulent, firm flesh. Plants should be supported with sticks or string, and are best grown outdoors in warm regions.

suitable for containers
late spring to early summer
some resistance
not hardy
summer to early fall

'Sungold'

'Sungold' is a heavy-cropping cherry variety that bears sweet, round, and attractive, golden-orange fruits. Plants can be cultivated in a greenhouse or can be grown outdoors; they have a vine habit, so will need support from sticks or string.

 suitable for containers
 late spring to early summer
 some resistance
not hardy
summer to early fall

'Balconi Red'

This variety has a trailing bush habit and is ideally suited for hanging baskets and ornamental containers. The plants grow fast, crop early, and are unusually prolific. The bright red fruits are attractive and delicious and will hang for a long time.

 suitable for containers
late spring to early summer
some resistance
not hardy
 summer to early fall

'Tumbling Tom Red'

The prolific, bright-red fruits of this variety are attractive and delicious, and hang for a long time. The plants grow fast, crop early, and are very robust. Their trailing bush habit is ideally suited for hanging baskets and other ornamental containers.

suitable for containers
late spring to early summer
 some resistance
not hardy
 summer to early fall

'Totem'

This dwarf, bush tomato is attractive and quick-growing. The well-flavored crimson fruits are produced abundantly and hang on the plant, enhancing its ornamental value. It is ideal for growing in patio containers, and support is often needed.

	suitable for containers
	late spring to early summer
	some resistance
	not hardy
	summer to early fall

'Legend'

This hybrid bush variety produces early crops of large, bright-red fruits that have some tolerance of late blight. Plants are best grown outdoors, but may need protection under cloches or other low-level protection, such as horticultural fleece.

	suitable for containers
	late spring to early summer
	good resistance
	not hardy
	summer to early fall

'Glacier'

This early-cropping variety bears numerous small, bright fruits, even in cool weather. It grows with aspects of both bush and vine habit, so is best trained roughly to a stick or string. Plants have potato-leafed foliage; they are best grown outdoors.

	suitable for containers
	late spring to early summer
	some resistance
	not hardy
	summer to early fall

'Tumbler'

This bush tomato has a compact trailing habit, which makes it ideal for hanging baskets and container-growing. The small fruits are well-flavored and abundant, and the plants are very robust and reliable, even when they are grown in hanging baskets.

 suitable for containers
 late spring to early summer
 some resistance
 not hardy
 summer to early fall

'Rutgers'

This long-established bush variety is capable of good outdoor crops in warm, sunny situations or in hot regions. Plants bear medium-sized, round, and slightly flattened, red fruits that have a good flavor and are ideal for cooking.

suitable for containers
late spring to early summer
some resistance
not hardy
summer to early fall

'Celebrity'

This compact bush tomato produces large, bright-red fruits. It is untroubled by many root diseases and pests that some varieties suffer from, and is best suited to warm regions. It is likely to require cloche or fleece protection in cooler areas.

 suitable for containers
late spring to early summer
good resistance
not hardy
 summer to early fall

'Juliet'

This hybrid vine variety needs supporting with string or sticks for cultivation outdoors or in the greenhouse. Fruits are small, elongated, and bright red, with a rich, succulent flavor. They hold well on the vine and are especially good for use in salads and sauces.

- 🪣 suitable for containers
- 🌱 late spring to early summer
- 🐞 some resistance
- ❄️ not hardy
- 🔒 summer to early fall

'Verde'

Closely related to tomatoes and grown in the same way, these bushy tomatillo plants are trouble-free and crop heavily. The green, sharply flavored fruits are used in Mexican cuisine and are also suited to relishes, when used in the same way as green tomatoes.

- 🪣 suitable for containers
- 🌱 late spring to early summer
- 🐞 some resistance
- ❄️ not hardy
- 🔒 summer to early fall

'Purple de Milpa'

Although it is grown as a tomato, this variety is actually a tomatillo, and needs a stout stake to support the tall, bushy plants. It produces large, purple, sharp-flavored fruits ideal for salsa sauces and for a wide range of pickles and chutneys.

- 🪣 suitable for containers
- 🌱 late spring to early summer
- 🐞 some reistance
- ❄️ not hardy
- 🔒 summer to early fall

'Black Russian'

Originally from Russia, this compact, beefsteak variety produces heavy crops of fairly large, deep-maroon fruits, which are succulent, with a hint of salt. Plants have a vine habit and will need support with sticks or string. Protect against blight in cool, wet regions.

 suitable for containers
 late spring to early summer
 some resistance
 not hardy
summer to early fall

'Tigerella'

Although flavor is fair and crops only reasonable, this vine variety is grown for its small, red- and green-striped, attractive fruits. Best-suited to greenhouse growing, it does crop outdoors in warm regions. Support plants with sticks or string.

 suitable for containers
late spring to early summer
some resistance
not hardy
summer to early fall

'Stupice'

This heavy-cropping vine tomato was originally bred in the Czech Republic. It bears heavy crops of bright-red, round fruits of good flavor, which ripen early, even in cooler regions. Plants should be grown up sticks or string, and can be grown indoors or out.

suitable for containers
 late spring to early summer
 some resistance
not hardy
summer to early fall

'Sweet Olive'

This vigorous, easy-to-grow vine variety bears heavy crops of small, bright-red, round- to plum-shaped tomatoes. Plants should be supported with sticks or string, and are suitable for both greenhouse growing and for growing outdoors.

	suitable for containers
	late spring to early summer
	some resistance
	not hardy
	summer to early fall

'Golden Sunrise'

This high-yielding vine variety bears small, round, golden-yellow fruits with excellent flavor. They are capable of good outdoor crops in warm sunny situations, and are reliable even in cooler regions. Support plants with sticks or string.

	suitable for containers
	late spring to early summer
	some resistance
	not hardy
	summer to early fall

'Arkansas Traveler'

This long-established variety comes from the South and bears large, red-pink fruits of very good flavor. It will need support from sticks or string, and is ideally suited to hot regions. It will need greenhouse protection in cooler areas.

	suitable for containers
	late spring to early summer
	some resistance
	not hardy
	summer to early fall

'Tomatoberry Garden'

This cascading vine variety produces long trusses of small, bright-red fruits with pointed bases and a good flavor. Plants should be supported with sticks or string and are suitable for growing indoors or outdoors. They are tolerant of late blight.

 suitable for containers
 late spring to early summer
 some resistance
 not hardy
 summer to early fall

'Moneymaker'

This vine variety is long established for greenhouse use and needs support with sticks or string. It produces moderate yields of bright-red, round fruits of fair flavor. Plants tolerate poor soil, and seed is inexpensive and widely available.

 suitable for containers
 late spring to early summer
 some resistance
 not hardy
 summer to early fall

'Spear's Tennessee Green'

This heirloom variety produces very large green fruits with good flavor. Plants should be supported with sticks or string. While best-suited to regions with hot summers, in cooler climates it should be grown in a greenhouse or in a warm, sunny position.

 suitable for containers
late spring to early summer
some resistance
not hardy
 summer to early fall

'Green Zebra'

The large and richly flavored fruits of the 'Green Zebra' variety are green- and yellow-striped, becoming a deeper yellow color as they ripen. Plants have a vine habit, and are best grown outdoors. They are well-suited to a mild, maritime climate.

- suitable for containers
- late spring to early summer
- some resistance
- not hardy
- summer to early fall

'Alicante'

A long-established vine variety, 'Alicante' bears heavy crops of medium size, round, red fruits with fair flavor. Capable of good outdoor crops in warm sunny situations, it is reliable even under difficult conditions. Support with sticks or string.

- suitable for containers
- late spring to early summer
- some resistance
- not hardy
- summer to early fall

'Roma'

This traditional, bush, plum tomato is originally from Italy. It produces heavy crops of bright red, solid, fruits. Plants must be protected from late blight in cool, wet regions, although 'Roma VF' is also available, and is resistant to fungal wilt diseases.

- suitable for containers
- late spring to early summer
- some resistance
- not hardy
- summer to early fall

'Yellow Perfection'

This long-established and high-yielding variety produces medium-sized, mild-flavored, pale-yellow fruits. Plants have a vine habit and should be grown up sticks or string. They are suitable for greenhouses or for growing outdoors in cooler regions.

 suitable for containers
late spring to early summer
some resistance
not hardy
summer to early fall

'Principe Borghese'

This heavy-cropping Italian plum variety produces bright-red, solid fruits that last well on the vine; the succulent, firm flesh is ideal for sauces. Plants should be supported with sticks or string, and plants need protection from late blight in cool, wet regions.

suitable for containers
late spring to early summer
some resistance
not hardy
summer to early fall

'Olivade'

This hybrid vine variety produces heavy crops of solid, well-flavored, bright-red plum fruits. Plants should be trained up sticks or string and are best grown in a greenhouse in cooler regions. They are robust and will perform well even in poor conditions.

suitable for containers
late spring to early summer
some resistance
not hardy
summer to early fall

'Amish Paste'

This traditional plum variety produces bright-red, full-flavored, large fruits that mature early and that are especially suitable for cooking. 'Amish Paste' plants will need to be supported with sticks or string and will crop well outdoors in warm regions.

- suitable for containers
- late spring to early summer
- some resistance
- not hardy
- summer to early fall

'Summer Sweet'

An early-maturing plum type that bears high yields of bright-red, good flavored, small-to-medium sized fruits. Plants have a vine habit so should be supported with sticks or string. They are suitable for growing in a greenhouse or for outdoors in warm regions.

- suitable for containers
- late spring to early summer
- some resistance
- not hardy
- summer to early fall

'Ramapo'

This beefsteak hybrid tomato produces heavy crops of large, well-flavored, bright-red fruits. Plants should be grown up sticks or string and lightly tied in since they are not fully indeterminate. They are ideal for regions with hot summers.

- suitable for containers
- late spring to early summer
- some resistance
- not hardy
- summer to early fall

'Carmello'

This heavy-cropping beefsteak tomato originated in France. It bears bright-red, flattened, ribbed fruits, with succulent, firm flesh. Available as either hybrid or non-hybrid seed, it is suitable for cooler regions and should be supported with sticks or string.

- suitable for containers
- late spring to early summer
- some resistance
- not hardy
- summer to early fall

'Summer Sweet'

'Black Krim'

This traditional, beefsteak tomato originates from Russia. 'Black Krim' bears heavy crops of large, dark, brown-red fruits, with succulent, firm flesh; it is ideal for stuffing. Support the vine plants with sticks or string, and protect it in cool wet regions to prevent late blight.

- 🪣 suitable for containers
- 🌱 late spring to early summer
- 🐛 some resistance
- ❄️ not hardy
- 🔒 summer to early fall

'Great White'

This beefsteak variety bears heavy crops of well-flavored, creamy-white fruits. Support plants with sticks or string. Best grown in warmer regions, it will also succeed quite well in cooler areas. Ripeness is detectable by a yellowish tinge at the flower end.

- 🪣 suitable for containers
- 🌱 late spring to early summer
- 🐛 some resistance
- ❄️ not hardy
- 🔒 summer to early fall

'Brandywine'

This beefsteak variety bears moderate crops of large, flat, red fruits that possess succulent, pink flesh and a potato-type foliage. The plants have a vine habit and need support with sticks or string; they can be grown indoors or out.

- 🪣 suitable for containers
- 🌱 late spring to early summer
- 🐛 some resistance
- ❄️ not hardy
- 🔒 summer to early fall

'Country Taste'

This beefsteak-type tomato has a vine habit, so should be grown up sticks or string, either indoors or out. It bears heavy, early-maturing crops of bright-red, flattened, ribbed fruits with succulent, firm flesh. Plants are more robust and heavier yielding than similar heirloom varieties.

 suitable for containers
 late spring to early summer
 some resistance
not hardy
summer to early fall

'Cherokee Purple'

This traditional beefsteak tomato bears heavy crops of pink to purple, flattened, ribbed fruits with red flesh and good flavor. The succulent, firm flesh is ideal for slicing or stuffing. Plants should be supported with sticks or string.

 suitable for containers
 late spring to early summer
some resistance
 not hardy
 summer to early fall

'Pineapple'

This traditional beefsteak tomato needs a warm, sunny site, and should be supported with sticks or string. It produces heavy crops of very large, bright-red- and green-striped, flattened, ribbed fruits. The succulent, firm flesh is ideal for slicing or stuffing.

 suitable for containers
 late spring to early summer
some resistance
 not hardy
 summer to early fall

SWEET AND CHILI PEPPERS

Capsicum anuum Longum Group and *C. anuum* Grossum Group

Amazingly diverse, peppers are available in a vivid range of shades, from green to red, purple, yellow, black, and orange. They can also be round, barrel-shaped, pointed, or flat. In addition to being good to eat—either sweet or intensely fiery—they are often highly ornamental, and are easy to grow as long as they have plenty of warmth.

	SPRING	SUMMER	FALL	WINTER
SOW/PLANT				
HARVEST				

SOWING

Peppers will thrive in containers, as long as these are large enough to sustain them and contain fertile soil. Before planting, dig in plenty of well-rotted manure or compost, and apply some general fertilizer.

Sow seed in early spring. Scatter it thinly and cover with a thin layer of soil; it will need a minimum temperature of around 64–77°F (18–25°C). Transfer the seedlings into individual pots as soon as they are large enough to be handled. They need warmth and light, must not get crowded, and will need liquid fertilizer when roots appear at the bottom of the container.

When the seedlings have filled their pots with roots, plant them

Plant peppers out after hardening off.

in a greenhouse or move them outside and protect with cloches or fleece, if necessary. Allow 15–18 in (38–45 cm) between plants.

CROP CARE

Water to keep the root zone moist. Plants usually branch naturally, but you will also need to pinch out the growing tips to induce bushy growth. Support plants with stakes and string,

to prevent plants toppling under the weight of their fruits.

HARVESTING
Peppers change color as they ripen, from green to a range of colors. Harvest them when green and unripe, or leave them to ripen fully. Ripe fruits have a richer, sweeter flavor, but leaving them can reduce the overall yield.

STORING
Less fleshy forms of pepper, especially hot chili peppers, can be dried for long-term storage. Otherwise, use sweet peppers as soon as possible after picking.

PESTS AND DISEASES

Peppers can be attacked by sap-sucking insects such as capsid bugs or aphids, or by caterpillars. Biological controls are effective in greenhouses but insecticides might be required outdoors. Pick off any caterpillars that you find and apply an appropriate insecticide, if necessary. Few diseases affect peppers, but fungal rots might require control. To ensure healthy plants, practice good garden hygiene and ensure that plants are kept well ventilated, especially if you are growing them in a greenhouse.

'Friggitello'

This excellent sweet pepper bears numerous long, thin, and horn-shaped fruits, which as they ripen change in color from green to red. The yield is moderate, but fruits have a very sweet flavor and pickle well. Plants may need greenhouse protection in cool regions.

	suitable for containers
	spring to summer
	some resistance
	not hardy
	late summer to early fall

'Lipstick'

This non-hybrid sweet pepper bears heavy crops of elongated, tapering, blocky fruits that ripen from deep green to rich red. Its flavor is good. The robust plants will thrive in warm regions and in cooler areas, if provided with greenhouse protection.

	suitable for containers
	spring to summer
	some resistance
	not hardy
	late summer to early fall

'Round of Hungary'

This sweet, Pimiento-type pepper produces highly ribbed, flattened, fleshy fruits that are similar in appearance to a beefsteak tomato. The flavor of this non-hybrid is very sweet and the fruits ripen to red from green. It does best in hot regions or warm sites.

	suitable for containers
	spring to summer
	some resistance
	not hardy
	late summer to early fall

'Mohawk'

Abundant, medium-sized fruits are borne on this variety's compact plants, which are ideally suited to growing in a container or on a windowsill. Peppers ripen from green to yellow with fair flavor, but tend to be thin-walled. Plants are reliable even in cooler regions.

 suitable for containers
 spring to summer
 some resistance
not hardy
late summer to early fall

'Giant Marconi Hybrid'

This non-hybrid sweet pepper bears elongated, large, blocky, tapering fruits that ripen from pale green to bright red; they are well-flavored and fleshy. Plants mature quickly and, although best in hot regions, have potential as a greenhouse crop in cooler areas.

 suitable for containers
 spring to summer
 some resistance
 not hardy
late summer to early fall

'Flavorburst'

This hybrid sweet pepper produces very large, blocky fruits that ripen from pale green to a warm yellow. The sweet, fleshy fruits are borne in abundance in hot regions, and if grown in a greenhouse, this pepper has potential even in cooler areas.

suitable for containers
spring to summer
some resistance
not hardy
late summer to early fall

'Gypsy'

This hybrid sweet pepper variety bears long, green, fleshy fruits that ripen to bright red. The quality and flavor are excellent and, in greenhouses or hot areas, yields are very good. The plants are compact and are well-suited to growing in greenhouses or containers.

- 🪴 suitable for containers
- 🡖 spring to summer
- ✴ some resistance
- ❄ not hardy
- 🔒 late summer to early fall

'Islander F1 (purple)'

This hybrid sweet pepper produces blocky fruits that ripen early, going from a most attractive purple to red, via orange. Flavor is good, but the fruits are thin-walled until fully ripe. Yields are good in hot regions, to which this variety is best-suited.

- 🪴 suitable for containers
- 🡖 spring to summer
- ✴ some resistance
- ❄ not hardy
- 🔒 late summer to early fall

'California Wonder'

This non-hybrid sweet pepper produces large, blocky, fleshy fruits that ripen from green to red. Plants are really best-suited to warm regions and may require protection in cooler areas in order to produce a good yield.

- 🪴 suitable for containers
- 🡖 spring to summer
- ✴ some resistance
- ❄ not hardy
- 🔒 late summer to early fall

'Bell Boy'

This conventional sweet pepper bears very heavy crops of blocky, fleshy fruits, which ripen from bright green to glistening red. Early, and with unusually good tolerance of cool conditions, this variety has very good cropping potential, both indoors and out.

 suitable for containers

spring to summer

some resistance

not hardy

late summer to early fall

'Ariane'

This hybrid sweet pepper produces heavy, early crops of sweet, fleshy, blocky fruits, which ripen from green to orange. Plants grow to 30 in (76 cm) tall, and have an open, easy-to-manage habit. They are well adapted to cooler regions.

 suitable for containers

spring to summer

some resistance

not hardy

late summer to early fall

'Alma Paprika'

This non-hybrid, paprika pepper is not sweet, but it is not burning hot either. The delightful round fruits have thick walls, and they ripen from creamy-white through orange into a deep red. The plants are best-suited to warmer regions.

suitable for containers

spring to summer

some resistance

not hardy

late summer to early fall

'Ferrari'

This hybrid sweet pepper bears good yields of medium-sized, blocky fruits that ripen red from green. The plants are tall and will require staking. This robust variety tolerates cool climates, but prefers warmer regions or greenhouse cultivation.

- suitable for containers
- spring to summer
- some resistance
- not hardy
- late summer to early fall

'Jimmy Nardello's'

This variety originated in Italy and produces long, thin, sweet peppers. The fruits ripen from green to deep red and have good flavor. Best-suited to regions with hot summers, it can do well in warm sunny sites in less favored areas.

- suitable for containers
- spring to summer
- some resistance
- not hardy
- late summer to early fall

'Carmen F1'

This hybrid sweet pepper bears long, horn-shaped fruits that ripen from green to red; the peppers are fleshy and sweet. In hot regions, the plants crop very heavily and, since they mature early, they have potential in cooler regions when grown in a greenhouse.

- suitable for containers
- spring to summer
- some resistance
- not hardy
- late summer to early fall

'Purple Beauty'

This non-hybrid sweet pepper produces medium-sized, blocky fruits that ripen early through purple to red. The plants are compact and bushy and the fruits fleshy and well-flavored. Since it is early maturing, this pepper can be grown in cool as well as hot regions.

 suitable for containers
spring to summer
some resistance
not hardy
late summer to early fall

'Valencia Hybrid'

This sweet hybrid pepper produces large, blocky fruits that mature from green to orange. The late-maturing, fleshy fruits have a sweet flavor. If grown in the warm regions that suit it best, the yields from this robust plant are good.

 suitable for containers
spring to summer
some resistance
 not hardy
late summer to early fall

'Red Knight'

This early, hybrid sweet pepper bears very large, blocky fruits, which ripen from dark green to strong red. Plants are a moderate size and have a higher than usual disease resistance. Best for hot regions, they may require a greenhouse in cooler areas.

 suitable for containers
spring to summer
some resistance
 not hardy
 late summer to early fall

'Cherry Bomb'

'Cherry Bomb' is a fast-growing variety that bears large, 2.5-in (6-cm) long, rounded fruits that ripen to red and have a moderately hot taste. The peppers are good for stuffing or using in cooking. The plants crop heavily and produce fruits early even in cooler regions.

- suitable for containers
- spring to summer
- some resistance
- not hardy
- late summer to early fall

'Aji Amarillo'

This non-hybrid chili is more a type than a variety, and originated in Peru. The plants are medium-sized and carry long, thin, very hot peppers, ripening from green through yellow to red. It is best-suited to hot regions or to greenhouses in cooler areas.

- suitable for containers
- spring to summer
- some resistance
- not hardy
- late summer to early fall

'Long Thin Cayenne'

This tall, non-hybrid chili produces long, thin, very hot fruits that ripen from green to glistening red. The peppers are attractive and excellent for drying. This variety does best in regions with hot summers, but is also reliable in cooler areas.

- suitable for containers
- spring to summer
- some resistance
- not hardy
- late summer to early fall

'Ring O' Fire'

The fiery, long, thin peppers of this variety ripen from green to bright red on tall, bushy plants. Quick-growing and prolific, the plants are tolerant of cooler conditions. 'Ring O' Fire' responds well to sun and warmth. Fruits dry well and have great ornamental value.

 suitable for containers
 spring to summer
 some resistance
not hardy
late summer to early fall

'Meek and Mild'

This non-hybrid chili produces large, deep-green fruits ripening to an equally deep red. The fruits have very little heat and some sweetness, so are good for stuffing or eating raw. The plants are reliable even in cooler climates, and suit container cultivation.

 suitable for containers
spring to summer
some resistance
not hardy
late summer to early fall

'Firecracker'

This very hot chili was named 'Firecracker' for a reason. It produces many upright peppers that ripen from white to purple, through orange, then finally red. The tall plants will need staking and are well-suited to container growing, even in cooler regions.

 suitable for containers
spring to summer
some resistance
not hardy
late summer to early fall

'Mariachi Hybrid'

This hybrid chili produces numerous medium-sized, conical fruits that have a low level of hotness. They ripen from pale green through creamy yellow to red on compact plants that are well-suited to container cultivation. They are robust and will grow in cooler regions.

- 🪣 suitable for containers
- 🌱 spring to summer
- 🐛 some resistance
- ❄ not hardy
- 🔒 late summer to early fall

'Super Chili'

This fiery hot chili bears huge numbers of small, very attractive fruits that ripen from pale green to bright red. The fruits are ideal for drying. The compact plant is highly ornamental and is well-suited to patio pots even in regions with cool summers.

- 🪣 suitable for containers
- 🌱 spring to summer
- 🐛 some resistance
- ❄ not hardy
- 🔒 late summer to early fall

'Tricolor Variegatum'

This variegated, non-hybrid chili bears green leaves splashed with cream and purple. The hot fruits are small and numerous, maturing from purple to orange and finally red. The plants are tall and suited to pots; they are good even in cooler regions.

- 🪣 suitable for containers
- 🌱 spring to summer
- 🐛 some resistance
- ❄ not hardy
- 🔒 late summer to early fall

'Apache'

This highly ornamental chili has a bushy habit and bears numerous small, fleshy, hot peppers that ripen from deep green to bright red. The fruits point outward from the stems and are very decorative. Plants are reliable even in cool regions.

- 🪣 suitable for containers
- 🌱 spring to summer
- 🐛 some resistance
- ❄ not hardy
- 🔒 late summer to early fall

'Super Chili'

'Prairie Fire'

These spreading, dwarf plants
thrive even in cooler regions,
producing prolific clusters of
small and fiery upright fruits,
ripening from white through
yellow and orange before finally
becoming red. The plants are
ideal for growing in containers
or on windowsills.

- suitable for containers
- spring to summer
- some resistance
- not hardy
- late summer to early fall

'Czech Black'

This non-hybrid chili bears small,
conical fruits on bushy plants.
The fleshy and moderately hot
peppers ripen from black to red,
giving the robust plants good
ornamental value. It suits a
greenhouse in cooler regions,
but thrives best in hot summers.

- suitable for containers
- spring to summer
- some resistance
- not hardy
- late summer to early fall

'Tabasco'

This bushy, traditional chili
bears numerous very small
but fiery-hot fruits that ripen
from pale green to a bright-
red color. The plants are
best-suited to regions that have
hot summers or, in cooler areas,
to greenhouse cultivation.

- suitable for containers
- spring to summer
- some resistance
- not hardy
- late summer to early fall

'Etna'

This compact, non-hybrid variety
bears prolific clusters of upright
peppers that mature from green
to fiery, glistening red, with
corresponding hotness. The
robust plants suit container
cultivation and will thrive in any
reasonably warm environment.

- suitable for containers
- spring to summer
- some resistance
- not hardy
- late summer to early fall

'Demon Red'

This non-hybrid chili is bred to grow in pots and even on windowsills. It has a very compact habit, but is covered in short, thin, pointed fruits that ripen from green to bright red, and are very hot. The plants are robust and reliable, even in cooler regions.

 suitable for containers
 spring to summer
 some resistance
 not hardy
 late summer to early fall

'Jalapeno'

This early-cropping chili is easy to grow and is reliable even in regions with cool, wet summers. The narrow, conical fruits ripen from clear green to fiery red, but their flavor is relatively mild; they can even be eaten raw. Yields are relatively modest.

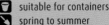 suitable for containers
spring to summer
some resistance
not hardy
late summer to early fall

'Anaheim'

This non-hybrid chili grows relatively tall and carries heavy crops of very large, bright-red fruits that ripen from green. They have mild heat and good flavor. It is best-suited to warm regions and greenhouse cultivation in cooler areas.

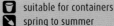 suitable for containers
 spring to summer
some resistance
not hardy
late summer to early fall

'Hungarian Hot Wax'

This non-hybrid chili variety
bears long, conical fruits,
which ripen from pale yellow
to bright red. The peppers have
moderate heat and are good for
stuffing or using in salads.
The plants tolerate cool growing
conditions and will perform well
in containers.

🪣	suitable for containers
🖊	spring to summer
🕷	some resistance
❄	not hardy
🔒	late summer to early fall

'Friar's Hat'

This hot, non-hybrid chili
bears highly unusual, bell-
shaped, lobed, medium-sized
fruits that ripen from green to
red and are exceptionally
eye-catching. The tall plants are
best-suited to hot regions; grow
in a greenhouse elsewhere.

🪣	suitable for containers
🖊	spring to summer
🕷	some resistance
❄	not hardy
🔒	late summer to early fall

'Habanero'

Strictly speaking, this chili
is a type rather than a variety.
It bears rounded, green fruits
with pointed ends, which
usually ripen to red, but are
sometimes orange or yellow.
The very hot fruits are borne
on medium-sized plants.

🪣	suitable for containers
🖊	spring to summer
🕷	some resistance
❄	not hardy
🔒	late summer to early fall

'Filius Blue'

This fiery, non-hybrid chili
bears white flowers, followed by
unusual, small, blue fruits that
ripen through pale green to
purple, finally becoming red.
The vigorous plants are medium-
sized and highly ornamental;
they are well-suited to cooler
regions and container growing.

- suitable for containers
- spring to summer
- some resistance
- not hardy
- late summer to early fall

'Padron'

Also known as 'Pimiento de
Padron', this traditional,
non-hybrid chili is originally
from Spain. The small fruits
ripen from green to red; some
can be very hot, although others
are on the mild side. It grows
best in regions with hot summers.

- suitable for containers
- spring to summer
- some resistance
- not hardy
- late summer to early fall

'Ciliegia Piccante'

Originating in Italy, this
attractive chili bears numerous,
cherry-sized fruits of moderate
heat, which reduce on cooking.
Fruits are prominently borne on
bushy plants, which are best in
hot regions, but also suit cooler
regions if grown in a greenhouse.

- suitable for containers
- spring to summer
- some resistance
- not hardy
- late summer to early fall

EGGPLANTS *Solanum melongena*

Also known as "aubergine" or "brinjal," these variable fruits come in a wide range of shapes, sizes, and colors. They are easy to grow but won't do well in cold conditions and will be killed by frost; in cool regions, they are best in a greenhouse. Although young plants are widely sold and are a good choice for gardeners without the warm conditions needed to raise seedlings, a wider range of varieties are offered as seed.

	SPRING	SUMMER	FALL	WINTER
SOW/PLANT				
HARVEST				

SOWING

Sow seed in late winter or early spring, ensuring a minimum temperature of between 64–77°F (18–25°C). For optimum growth, seedlings need ample warmth and light and must not get crowded. Plant them out into individual containers as soon as possible.

Before transplanting, enrich soil, indoors or out, by digging in a 2 in (5 cm) layer of rotted organic matter and, in addition, in poor soils apply a generous amount of a balanced fertilizer. A warm, sheltered, sunny site is essential outdoors, and young seedlings may need protection with a cloche or a layer of horticultural fleece. Eggplants thrive in containers,

Plant out seedlings after hardening off.

and fruit set is often enhanced if these are not too large.

CROP CARE

During growth, pinch out the growing tips to induce bushy growth. Plants can produce large numbers of fruits, so support them with string and stakes to prevent damage. Plants are self-pollinating and do not require any assistance to set fruits.

Greenhouse crops respond to warmer conditions than other tender plants, and benefit from being grown under a fleece tent. Water plants during dry periods. They will need an application of liquid fertilizer as they grow.

HARVESTING

Gather fruits once they have attained their full color and stopped growing in size. If left too long, they cease to be glossy and lose their color; overripe peppers nearby may suppress the formation of subsequent fruits. They are vulnerable to rotting if conditions are humid and cool.

PESTS AND DISEASES

Pests such as whitefly, red spider mite, or caterpillars may be troublesome in greenhouses. Pick off any caterpillars as you see them. Outdoors, you may need to apply an appropriate insecticide.

Soil-grown plants are at risk from verticillium wilt. This disease causes wilting and eventual death. Remove and destroy any infected plant material. To reduce the risk of infection, buy plants grafted onto disease-resistant tomato rootstock and practice good garden hygiene.

'Fairy Tale'

This unusual hybrid plant bears long, thin fruits, striped with white and purple; they are often carried in clusters. The compact plants are well-suited to growing in containers, grow bags, and pots on the patio, and often do well in cooler regions.

🪣	suitable for containers
🍃	spring
✳️	some resistance
❄️	not hardy
🔒	summer

'Bonica'

This tall, hybrid standard-type plant has excellent vigor and is highly productive, even in cooler regions. The lofty plants produce excellent-quality fruits and are suitable for container or soil cultivation, indoors or outdoors, but will need supports.

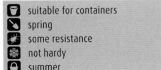

🪣	suitable for containers
🍃	spring
✳️	some resistance
❄️	not hardy
🔒	summer

'Moneymaker'

This very robust and cold-tolerant hybrid eggplant bears slightly elongated and rather pointed fruits of good flavor. It is well-suited to both cool and warm regions, and can yield well outdoors in hot summers. It is best-suited to greenhouse use.

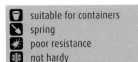

🪣	suitable for containers
🍃	spring
✳️	poor resistance
❄️	not hardy
🔒	summer

'Mini Bambino'

This novelty plant produces numerous glossy, dark, attractive fruits. Although the small size and limited yield make it a poor choice for the kitchen, it is a decorative, highly ornamental vegetable and is especially loved by children. It is suited to both soil and pot growing.

 suitable for containers

 spring

 poor resistance

not hardy

summer

'Turkish Orange'

This traditional non-hybrid type produces highly unusual fruits that are small but numerous and have a sweet flavor. This variety is only suitable for warm conditions so grow it under plastic or glass in cold regions, or outdoors in hot areas.

 suitable for containers

spring

poor resistance

 not hardy

 summer

'Little Finger'

This non-hybrid cultivar bears many slim, long, dark-purple fruits of good texture and flavor, which are carried on vigorous plants. It has great ornamental and curiosity value, and is good for culinary use in warm regions or for indoor cultivation.

 suitable for containers

spring

 some resistance

 not hardy

 Summer

'Applegreen'

This novelty, heirloom, non-hybrid variety produces moderate yields of egglike, apple-green fruits even when conditions are not ideal. The small fruits are tender and of good flavor. It does best in hot regions and should be grown in greenhouses elsewhere.

- suitable for containers
- spring
- poor resistance
- not hardy
- summer

'Prosperosa'

This non-hybrid, traditional eggplant originates in Italy. The fruits are small and almost spherical. They are of good quality and their pale purple color is unusual and well worth growing for its ornamental value. Greenhouse cultivation is best in areas without hot summers.

- suitable for containers
- spring
- poor resistance
- not hardy
- summer

'Galine'

This hybrid standard-type bears heavy crops of large, attractively glossy, purple fruits. It is best suited to indoor cultivation in cooler areas. Plants are relatively compact and easily managed, although some staking is required.

- suitable for containers
- spring
- some resistance
- not hardy
- summer

'Long Purple'

This long-established, rather variable, non-hybrid eggplant is sold widely and inexpensively and has stood the test of time. Although it is not the heaviest cropper, it is reliable, producing long, good-quality violet rather than purple fruits.

- suitable for containers
- spring
- poor resistance
- not hardy
- Summer

'Rosa Bianca'

This non-hybrid variety bears round, almost ball-shaped fruits that become pinkish-purple in color and have a good flavor and texture. It is best grown in warm regions or indoors, and being highly ornamental, it is very good for container cultivation.

 suitable for containers
 spring
 poor resistance
 not hardy
 summer

'Snowy'

This non-hybrid variety bears medium-sized, white fruits that are highly ornamental but also have good flavor and texture. 'Snowy' can be grown indoors in cool regions or outside in warmer areas. It is highly suited to growing in containers.

 suitable for containers
 spring
 poor resistance
 not hardy
 summer

'Dancer'

This robust hybrid plant bears appetizing green fruit leaves, and medium size, bright pink fruits that are well-flavored with a good texture. 'Dancer' is suited to outdoor cultivation in warm areas, but better grown indoors in cool regions.

 suitable for containers
 spring
 some resistance
 not hardy
 summer

'Slim Jim'

This non-hybrid variety produces long, thin, glossy purple fruits of good flavor and texture. They are borne in abundance if grown in warm conditions. 'Slim Jim' is best grown indoors in cool regions, but is well-suited to outdoor growing in hot areas.

- suitable for containers
- spring
- poor resistance
- not hardy
- summer

'Falcon'

This early, hybrid standard-type variety bears heavy crops of large, smooth, spine-free fruits of a deep purple, almost black, color. It is best-suited to indoor cultivation but grows outdoors in warmer regions. The compact plants require staking.

- suitable for containers
- spring
- some resistance
- not hardy
- summer

'Listada de Gandia'

This traditional, non-hybrid eggplant from Italy carries rounded, white- and purple-streaked, well-flavored fruits on medium-sized plants. These attractive ornamental plants should be grown indoors in areas with cool summers.

- suitable for containers
- spring
- poor resistance
- not hardy
- summer

'Black Beauty'

This standard-type plant produces good-quality, pear-shaped dark fruits of good texture and flavor. Being non-hybrid it has modest yields and vigor, and although it will grow in all situations, it is best-suited for warm regions or indoor cultivation.

 suitable for containers

spring

poor resistance

not hardy

summer

'Violetta Lunga'

This non-hybrid, standard-type eggplant bears large, glossy, purple fruits with attractive leaves. Plants are robust and medium-sized, and suitable for indoor cultivation in cool regions or outdoors in warm areas. It is well-suited for containers.

 suitable for containers

spring

poor resistance

not hardy

summer

'Thai Green'

This non-hybrid variety produces unusual, long, green fruits often used in Thai cuisine. It is suitable for soil or container cultivation but requires warm conditions. It will only grow under glass or plastic in all but the warmest, sunniest regions.

 suitable for containers

spring

poor resistance

not hardy

summer

CORN *Zea mays*

Corn grows easily in warm regions, but good crops are possible in cooler areas if seed is sown under cover. Standard or sugary (su) varieties have been largely supplanted by supersweet (Sh2) corn, which retains its very sweet flavor after picking. Sugar enhanced types (se) are also very sweet, and widely grown; hybrid synergistic corn combines traits from both. Baby corn can be grown on closely spaced plants or by using special varieties.

	SPRING	SUMMER	FALL	WINTER
SOW/PLANT				
HARVEST				

SOWING

Any fertile garden soil in full sun is suitable. Dig in plenty of well-rotted manure before planting, and supplement this with an application of balanced liquid fertilizer. Add lime, too, if soils are acidic. Being wind pollinated, it is best raised in squares rather than rows.

Plant out seedlings from late spring.

Raise early crops by sowing seed under cover, two seeds per small container, at a depth of 1–1.5 in (2.5–4 cm), keeping them at a minimum temperature of 70–80°F (20–27°C). Seedlings can be singled out once they have started to develop. Plant them out in late spring or early summer, and protect them with cloches or fleece if the weather is cold. Ensure that plants have enough space—about 16 in (40 cm) between plants in the case of full-sized corn. Where baby corn is being grown, allow 6 in (15 cm) between plants, and 12 in (30 cm) between rows.

If sowing directly into the ground, wait until days are warm and night temperatures are above 50°F (10°C). Sow three seeds for each plant and thin out later, if required. Subsequent crops can be

sown every two weeks until early summer. Cross pollination from nearby agricultural or ornamental corns, or between standard and sweeter types of corn, will lead to a loss of sweetness.

CROP CARE

Keep plants well weeded, and ensure that they are given plenty of water in dry spells, particularly once flowering begins.

HARVESTING

Gather cobs once the silky parts brown and the kernels exude a milky juice when split. Once harvested, use as soon as possible.

PESTS AND DISEASES

Exclude birds from developed cobs using netting or by covering individual cobs with plastic bags. Large mammals may trample plants and eat the cobs. Smut disease can cause distorted cobs. Protect after sowing, since birds or mice may eat ungerminated seeds.

Protect cobs to prevent attack.

'Marshall's Honeydew'

This extra-tender variety produces medium-sized, sturdy plants, bearing strong foliage, and medium-sized, well-filled cobs of good texture and flavor. They mature in the mid- to late season period. Suitable for cooler regions and all good garden soils.

- unsuitable for containers
- spring
- some resistance
- not hardy
- summer to early fall

'Mirai 302BC'

Also referred to as 'Mirai Bicolor M302', this hybrid supersweet variety has an unusual mixture of white and yellow kernels. It has good sweetness, tenderness, and flavor. Plants are tall and vigorous, so are not best-suited to windy locations.

- unsuitable for containers
- spring
- some resistance
- not hardy
- summer to early fall

'Lapwing'

This heavy-cropping, tendersweet type bears very sweet and tender, bright-yellow kernels in large, elongated, well-filled cobs. The fruits mature early to midseason. Plants are robust and have a good tolerance to a wide range of growing conditions.

- unsuitable for containers
- spring
- some resistance
- not hardy
- summer to early fall

'Sundance'

This standard-type variety matures early and is well-suited to cooler regions and to areas where the growing season is short. The long cobs have a sweet flavor, good texture, and are filled with cream-colored kernels. Plants are short but have a sturdy constitution.

- unsuitable for containers
- spring
- some resistance
- not hardy
- summer to early fall

'Northern Extra Sweet'

This exceptionally early-maturing, supersweet type is also called 'Northern Xtra Sweet'. It bears long cobs with large, flavorful kernels, and is excellent for cool locations, and for early crops in warm regions. It is of medium height, so is suited to exposed sites.

- unsuitable for containers
- spring
- some resistance
- not hardy
- summer to early fall

'Double Standard'

Strong germination in cool soil makes this corn ideal for northern gardens. At 5 ft (1.5 m), 'Double Standard' is fairly compact, and its ears ripen over several weeks rather than at once. Seeds can be saved and planted; white kernels produce all-white ears.

- unsuitable for containers
- late spring
- some resistance
- not hardy
- mid- to late summer

'Serendipity Hybrid'

A mid-season hybrid, this variety is well-suited to cultivation in regions with hot summers. The white and yellow kernels are carried in large heads and combine the sugary sweetness of supersweets with the succulent texture of sugar-enhanced types.

- 🪣 unsuitable for containers
- 🌱 spring
- 🕷 some resistance
- ❄ not hardy
- 🔒 summer to early fall

'Dynasty'

This tall, supersweet variety produces sturdy growth, strong foliage, and long, large, well-filled cobs that have both a good texture and a good flavor. 'Dynasty' matures in the mid- to late season period, thus making it suitable for cooler regions.

- 🪣 unsuitable for containers
- 🌱 spring
- 🕷 some resistance
- ❄ not hardy
- 🔒 summer to early fall

'Incredible'

This sugar-enhanced, midseason variety can produce heavy crops when grown in a wide range of conditions. The cobs are large and sweet, although less so than the supersweets. It is well-suited to sowing in colder regions since it will tolerate cool soils.

- 🪣 unsuitable for containers
- 🌱 spring
- 🕷 poor resistance
- ❄ not hardy
- 🔒 summer to early fall

'Honey Select Hybrid'

This midseason hybrid combines the sugary sweetness and full flavor of supersweets with the tender crunchiness of sugar-enhanced corn. Cobs have yellow grains and are outstandingly sweet and tender. This variety is best suited to hot regions.

- 🪣 unsuitable for containers
- 🌱 spring
- 🕷 some resistance
- ❄ not hardy
- 🔒 summer to early fall

'Minipop'

This specialized variety is grown for the sole purpose of producing baby corn, and is therefore unsuitable for other uses. Several cobs are produced on these vigorous, easy-to-grow plants, which often produce more than one stem. The seeds should be sown closely together.

 unsuitable for containers
spring
some resistance
not hardy
summer to early fall

'Sugar Buns Hybrid'

This early-maturing hybrid variety produces long ears filled with large, yellow kernels, carried on tall, vigorous plants. The cobs have the excellent, sweet flavor and tender texture typical of this type, and do well in regions with warm summers.

 unsuitable for containers
spring
some resistance
not hardy
summer to early fall

'Prelude'

This medium-sized, supersweet variety has exceptionally vigorous, sturdy growth and produces high yields of large, well-filled cobs of excellent texture and flavor. Maturing in the midseason period, it suits a wide range of conditions.

 unsuitable for containers
spring
some resistance
not hardy
summer to early fall

'Country Gentleman'

This late-maturing, non-hybrid variety has long been grown in warmer regions, where it thrives best. It produces creamy-white kernels, which have a relatively moderate sweetness. In the right climate, it will produce more than one shoot, each of which bears one cob.

- unsuitable for containers
- spring
- some resistance
- not hardy
- summer to early fall

'Strawberry Popcorn'

This charming ornamental plant bears small, round, and attractive cobs of rich, red grains that look similar to strawberries. The dried cobs make good ornaments and the grains can be popped. This variety should be grown away from other varieties.

- unsuitable for containers
- spring
- some resistance
- not hardy
- summer to early fall

'Brocade F1'

This midseason, sugar-enhanced 'F1' variety produces long, heavy cobs full of tender, sweet, and flavorful kernels. Plants are tall and vigorous, and grow best in warmer regions, where their disease tolerance comes in especially useful.

- unsuitable for containers
- spring
- good resistance
- not hardy
- summer to early fall

'Luscious F1'

This hybrid, sugar-enhanced corn produces heavy, very sweet and tender heads, filled with yellow and white kernels. Plants are tall and vigorous and suit regions with hot summers; they tolerate the leaf diseases often found in these areas.

- unsuitable for containers
- spring
- some resistance
- not hardy
- summer to early fall

'Strawberry Popcorn'

'Jubilee'

This excellent-quality variety produces large cobs that grow up to 8 in (20 cm) in length, and are filled with sweet, tender, and vibrantly colored yellow kernels. The delicious cobs freeze well, and they are borne on tall plants that ripen quickly.

- unsuitable for containers
- spring
- some resistance
- not hardy
- summer to early fall

'How Sweet It Is'

This is the first white, supersweet hybrid to earn an All-America Selections Award. It produces 8-in (20-cm) ears full of crisp, tender kernels. The plants must be isolated from other corn types to prevent cross-pollination, which degrades kernel quality.

- unsuitable for containers
- late spring
- some resistance
- not hardy
- late summer

'Butterscotch'

This is as early-maturing, supersweet-type 'F1' hybrid, producing tender kernels that retain their excellent qualities, even after freezing. Growing to just 5 ft (1.5 m) tall, it is suitable for cooler, exposed gardens. Grow in good, free-draining soil.

- unsuitable for containers
- spring
- some resistance
- not hardy
- summer to fall

'Ambrosia'

This sugar-enhanced bicolor is known for seedling vigor, wilt resistance, and superior flavor. Favored by gardeners in cool climates, 'Ambrosia' bears 8-in (20-cm) ears filled with plump white and yellow kernels 75 days after seeds are sown.

- unsuitable for containers
- late spring
- good resistance
- not hardy
- mid- to late summer

'Swift'

An extra-tender type, this variety produces medium-sized heads filled with succulent, sweet, and bright-yellow grains. The robust plants mature especially early, and they reliably bear heavy crops, even in cooler regions and under a wide range of conditions.

  unsuitable for containers
spring
some resistance
not hardy
summer to early fall

'Inca Rainbow'

This is an unusual, heritage variety that produces distinctive single- or multicolored cobs, made up of red, white, yellow, and purple kernels. It reaches 8 ft (2.4 m) high and needs a long, hot growing season for the best crop. Treat it as a novelty.

unsuitable for containers
spring
some resistance
not hardy
summer to fall

'Bodacious Hybrid'

This sugar-enhanced variety is early-maturing and carries long, good-quality cobs filled with sweet, yellow, especially tender grains. It has good rust tolerance and is suitable for cooler regions, and where the growing season is short.

unsuitable for containers
spring
some resistance
not hardy
summer to early fall

'Sugar Pearl Hybrid'

This synergistic hybrid combines the sweet, full flavor of supersweet types with the tender succulence of sugar-enhanced corn in its white kernels. Best-suited for regions with hot summers, the tall vigorous plants mature late in the season.

- unsuitable for containers
- spring
- some resistance
- not hardy
- summer to early fall

'Earlibird'

This tall, supersweet type produces sturdy growth, strong foliage, and even, well-filled cobs of good texture and flavor. Despite its name, 'Earlibird' matures in the mid- to late season period. It is especially suitable for cooler regions.

- unsuitable for containers
- spring
- some resistance
- not hardy
- summer to early fall

'Stowell's'

This standard-type variety is well-suited to regions with hot summers. It matures late and has sweet, tender, and white kernels. Cobs remain milky for a prolonged period; the variety is therefore sometimes referred to as 'Stowell's Evergreen.'

- unsuitable for containers
- spring
- some resistance
- not hardy
- summer to early fall

'Mirai 421W'

This supersweet type, also called 'Mirai White M421', produces long ears filled with white kernels of a high sugar content and exceptional flavor and tenderness. Plants are early-maturing, vigorous, tall, and leafy. Plant in full sun and give them plenty of warmth.

- unsuitable for containers
- spring
- some resistance
- not hardy
- summer to early fall

'Seville'

This tall, supersweet, late-season variety produces vigorous, sturdy growth, strong foliage, and excellent, large, well-filled cobs. Kernels are small and of good texture and flavor. It is suitable for cooler regions, but fertile soils are required for the best cobs.

 unsuitable for containers
 spring
 some resistance
not hardy
summer to early fall

'Early Sunglow Hybrid'

This early-maturing, hybrid variety produces heads of yellow grains, with moderate sweetness and storage ability, but good tenderness. Satisfactory for cooler regions but best in warm areas, plants are robust with strong green foliage and husks.

 unsuitable for containers
spring
some resistance
not hardy
summer to early fall

'Conqueror'

This tall, vigorous, supersweet variety of corn produces long cobs with sweet and tender kernels. It copes well with a wide range of conditions and, despite being late-maturing, it is especially well-adapted to cooler regions.

 unsuitable for containers
 spring
 some resistance
not hardy
 summer to early fall

'Avalon Hybrid'

This hybrid bears large cobs and combines the best of supersweet and sugar-enhanced corns, resulting in very sweet, tender kernels. Like supersweets, the flavor is retained well after harvest, but like sugar-enhanced, the ears need gentle handling.

- unsuitable for containers
- spring
- some resistance
- not hardy
- summer to early fall

'Lark'

This tall, midseason, tendersweet variety produces sturdy growth, strong foliage, and medium-sized, well-filled cobs. Kernels are bright yellow in color and of excellent texture and flavor. Suitable for cooler regions and grows in all good garden soils.

- unsuitable for containers
- spring
- some resistance
- not hardy
- summer to early fall

'Silver Queen Hybrid'

This standard-type hybrid produces exceptionally long, heavy ears that mature early and are filled with glistening white kernels. It is especially well-suited to regions with hot summers, having resistance to diseases common in these areas.

- unsuitable for containers
- spring
- some resistance
- not hardy
- summer to early fall

'Sparrow'

This is a stocky, midseason tendersweet type. It produces sturdy growth, strong foliage, and medium size, well-filled cobs of excellent texture and flavor. Suitable for a wide range of conditions, this variety will thrive in cooler regions.

- unsuitable for containers
- spring
- some resistance
- not hardy
- summer to early fall

'Lark'

Cucumbers and Squashes

- Cucumbers
- Zucchini, Marrow squashes, and Summer squashes
- Pumpkins and Winter squashes

CUCUMBERS *Cucumus sativus*

You can grow a cucumber no matter how small your garden: if you have limited space, grow a trailing outdoor variety in a container. Outdoor cucumbers are hardier than their indoor relatives, with a thicker, more knobbled skin, and are excellent pickled. If you have the luxury of a greenhouse, you can grow indoor varieties, too, which are longer, with thinner skins, and are good for use in salads or sandwiches.

	SPRING	SUMMER	FALL	WINTER
SOW/PLANT				
HARVEST				

SOWING

Most modern greenhouse varieties are all-female and it is important that they are grown where they cannot be pollinated by male flowers, since this results in bitter fruits. Site plants carefully, and pinch out any male flowers that appear on indoor types.

Be careful not to damage the roots.

Outdoor cucumbers grow best in a warm, sunny site, and will thrive in containers or growing bags, indoors or out. They need a rich, well-drained soil, so dig in well-rotted manure or compost before sowing or planting out.

Seed can be sown indoors from early spring onward; it needs a minimum temperature of 68°F (20°C) to germinate. Harden off and plant out seedlings when they reach about four weeks old,

taking care not to damage the roots. Space them 18 in (45 cm) apart, allowing more room if plants are to trail.

Alternatively, warm the soil with a cloche or cold frame and sow directly into the ground from early summer, once the danger of frosts has passed. Sow two or three seeds together every 18 in (45 cm) and thin out the weakest as they develop.

CROP CARE

Trailing types will need support, so construct bamboo cane structures or use netting. Give them plenty of water during growth, especially while fruits are developing, and feed them every two weeks with a balanced liquid fertilizer. You will need to hand-pollinate outdoor types yourself (see p.532).

HARVESTING AND STORING

Harvest while young, since leaving cucumbers too long can spoil the flavor of those left on the plant. Cucumbers do not store, but small ones can be pickled.

PESTS AND DISEASES

Discourage the spread of common diseases such as powdery mildew and cucumber mosaic virus by keeping plants well-watered and well-ventilated. Red spider mite or whitefly may be troublesome under glass. Guard young plants against slugs.

Red spider mite may mottle leaves.

'Bella'

This strong and vigorous F1 cultivar produces healthy foliage that is resistant to both powdery mildew and downy mildew. It produces a heavy yield of long, and slightly ribbed, good-quality fruits that are dark green in color.

🪣	suitable for containers
🌱	early to mid-spring
🕷️	good resistance
❄️	not hardy
🔒	late summer to mid-fall

'Emilie'

This cultivar produces fruits that have attractive, smooth, dark-green skin, crisp white flesh, and a good flavor. They are a useful size, growing to around 8 in (20 cm), which means they provide enough for a meal, without leftovers.

🪣	suitable for containers
🌱	early to mid-spring
🕷️	good resistance
❄️	not hardy
🔒	late summer to mid-fall

'Tanja'

A robust cultivar, 'Tanja' produces heavy yields and crops well over a long period. The fruits are 12 in (30 cm) long (or more), with dark-green, smooth, shiny skin, and an appetizing flavor. This is a good choice for containers.

🪣	suitable for containers
🌱	early to mid-spring
🕷️	poor resistance
❄️	not hardy
🔒	late summer to mid-fall

'Marketmore'

This very popular cultivar is normally grown outdoors to produce good yields of medium-sized, attractive, dark-green fruits with a few white spines. It is reliable, performing well even in a poor season, and is resistant to powdery and downy mildew.

 suitable for containers
early to mid-spring
good resistance
not hardy
late summer to mid-fall

'Eureka Hybrid'

This strong, indeterminate hybrid has extremely good disease resistance, with high yields of 2–7-in (5–18-cm), very dark-green slicing or pickling cucumbers. Plants are monoecious and trouble-free, and can be grown on a trellis for easy harvesting.

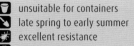 unsuitable for containers
late spring to early summer
excellent resistance
not hardy
midsummer to early fall

'Palermo'

An F1 hybrid cultivar, 'Palermo' has good resistance to powdery mildew. It makes a good choice for growing in an unheated greenhouse, and produces long, juicy, dark-green fruits that are equally good in sandwiches or salads.

suitable for containers
early to mid-spring
some resistance
not hardy
late summer to mid-fall

'Cucino'

This cultivar produces mini cucumbers 3–4 in (7.5–10 cm) long, making them ideal for snacks and lunch boxes. The fruits are uniform with thin, smooth, dark-green skin and tasty, green flesh. It is highly productive, yielding double the fruits of many other cultivars.

- suitable for containers
- early to mid-spring
- some resistance
- not hardy
- late summer to mid-fall

'Picolino'

This heavy-cropping F1 cultivar produces medium-sized, crisp, juicy cucumbers around 6–7 in (15–18 cm) long. A relatively healthy variety, it should be grown under cover, and has good resistance to both powdery and downy mildew.

- suitable for containers
- early to mid-spring
- good resistance
- not hardy
- late summer to mid-fall

'Boothby's Blonde'

This heirloom cultivar originated in Maine. The fruits have creamy-white skins flushed with yellow or green and a scattering of black spines. They are short and fat, best picked at 3–4 in (7.5–10 cm) long, and may be used fresh or pickled.

- suitable for containers
- early to mid-spring
- poor resistance
- not hardy
- late summer to mid-fall

'Crystal Apple'

This interesting, easy-to-grow cultivar produces a large crop of pale, yellow-green, spherical cucumbers that turn a deeper shade of yellow as they age. The unusual fruits are particularly flavorful and juicy, but they can be a little bit seedy in the center.

	suitable for containers
	early to mid-spring
	poor resistance
	not hardy
	late summer to mid-fall

'Rocky'

This is an unusually compact cultivar, producing clusters of baby cucumbers that are close to the main stem. It is an early maturing variety and likes plenty of warmth, so would be a good choice for a container on a sunny patio.

	suitable for containers
	early to mid-spring
	some resistance
	not hardy
	late summer to mid-fall

'Naomi'

This cultivar produces long, straight, and slightly ribbed fruits that have attractive, dark-green skin and a good flavor. It has some resistance to a number of fungal diseases that can affect foliage, including powdery mildew.

	suitable for containers
	early to mid-spring
	some resistance
	not hardy
	late summer to mid-fall

'Masterpiece'

An outdoor, ridge-type cucumber, 'Masterpiece' produces heavy yields of dark-green, slightly spiny, medium-sized fruits that have a crisp, white flesh. It is a very reliable cropper, with healthy foliage, and would be a good choice for growing in a large container.

🪣	suitable for containers
🌱	early to mid-spring
🐞	some resistance
❄️	not hardy
🔒	late summer to mid-fall

'White Wonder'

This old, dual-purpose cultivar dates back to the 1800s and was traditionally used for pickling, although it can also be eaten fresh. It starts to crop early in the season, producing creamy-white fruits that are best picked before they exceed 6 in (15 cm).

🪣	suitable for containers
🌱	early to mid-spring
🐞	poor resistance
❄️	not hardy
🔒	late summer to mid-fall

'Salad Bush Hybrid'

Bush cucumbers, like 'Salad Bush' and 'Spacemaster', are good for small gardens or containers: they take up one-third of the space of typical vines. Disease resistance and plentiful 8-in (20-cm) slicers earned this hybrid a 1988 All-America Selections award.

🪣	suitable for containers
🌱	late spring to early summer
🐞	good resistance
❄️	not hardy
🔒	midsummer to early fall

'Green Fingers'

This F1 hybrid cultivar produces lots of mini cucumbers that are just 3–4 in (7.5–10 cm) in length. They have very thin skins, green flesh, a firm, crunchy texture, and are packed with flavor. The plants are resistant to powdery mildew as well as downy mildew.

- suitable for containers
- early to mid-spring
- good resistance
- not hardy
- late summer to mid-fall

'Tasty King'

A Japanese-bred F1 hybrid cultivar, 'Tasty King' can be grown in an unheated greenhouse or outdoors. It produces a heavy crop of good-looking, tasty fruits that are longer than average, reaching 16 in (40 cm) or more.

- suitable for containers
- early to mid-spring
- poor resistance
- not hardy
- late summer to mid-fall

'Lemon'

Small, round, 2–4-in (5–10-cm) cucumbers are ready to harvest 68 days after sowing, and turn from pale greenish-yellow to lemon yellow when they reach the best eating stage. This specialty heirloom is prized for the crisp, mild flavor of its unusual fruits.

- suitable for containers
- late spring to early summer
- no resistance
- not hardy
- midsummer to early fall

'Tiffany'

This F1 hybrid cultivar produces a uniform crop of long fruits that are slightly ribbed. The "Tiffany' fruits have an attractive appearance, with dark-green skin and a nice and even shape, which could make them a winner on the show bench.

- suitable for containers
- early to mid-spring
- some resistance
- not hardy
- late summer to mid-fall

'Burpless Tasty Green'

A Japanese cultivar, 'Burpless Tasty Green' was specially bred to be easy to digest. It has tender skin and no bitterness. Resistant to powdery mildew, 'Burpless Tasty Green' produces medium-to-long, dark-green fruits with crisp, tasty flesh.

- suitable for containers
- early to mid-spring
- some resistance
- not hardy
- late summer to mid-fall

'Socrates'

'Socrates' is a reliable cultivar that produces an early and prolific crop of small, narrow fruits that are about 6 in (15 cm) in lengh, making it good for containers. It is a strong and vigorous grower, and the fruits have smooth, shiny skins and a good flavor.

- suitable for containers
- early to mid-spring
- some resistance
- not hardy
- late summer to mid-fall

'Passandra'

This cultivar bears prolific crops of high-quality, half-sized fruits that ideal for picking at around 6–8 in (15–20 cm); they have smooth, dark skin and crisp, white flesh. Plants show good resistance to powdery and downy mildews and cucumber mosaic virus.

 suitable for containers
 early to mid-spring
 good resistance
 not hardy
 late summer to mid-fall

'Tyria'

This F1 hybrid cultivar is suitable for growing outdoors or in an unheated greenhouse. It produces long, dark-green, and slightly ribbed, seedless fruits. The plants are resistant to powdery mildew, scab, and leaf spot.

 suitable for containers
early to mid-spring
excellent resistance
 not hardy
 late summer to mid-fall

'Cool Breeze Hybrid'

This parthenocarpic French cornichon hybrid is disease-resistant and needs no pollination. Vines can be protected from insects with row covers. Almost 100 percent female, the flowers mature early, yielding dark-green seedless, 4–5-in (10–13-cm) fruits.

unsuitable for containers
late spring to early summer
 good resistance
not hardy
 midsummer to early fall

'Mini Munch'

A highly productive cultivar, 'Mini Munch' produces abundant, small fruits, which are just 4 in (10 cm) in length. They are shiny-skinned, with a crunchy texture and good flavor. They make a great snack and are an excellent choice for packed lunches.

- suitable for containers
- early to mid-spring
- some resistance
- not hardy
- late summer to mid-fall

'La Diva'

This cultivar produces a crop of sweet, tender, and crisp fruits that have a smooth, thin skin. They average about 6 in (15 cm) in length, and have no seeds. With better-than-average cold tolerance, this is a good variety for growing outdoors in cooler areas.

- suitable for containers
- early to mid-spring
- poor resistance
- not hardy
- late summer to mid-fall

'Alibi Hybrid'

This dual-purpose hybrid produces high yields of 2–4-in (5–10-cm) dark-green fruits that are excellent fresh or pickled. The vines are more compact than typical varieties, and are resistant to powdery and downy mildew, scab, and mosaic virus.

- suitable for containers
- late spring to early summer
- good resistance
- not hardy
- midsummer to early fall

'Suyo Long'

This Asian heirloom produces 15-in (38-cm), slim, "burpless," sweet cucumbers with a crisp texture. Hardy and productive, even under adverse conditions, 'Suyo Long' is recommended for hot, humid climates. Trellising prevents fruit ends from curling.

- suitable for containers
- early to mid-spring
- some resistance
- not hardy
- midsummer to early fall

'La Diva'

ZUCCHINI, MARROW SQUASHES, AND SUMMER SQUASHES *Cucurbita pepo*

Fast and easy to grow, these reliable vegetables are prolific croppers.
Not all types are long and green—they come in a range of colors and
unusual shapes, many of which are highly decorative. Although all types
will grow to marrow squash size, harvest zucchini and squashes when small.

	SPRING	SUMMER	FALL	WINTER
SOW/PLANT				
HARVEST				

SOWING

Zucchini, summer squashes,
and marrow squashes all do best
in a sunny, open site, with rich,
well-drained soil. Dig in some
well-rotted manure or compost
before sowing or planting.

Seed can be sown from mid-
spring onward: if sowing early,
do so in a greenhouse or under
cover. Later seed can be sown in
pots or in the ground but will
need protection with a cloche or
cold frame. Sow seed 18 in (45 cm)
apart, and 1 in (2.5 cm) deep.

CROP CARE

Developing fruits need regular
watering and should not be
allowed to dry out, especially
when they are flowering, or while
the fruits are swelling. They may

It may help to pollinate by hand.

benefit from an application of
general fertilizer during growth.

If you are growing under glass,
your crops may lack insect
pollinators so you may need to
pollinate them by hand. Identify
a female flower, one that has
the thickened stem of the
developing fruit, and transfer
pollen from a male flower's
stamens onto the stigma, by
touching the flowers together.

HARVESTING

Zucchini and summer squashes should be harvested when they are small, at about 4 in (10 cm) long, when they are at their most flavorful. Regular picking will encourage the plants to produce a greater number of fruits.

Marrow squashes can be harvested when they are about 6 in (15 cm) long. They can be left to grow much larger, and will develop a thick, protective skin.

STORING

Allow marrow squashes to develop a thick skin, and store undamaged crops in a warm, dry place.

PESTS AND DISEASES

Ensuring that plants are well-watered and well-ventilated will help to prevent the most common diseases:, such as powdery mildew and cucumber mosaic virus. You may need to support plants carefully to prevent fruits from becoming cramped. Remove and destroy any infected plant material and, if necessary, apply an appropriate insecticide. Seedlings and developing plants are vulnerable to slugs and snails. Use pellets, set up traps, or lay a line of sand or grit, or copper tape, around the base of your plants.

'Custard White'

A patty-pan-type, this American heirloom cultivar produces creamy-white fruits shaped like a flying saucer with scalloped edges. They have firm flesh and can be picked from 2 in (5 cm) for slicing, or up to 5 in (12 cm) for stuffing or baking whole.

🪣 suitable for containers
🌱 early to late spring
🦟 poor resistance
❄️ not hardy
🔒 midsummer to early fall

'Seneca'

Ripening in just 42 days, 'Seneca' is a good choice for cool-summer regions, such as the Pacific Northwest, where growing squash can be difficult. The bush-type hybrid produces heavy yields of fruits that are most tender when picked at 6–8 in (15–20 cm).

🪣 unsuitable for containers
🌱 late spring
🦟 some resistance
❄️ not hardy
🔒 mid- to late summer

'Cocozelle Bush'

This Italian heirloom zucchini-type squash produces attractive dark-green fruits with light stripes that are at their tender best when harvested at 12 in (30 cm) or less. The compact, bushy plants are very prolific, and the flavorful fruits ripen in just 50 days.

🪣 unsuitable for containers
🌱 late spring
🦟 poor resistance
❄️ not hardy
🔒 mid to late summer

'Gold Rush'

This F1 hybrid, standard zucchini-type cultivar produces golden-yellow fruits with green stems that look good both in the garden and on the plate. The striking color makes them easy to spot. For best taste, the fruits should be picked before they get too large.

 suitable for containers
early to late spring
poor resistance
not hardy
midsummer to early fall

'Yellow Scallopini'

A patty-pan-type, this F1 hybrid cultivar is resistant to powdery mildew. It produces early and prolific crops of saucer-shaped fruits with scalloped edges. They are golden-yellow with a green disk at the blossom end. Harvest when 1.5–3 in (4–7.5 cm) across.

suitable for containers
early to late spring
some resistance
not hardy
midsummer to early fall

'Magda'

A club-shaped zucchini-type, this F1 hybrid cultivar produces creamy-green fruits with white flesh. They are best picked when small, at around 3–4 in (7.5–10 cm). At this size, they are very tender and are perfect for Middle Eastern cooking.

suitable for containers
early to late spring
poor resistance
not hardy
midsummer to early fall

'One Ball'

A ball-shaped zucchini-type, this bushy, F1 hybrid cultivar produces a good yield. The fruits are golden yellow, often marked with a green ring or star around the stalk or at the end of the blossom. They are perfect either roasted whole or cooked with stuffing.

- 🪴 suitable for containers
- 🌱 early to late spring
- ✳️ poor resistance
- ❄️ not hardy
- 🔒 midsummer to early fall

'Greyzini'

A standard zucchini-type, this very high-yielding F1 hybrid cultivar produces light-green fruits with unusual grayish mottling and faint stripes. Pick when medium-sized for the best flavor, and use sliced and grilled, steamed, or stir-fried.

- 🪴 suitable for containers
- 🌱 early to late spring
- ✳️ poor resistance
- ❄️ not hardy
- 🔒 midsummer to early fall

'Yellow Crookneck'

A crookneck-type, this cultivar tends to be late-cropping and needs warm conditions to do well. The fruits are bright yellow when mature, with knobbly, warty skin. Pick young to use like zucchini, or allow them to mature for baking whole.

- 🪴 unsuitable for containers
- 🌱 early to late spring
- ✳️ poor resistance
- ❄️ not hardy
- 🔒 midsummer to early fall

'Jemmer'

This high-yielding, F1-hybrid, zucchini-type cultivar produces slim, pale-yellow fruits on vigorous, upright, and compact plants. The attractive fruits are easy to see for picking and look equally good in the garden, or in salads or cooked dishes.

 suitable for containers

 early to late spring

 poor resistance

 not hardy

 midsummer to early fall

'Sungreen'

Hybrid 'Sungreen' offers high yields in limited space, and unequaled virus disease resistance. Bush-type plants are compact, yet open for easy harvest, and produce glossy, straight, dark-green fruits ready for harvest at 8 in (20 cm) or less.

 unsuitable for containers

late spring

good resistance

not hardy

mid- to late summer

'Dark Green'

Open-pollinated 'Dark Green' produces smooth, straight fruits with dark-green mottled skins. When harvested young, at 8 in (20 cm) or less, the green-tinted white flesh is firm and delicately flavored. The vigorous bush-type plants produce in 50 to 60 days.

 unsuitable for containers

late spring

poor resistance

not hardy

mid- to late summer

'Sunburst'

A patty-pan-type, this F1 hybrid cultivar produces attractive, glossy, bright-yellow fruits that have scalloped edges. They are at their best when harvested while still small, at around 2 in (5 cm). At this size, they are suitable for use either raw or cooked.

- suitable for containers
- early to late spring
- some resistance
- not hardy
- midsummer to early fall

'Raven'

The very dark skin on this hybrid, zucchini-type squash indicates high levels of lutein, an antioxidant linked to eye health. Growing just 3 ft (1 m) wide, 'Raven' produces a steady yield over a long period. Fruits are best harvested at 6–8 in (15–20 cm).

- unsuitable for containers
- late spring
- some resistance
- not hardy
- mid- to late summer

'Italiano Largo'

A standard zucchini-type, this F1 hybrid variety produces long, thin, slightly curved fruits that have distinct ribs running down their length. It develops few seeds, even when allowed to grow large, so more of the flesh can be used.

- suitable for containers
- early to late spring
- poor resistance
- not hardy
- midsummer to early fall

Zucchini

This prolific squash variety starts cropping early on in the season and continues to crop throughout it, producing a very heavy yield. The fruits are dark green in color and have a tender, pleasing texture that is matched by a good flavor.

 suitable for containers
 early to late spring
 poor resistance
 not hardy
 midsummer to early fall

'Zephyr'

A straightneck-type, this F1 hybrid cultivar produces slender fruits with a bulbous end. They have a distinctive appearance, with pale-yellow skin changing abruptly to pale green toward the blossom end. The flesh is firm with a delicious, nutty flavor.

suitable for containers
early to late spring
poor resistance
not hardy
midsummer to early fall

'Goldy'

This hybrid zucchini-type squash produces long, slender, bright-yellow fruits with white flesh in 50 to 55 days. The fruits keep their color, unlike similar varieties, and are tender and delicious raw or steamed. Plants are vigorous, compact, and prolific.

 unsuitable for containers
 late spring
 some resistance
 not hardy
 mid- to late summer

'Black Forest'

Most zucchini-type cultivars produce short, bushy plants but this F1 hybrid is a trailer, so it can be trained up supports to save space and make picking easier. The dark-skinned fruits are of good quality, with tender flesh. It is also suitable for containers.

	suitable for containers
	early to late spring
	poor resistance
	not hardy
	midsummer to early fall

'Benning's Green Tint'

A patty-pan type, this American cultivar is more than 100 years old. The sprawling, bush-type plants produce pale-green, flat, scalloped-edge fruits, that are best picked at around 3 in (7.5 cm), when the white flesh has a fine, creamy texture and good flavor.

	suitable for containers
	early to late spring
	poor resistance
	not hardy
	midsummer to early fall

'Sunny Delight'

A patty-pan-type, this F1 hybrid cultivar develops into an upright, semi-bush plant. It starts cropping early, producing attractive, pure-yellow fruits with no green markings, which are best when picked at 2.5–3 in (6–7.5 cm) across.

	suitable for containers
	early to late spring
	poor resistance
	not hardy
	midsummer to early fall

'Defender'

A standard zucchini-type, this F1 hybrid cultivar produces an abundant crop of slender, and very slightly flecked fruits that are mid-green in color throughout the entire season. The plants show a fair degree of resistance to cucumber mosaic virus.

 suitable for containers

 early to late spring

 some resistance

not hardy

midsummer to early fall

'Fancycrook'

A crookneck-type, this F1 hybrid variety produces a high yield on vigorous, open plants that are resistant to powdery mildew. The fruits are buttery yellow and bulbous, with a thin, curved neck. They are best picked at around 5 in (13 cm) long.

 unsuitable for containers

early to late spring

some resistance

not hardy

midsummer to early fall

'Segev'

A club-shaped zucchini, this F1 hybrid cultivar sets its pale-green, tapered fruits without pollination, so still crops well in poorer weather, or if insects are scarce. The plants are resistant to powdery mildew and have few spines, making picking easier.

 suitable for containers

 early to late spring

some resistance

not hardy

midsummer to early fall

'Parador'

This F1 hybrid, zucchini-type cultivar starts to crop early and continues to be productive all season. The fruits are an attractive, shiny, golden-yellow color that is hard to overlook, and the flavor is good as well. It is a good choice for growing in containers.

- suitable for containers
- early to late spring
- poor resistance
- not hardy
- midsummer to early fall

'Giambo'

This early cultivar produces short, fat fruits on a compact, bushy plant. A good choice to use for stuffed flowers, the fruits are best picked before they reach 6 in (15 cm) long, by which time flowers will be about 3 in (7.5 cm) wide.

- suitable for containers
- early to late spring
- poor resistance
- not hardy
- midsummer to early fall

'Success PM'

A straightneck-type, this high-yielding cultivar produces prolific crops on healthy plants (the "PM" stands for "powdery mildew resistance"). The fruits have pale-yellow, smooth skins with a bulbous base, and are best picked at about 6 in (15 cm) long.

- suitable for containers
- early to late spring
- some resistance
- not hardy
- midsummer to early fall

'Tiger Cross'

An F1 hybrid, this prolific cultivar produces long marrow squashes that are mid-green in color with cream-colored stripes; they are uniform in shape and excellent for use in the kitchen. The plants have a bushy habit and are resistant to cucumber mosaic virus.

 unsuitable for containers
 mid-spring to early summer
 some resistance
 not hardy
 midsummer to fall

'Long Green Trailing'

Producing large, dark-green, pale-striped, very flavorful marrow squashes, this cultivar is an excellent choice for the garden, but requires a large growing space to accommodate its spreading habit and plentiful yield. Fruits store well over winter.

 unsuitable for containers
 mid-spring to early summer
poor resistance
not hardy
midsummer to fall

'Bush Baby'

This F1 hybrid cultivar is a good choice for containers, producing a good crop of three-quarter size squashes on compact, bushy plants. The fruits are dark green with narrow, pale-green stripes, and have a good flavor.

 suitable for containers
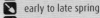 early to late spring
poor resistance
not hardy
 midsummer to early fall

PUMPKINS AND WINTER
SQUASHES *Cucurbita maxima, C. moschata* and *C. pepo*

Round, orange pumpkins are used as jack-o'-lanterns at Halloween, but they, and their close relatives winter squashes, are also found in a variety of unusual shapes, colors, and sizes. Delicious cooked, especially baked in pies, they store well, and are an excellent winter crop.

	SPRING	SUMMER	FALL	WINTER
SOW/PLANT				
HARVEST				

SOWING

Pumpkins and winter squashes grow best in fertile, well-drained soil, in a sunny, open site. Since plants will spread and become quite large, plan carefully to allow them plenty of space; they will need about 3–5 ft (1–1.5 m) between plants. Sow seed under cover in mid-spring for planting out later.

CROP CARE

Seedlings should be planted out in deep, very fertile soil, once all risk of frost has passed.

Your crops will need slightly different care, depending on their growing habit. Trailing types can be trained up supports to keep them well-ventilated and off the ground, and to minimize

Plant seedlings in rich, well-mulched soil.

their growing space. Bear in mind that heavy fruits may need support with netting in the same way that melons do (see p.159). Mulch around the plants, and thin fruits to two or three per plant if you want large specimens.

Pumpkins and winter squashes need to be watered well, and benefit from regular supplementary feeding with a tomato fertilizer.

HARVESTING

Harvest pumpkins and winter
squashes when they have grown
to full size and their stems start
to crack. It is preferable to leave
them growing for as long as
possible to allow their skins
to harden well. Cut them from
the plant with a sharp knife,
with a length of stalk attached.

STORING

Pumpkins and winter squashes
will store well over the winter
months. Harvest them when they
are fully ripe and prepare them
for storage by hardening their
skins for a few weeks in the sun.

PESTS AND DISEASES

Guard your crop against slugs and
snails, which will target young plants.
Use pellets if they attack, or deter
them by setting up beer traps or
laying a line of sand, grit, or copper
tape around the base of plants.

Ensure that plants are well-watered
and well-ventilated to discourage the
spread of diseases such as powdery
mildew and cucumber mosaic virus,
which is especially serious, since it is
incurable and will stunt and kill plants.
Remove and destroy infected crops
to prevent the spread of disease.

'Sweet Dumpling'

A very pretty squash, the small fruits are cream with green stripes and splashes, and shaped like a green pepper. They have sweet, well-flavored flesh and are delicious baked whole. The plants are compact trailers, so are good for training up supports.

	suitable for containers
	early to late spring
	some resistance
	not hardy
	late summer to mid-fall

'Honey Bear'

This modern, F1-hybrid, acorn-squash cultivar has resistance to powdery mildew. The plants are compact, and the fruits small and ridged, with very dark green skin and tasty orange flesh. Halved and baked they are ideal for two with no waste.

	suitable for containers
	early to late spring
	some resistance
	not hardy
	late summer to mid-fall

'Table Gold'

This productive bush-type acorn squash produces 1.5-lb (700-g) fruits, which can be harvested when light yellow in about 65 days and used as summer squash, or allowed to ripen to a deep gold. The flesh is nutty and tender, and perfect for soups.

	unsuitable for containers
	late spring to early summer
	none
	not hardy
	late summer to fall

'Crown Prince'

This Australian cultivar is one of the finest variety of squash available on the market. The large fruits are a flattened-pumpkin shape, steel-gray in color, with richly flavored, dense, orange-yellow flesh. They will store for six months or more.

 suitable for containers

 early to late spring

 poor resistance

not hardy

late summer to mid-fall

'Sweet REBA Bush'

REBA stands for Resistant Early Bush Acorn, which concisely describes this powdery mildew-resistant winter squash. Plants are open-pollinated, compact, and high yielding, and the 2-lb (1-kg) fruits begin to ripen as quickly as 70 days from sowing.

suitable for containers

late spring to early summer

good resistance

not hardy

late summer to fall

'Butternut'

This is the original butternut cultivar and bears the buff-skinned, pear-shaped fruits typical of this group. They have rich, dense, orange flesh and only a small seed cavity, so there is little waste. They keep well if fully ripened first.

suitable for containers

early to late spring

poor resistance

not hardy

late summer to late fall

'Queensland Blue'

This old Australian cultivar is blocky in shape, narrower at the base than at the top, and deeply ribbed; the skin is jade green in color with darker mottling. The sweet, golden flesh is useful for roasting, soups, and pumpkin pie, and the very large fruits also keep well.

🪣	unsuitable for containers
🍃	early to late spring
🕷	poor resistance
❄	not hardy
🔒	late summer to mid-fall

'Bon Bon'

This is a trailing, buttercup-type cultivar, producing high yields of uniform, medium-sized, blocky fruits with a flattened top and base. The fruits' skin is deep green, and the flesh yellow-orange. They can be stored until midwinter.

🪣	suitable for containers
🍃	early to late spring
🕷	poor resistance
❄	not hardy
🔒	late summer to mid-fall

'Harrier'

This is a butternut-type squash producing medium-sized fruits on large, semi-trailing plants. The fruits are pear-shaped with buff skin and orange flesh. Very early maturing, the fruits develop close to the main stem, so are easy to find and harvest.

🪣	unsuitable for containers
🍃	early to late spring
🕷	poor resistance
❄	not hardy
🔒	late summer to late fall

'Burgess'

'Burgess' is a highly praised, semi-vigorous cultivar, with excellent flavor and sweet, orange flesh. It produces round, dark-green fruits, which have a light-green "button" on the underside. In addition to the fruits being easy to peel, they also keep well.

 unsuitable for containers
 early to late spring
 poor resistance
 not hardy
late summer to mid-fall

'Spaghetti'

This cultivar is one of a kind. It is shaped like a fat marrow squash and is dull beige in color, but once baked or boiled and cut open, the flesh pulls away into long, spaghetti-like strands that are ideal with cheese, meat, or tomato sauce.

 unsuitable for containers
early to late spring
 poor resistance
 not hardy
late summer to mid-fall

'Uchiki Kuri'

Also known as 'Red Kuri' and 'Onion Squash', this cultivar produces medium-sized, onion-shaped fruits in a stunning, rich red-orange color. The deep orange flesh is smooth and dry with a rich, sweet, nutty flavor.

unsuitable for containers
early to late spring
 poor resistance
 not hardy
 late summer to mid-fall

'Turk's Turban'

This is a uniquely decorative variety of squash, featuring a riotous mixture of orange, green, and white fruits. They are medium in size and resemble a large and small pumpkin stacked together. The orange flesh is moist, and the fruits store well.

- unsuitable for containers
- early to late spring
- poor resistance
- not hardy
- late summer to mid-fall

'Golden Hubbard'

This American heirloom cultivar produces very large fruits that are roughly oval in shape and store well. The skin is a deep, dull, orange-red, mottled with lighter orange. The golden flesh is dry and fine-textured with a good flavor.

- unsuitable for containers
- early to late spring
- poor resistance
- not hardy
- late summer to mid-fall

'Hunter'

This productive, F1 hybrid cultivar produces very large crops of medium-to-large, butternut-type fruits. They are pear-shaped and long, with buff skin and golden-orange flesh. The fruits mature early, and develop close to the main stem, making picking easy.

- unsuitable for containers
- early to late spring
- some resistance
- not hardy
- late summer to late fall

'Delicata'

This American heirloom cultivar produces small, peanut-shaped fruits that are bright and creamy-white with fine, green stripes and speckles. The flesh is pale yellow and has a sweet, delicate flavor. Fruits are thin-skinned and as such do not keep well.

 suitable for containers

 early to late spring

 poor resistance

not hardy

late summer to mid-fall

'Table Queen Bush'

These compact, non-vining plants bear early-maturing, dark-green acorn squash, making them good for small gardens. The open-pollinated plants produce about five 1.5-lb (700-g) fruits each. They are excellent baked, and can be stored for several months.

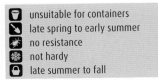

unsuitable for containers

late spring to early summer

no resistance

not hardy

late summer to fall

'Honey Nut'

This mini butternut squash was bred to be resistant to powdery mildew, which keeps it productive over a long period. The 4–5-in (10–13-cm) fruits have sweet, deep-orange flesh and rich in vitamins A and C. They ripen in about 100 days.

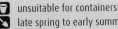

unsuitable for containers

late spring to early summer

good resistance

not hardy

fall

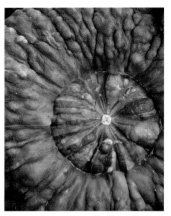

'Marina di Chioggia'

This heirloom cultivar, which was developed in northern Italy, bears very large pumpkin-shaped fruits that have very warty and knobbled skin, which is a mid-green color. The deep-yellow flesh is rich and sweet in flavor and the fruits will store for many months.

- 🪣 unsuitable for containers
- 🌱 early to late spring
- ✳️ poor resistance
- ❄️ not hardy
- 🔒 late summer to mid-fall

'Tennessee Sweet Potato'

This American heirloom cultivar produces large, pear-shaped fruits that have creamy-white skin, which is faintly lined with green. It crops well in cool weather, and is also a good keeper, with fairly dry flesh and a pleasant flavor.

- 🪣 unsuitable for containers
- 🌱 early to late spring
- ✳️ poor resistance
- ❄️ not hardy
- 🔒 late summer to mid-fall

'Sunshine'

This high-yielding, 'F1' hybrid cultivar produces attractive, medium size fruits on relatively compact, trailing plants. The fruits are smooth, shaped like a slightly flattened ball, with shiny, orange skin, a rich orange flesh, and a sweet and nutty flavor.

- 🪣 unsuitable for containers
- 🌱 early to late spring
- ✳️ poor resistance
- ❄️ not hardy
- 🔒 late summer to mid-fall

'Jack O' Lantern'

This cultivar produces pumpkins that are the perfect size and shape for carving. They are orange, with a slight greenish tinge, smoothly spherical, and about 10 in (25 cm) across. They also store well, and can be used for making pies, soups, and stews.

 unsuitable for containers

early to late spring

poor resistance

not hardy

late summer to mid-fall

'Long Island Cheese'

Shaped like a buff-colored 10-lb (4.5-kg) wheel of cheese, this heirloom winter squash is prized by gardeners for its sweet orange flesh, and is used for making delicious pies. 'Long Island Cheese' fruits ripen in about 100 days, and store well.

 unsuitable for containers

late spring to early summer

poor resistance

not hardy

fall

'Howden'

'Howden' is the picture-perfect standard for a jack-o-lantern pumpkin: plump, ribbed, and bright orange, with a strong "handle." The easy-to-grow, rambling plants yield a big crop of 20–30-lb (9–13.6-kg) fruits with thick, solid flesh.

 unsuitable for containers

late spring to early summer

no resistance

not hardy

fall

'Becky'

This 'F1' hybrid cultivar produces small, attractive-looking pumpkins that are ideal for use as decoration. They have smooth, lightly ribbed, yellow-orange skin and light orange flesh. In addition to being decorative, they are a handy size for cooking whole.

 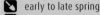

 unsuitable for containers
early to late spring
poor resistance
not hardy
late summer to mid-fall

'Atlantic Giant'

This is the cultivar to grow if you want to produce a record beater: it is the current world record holder for the heaviest pumpkin. It can produce vast, oval-shaped specimens without any special treatment, but the flavor is bland.

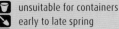

 unsuitable for containers
early to late spring
poor resistance
not hardy
late summer to mid-fall

'Rouge Vif d'Etampes'

This French heirloom cultivar produces classic, Cinderella's coach-style pumpkins that have a beautiful, rich orange-red skin, a squashed-globe shape, and deep ribs. They store well and may be used for decoration, but are also useful for culinary purposes.

 unsuitable for containers
 early to late spring
 poor resistance
 not hardy
 late summer to mid-fall

'Jack Be Little'

The 'Jack Be Little' cultivar is aptly named, producing tiny, ribbed pumpkins that are just 4 in (10 cm) across, with yellow-orange skin and yellow flesh. They are excellent halved and roasted, stuffed, or just used for decoration.

 suitable for containers
 early to late spring
 poor resistance
not hardy
late summer to mid-fall

'Winter Luxury Pie'

This 6–8-lb (2.7–3.6-kg) winter squash has been featured in sweet, velvety pumpkin pies for more than 100 years. Typically pumpkin-shaped, but overlaid with a fine-grained netting, the orange fruits grow to about 8–10 in (20–25 cm) in diameter.

 unsuitable for containers
late spring to early summer
 poor resistance
 not hardy
fall

SUPPLIER LIST

Adams County Nursery
26 Nursery Road
P.O. Box 108
Aspers, PA 17304
717-677-8105
www.acnursery.com
(Fruit trees)

Baker Creek Heirloom Seed
2278 Baker Creek Road
Mansfield, MO 65704
417-924-8917
www.RareSeeds.com.com
(Large selection of heirloom
vegetable and herb seeds)

Big Horse Creek Farm
P.O. Box 70
Lansing, NC 28643
www.bighorsecreekfarm.com
(Heirloom apple trees)

Burnt Ridge Nursery
& Orchards
432 Burnt Ridge Road
Onalaska, WA 98570
360-985-2873
www.burntridgenursery.com
(Fruiting plants and nut trees)

Cummins Nursery
1408 Trumansburg Road
Ithaca, NY 14456
607-227-6147
www.cumminsnursery.com
(Fruit trees)

Double A Vineyards
10277 Christy Road
Fredonia, NY 14063
716-672-8493
www.rakgrape.com
(Grapes, berries, and rhubarb)

Edible Landscaping Online
361 Spirit Ridge Lane
Afton, VA 22920
434-361-9134
www.eat-it.com
(Fruit trees, vines, and bushes)

Fedco Seeds and Trees
P.O. Box 520
Waterville, ME 04903
207-873-7333
www.fedcoseeds.com
(Vegetable seeds, fruit trees,
and berries)

Forestfarm
990 Tetherow Road
Williams, OR 97544
541-846-7269
www.forestfarm.com
(Fruit trees and plants)

Gourmet Seed International
HC 12 Box 510
178 Murphy's Chapel Lane
Tatum, NM 88267
575-398-6111
www.gourmetseed.com
(Vegetable and flower seeds,
including many imports)

Grandpa's Nursery
P.O. Box 773
Coloma, MI 49038
877-800-0077
www.grandpasorchard.com
(Fruit trees)

Hidden Springs Nursery
170 Hidden Springs Lane
Cookeville, TN 38501
931-268-2592
www.hiddenspringsnursery.com
(Organically grown fruit trees)

High Mowing Organic Seeds
76 Quarry Road
Wolcott, VT 05680
802-472-6174
www.highmowingseeds.com
(Organic vegetable, flower,
and herb seeds)

Johnny's Selected Seeds
955 Benton Avenue
Winslow, ME 04901
877-564-6697
www.johnnyseeds.com
(Vegetable and flower seeds,
including heirloom varieties and
organic seeds)

Kitchen Garden Seeds
23 Tulip Drive
P.O. Box 638
Bantam, CT 06750
860-567-6086
www.kitchengardenseeds.com
(Vegetable seeds and potato slips)

Logee's Greenhouses
141 North Street
Danielson, CT 06239
888-330-8038
www.logees.com
(Tropical fruit trees and vines)

Miller Nurseries
5060 West Lake Road
Canandaigua, NY 14424
800-836-9630
www.millernurseries.com
(Fruit trees and vines)

Nolin River Nut Tree Nursery
797 Port Wooden Road
Upton, KY 42784
270-369-8551
www.nolinnursery.com
(Nut trees)

Nourse Farms
41 River Road
South Deerfield, MA 01373
413-665-2658
www.noursefarms.com
(Berries and rhubarb)

Park Seed Company
1 Parkton Avenue
Greenwood, SC 29647
800-213-0076
www.parkseed.com
(Vegetable, herb, and flower seeds)

Pense Nursery
2318 Highway 71NE
Mountainburg, AR 72946
479-369-2494
www.alcasoft.com/pense
(Berries and grapevines)

Raintree Nursery
391 Butts Road
Morton, WA 98356
800-391-8892
www.raintreenursery.com
(Fruit trees and unusual fruits)

Sand Hill Preservation Center
1878 230th Street
Calamus, IA 52729
563-246-2299
www.sandhillpreservation.com
(Heirloom seeds and plants, and sweet potato slips)

Seeds of Change
P. O. Box 15700
Santa Fe, NM
888-762-7333
www.seedsofchange.com
(Certified organic vegetable seeds)

Seed Savers Exchange
3094 North Winn Road
Decorah, IA 52101
563-382-5990
www.seedsavers.org
(Heirloom vegetable seeds)

St. Lawrence Nurseries
325 State Highway 345
Potsdam, NY 13676
315-265-6739
www.sln.potsdam.ny.us
(Fruit and nuts for northern gardens)

The Strawberry Store
107 Wellington Way
Middletown, DE 19709
302-378-3633
www.thestrawberrystore.com
(Alpine and heirloom strawberries)

Territorial Seed Company
P.O. Box 158
Cottage Grove, OR 97424
800-626-0866
www.territorialseed.com
(Unusual and heirloom fruit and vegetables seeds and plants)

Trees of Antiquity
20 Wellsona Road
Paso Robles, CA 93446
805-467-9909
www.treesofantiquity.com
(Heirloom fruit trees)

Victory Seeds
P.O. Box 192
Molalla, OR 97038
503-829-3126
www.victoryseeds.com
(Open-pollinated seeds)

Whitman Farms
3995 Gibson Road NW
Salem, OR 97304
503-510-0486
www.whitmanfarms.com
(Berry bushes)

Womack Nursery Company
2551 State Hwy 6
De Leon, TX 76444
254-893-6497
www.womacknursery.com
(Fruit and nut trees)

ACKNOWLEDGMENTS

The publisher would like to thank the following for their kind permission to reproduce their photographs:
(Key: t-top; b-bottom)

Alamy Images: Eelco Nicodem 163; The Garden Picture Library 58t; **Dorling Kindersley:** Elaine Hewson 5tl, 416, 422t; Mel Shackleton: 238; Rebecca Tennant 118b, 302; **FLPA:** Nigel Cattlin 307b; **GAP Photos:** Maxine Adcock; 323t, 451t, 474t, 549t; Matt Anker 335t; BBC Magazines Ltd 547t; Pernilla Bergdahl 423t; Dave Bevan 319t, 425; Richard Bloom 262t; Christina Bollen 56b; Mark Bolton 553t; Elke Borkowski 113t, 207t, 305t, 344t, 400t, 465t, 499t, 535t; Jonathan Buckley 233t, 334t, 534t; Paul Debois 218t; FhF Greenmedia 186t, 216, 402t, 435; Flora Press 449t; Tim Gainey 161t; Charles Hawes 551t; Michael Howes 268b; Martin Hughes-Jones 178t, 224t, 311t, 427t, 491, 506t; Lynn Keddie 444, 493t; Michael King; 345t; Jenny Lilly; 324t; Clive Nichols 88t, 464t; Howard Rice 253; S&O 194t; SandO 271t; J.S. Sira 255t; Gary Smith 497, 528t; Friedrich Strauss 298b, 304t; Graham Strong 312t, 482t, 487t, 540t; Maddie Thornhill 428t; Tommy Tonsberg 356; Visions 235, 461t; Juliette Wade 365; Jo Whitworth 93t, 293t, 511, 517; Rob Whitworth 486t; **Garden Exposures Photo Library:** Andrea Jones 181t, 227t, 376t, 455t; **Garden World Images:** Dave Bevan 217b, 303b, 382, 501t; Francoise Davis 149b; Flowerphotos/Carol Sharp 217t; GWI/MAP/F.Didillon; 81t; Andrea Jones 18-19; MAP/Frédéric Didillon 10-11; Cora Niele 379; Trevor Sims 160t; Lee Thomas 6-7; **The Garden Collection:** Torie Chugg 443t, 464b, 472t, 485t, 489t, 541t, 554t; Michelle Garrett 548t, 555t; Andrew Lawson 84b; Marie O'Hara 310; Derek St Romaine 442t, 495t; Neil Sutherland 16, 177t, 470t, 471t; **Keepers Nursery:** 46t, 60t; **Marianne Majerus Garden Images:** 263t, 281t, 325t, 483t, 536t, 552t, 554b; Andrew Lawson 28b;

Marshalls Seeds: 80t, 92t, 174t, 176t, 178b, 179t, 182t, 200t, 208t, 249t, 250b, 250t, 251t, 254b, 254t, 256t, 275t, 282t, 300t, 308t, 313t, 318t, 320t, 336t, 359t, 360t, 380t, 473t, 475t; **Clive Nichols:** 468t, 498t, 502t; **Photolibrary:** David Askham 399t; David Cavagnaro 160b; Michael Gadomski 190t; Claire Higgins 69t, 120, 125t; Andrea Jones 165t; Cora Niele 369; Graham Salter 115; Richard Shiell 68t; Gary K. Smith 221t; Jo Whitworth 259; **Royal Horticultural Society, Wisley:** Jacquie Gray 38t, 112t, 180t, 223t, 264t, 294t, 450t; **Derek St Romaine:** 299t, 309t; **Suttons Seeds:** 88b, 103, 122t, 131b, 139t, 144t, 187t, 188t, 189t, 191t, 195t, 198t, 199t, 201t, 206t, 209t, 218t, 219t, 222t, 230t, 231t, 232t, 257b, 265t, 270t, 272t, 282t, 292t, 329t, 336b, 337t, 338t, 339t, 371t, 381t, 387t, 389t, 392t, 393t, 395t, 397t, 413t, 453, 507t, 509t, 513t, 522t, 523t, 524t, 539t, 543t; **Victoriana Nursery Gardens:** Stephen Shirley 15, 40t, 47t, 50t, 79, 96t, 97t, 98t, 99t, 100l, 100r, 130t, 135t, 138t, 145t, 157, 164t, 193t, 197, 203t, 211t, 236t, 237t, 240, 277t, 287t, 291t, 297t, 303t, 322t, 358t, 373t, 377t, 378, 388t, 391, 408t, 409t, 412t, 419, 420b, 452, 463t, 466t, 467t, 478t, 503t, 505t, 515t, 525t, 527t, 529t, 531, 537t, 545.

RHS Consultants: Jim Arbury and Guy Barter
RHS Editors: Rae Spencer-Jones and Simon Maughan

Dorling Kindersley would also like to thank the following: Stephen and Serena Shirley, Ian Midson, Colette Sadler, Chauney Dunford, Annabel Spilling, Laura Evans, and Jenny Baskaya.

All other images © Dorling Kindersley
For further information see:
www.dkimages.com